Hadoop Operations

Eric Sammer

O'REILLY®

Beijing · Cambridge · Farnham · Köln · Sebastopol · Tokyo

Hadoop Operations

by Eric Sammer

Published by O'Reilly Media, Inc., 1005 Gravenstein Highway North, Sebastopol, CA 95472.

O'Reilly books may be purchased for educational, business, or sales promotional use. Online editions are also available for most titles (*http://my.safaribooksonline.com*). For more information, contact our corporate/institutional sales department: 800-998-9938 or *corporate@oreilly.com*.

Editors: Mike Loukides and Courtney Nash
Production Editor: Melanie Yarbrough
Copyeditor: Audrey Doyle

Indexer: Jay Marchand
Cover Designer: Karen Montgomery
Interior Designer: David Futato
Illustrator: Robert Romano

September 2012: First Edition.

Revision History for the First Edition:
2012-09-25   First release
See *http://oreilly.com/catalog/errata.csp?isbn=9781449327057* for release details.

ISBN: 978-1-449-32705-7

[LSI]

1348583377

For Aida.

Table of Contents

Preface

Conventions Used in This Book

The following typographical conventions are used in this book:

Italic
> Indicates new terms, URLs, email addresses, filenames, and file extensions.

`Constant width`
> Used for program listings, as well as within paragraphs to refer to program elements such as variable or function names, databases, data types, environment variables, statements, and keywords.

`Constant width bold`
> Shows commands or other text that should be typed literally by the user.

`Constant width italic`
> Shows text that should be replaced with user-supplied values or by values determined by context.

 This icon signifies a tip, suggestion, or general note.

 This icon indicates a warning or caution.

Using Code Examples

This book is here to help you get your job done. In general, you may use the code in this book in your programs and documentation. You do not need to contact us for permission unless you're reproducing a significant portion of the code. For example, writing a program that uses several chunks of code from this book does not require permission. Selling or distributing a CD-ROM of examples from O'Reilly books does require permission. Answering a question by citing this book and quoting example code does not require permission. Incorporating a significant amount of example code from this book into your product's documentation does require permission.

We appreciate, but do not require, attribution. An attribution usually includes the title, author, publisher, and ISBN. For example: "*Hadoop Operations* by Eric Sammer (O'Reilly). Copyright 2012 Eric Sammer, 978-1-449-32705-7."

If you feel your use of code examples falls outside fair use or the permission given above, feel free to contact us at *permissions@oreilly.com*.

Safari® Books Online

Safari Safari Books Online (*www.safaribooksonline.com*) is an on-demand digital library that delivers expert content in both book and video form from the world's leading authors in technology and business.

Technology professionals, software developers, web designers, and business and creative professionals use Safari Books Online as their primary resource for research, problem solving, learning, and certification training.

Safari Books Online offers a range of product mixes and pricing programs for organizations, government agencies, and individuals. Subscribers have access to thousands of books, training videos, and prepublication manuscripts in one fully searchable database from publishers like O'Reilly Media, Prentice Hall Professional, Addison-Wesley Professional, Microsoft Press, Sams, Que, Peachpit Press, Focal Press, Cisco Press, John Wiley & Sons, Syngress, Morgan Kaufmann, IBM Redbooks, Packt, Adobe Press, FT Press, Apress, Manning, New Riders, McGraw-Hill, Jones & Bartlett, Course Technology, and dozens more. For more information about Safari Books Online, please visit us online.

How to Contact Us

Please address comments and questions concerning this book to the publisher:

O'Reilly Media, Inc.
1005 Gravenstein Highway North
Sebastopol, CA 95472
800-998-9938 (in the United States or Canada)
707-829-0515 (international or local)
707-829-0104 (fax)

We have a web page for this book, where we list errata, examples, and any additional information. You can access this page at *http://oreil.ly/hadoop_operations*.

To comment or ask technical questions about this book, send email to *bookquestions@oreilly.com*.

For more information about our books, courses, conferences, and news, see our website at *http://www.oreilly.com*.

Find us on Facebook: *http://facebook.com/oreilly*

Follow us on Twitter: *http://twitter.com/oreillymedia*

Watch us on YouTube: *http://www.youtube.com/oreillymedia*

Acknowledgments

I want to thank Aida Escriva-Sammer, my wife, best friend, and favorite sysadmin, for putting up with me while I wrote this.

None of this was possible without the support and hard work of the larger Apache Hadoop community and ecosystem projects. I want to encourage all readers to get involved in the community and open source in general.

Matt Massie gave me the opportunity to do this, along with O'Reilly, and then cheered me on the whole way. Both Matt and Tom White coached me through the proposal process. Mike Olson, Omer Trajman, Amr Awadallah, Peter Cooper-Ellis, Angus Klein, and the rest of the Cloudera management team made sure I had the time, resources, and encouragement to get this done. Aparna Ramani, Rob Weltman, Jolly Chen, and Helen Friedland were instrumental throughout this process and forgiving of my constant interruptions of their teams. Special thanks to Christophe Bisciglia for giving me an opportunity at Cloudera and for the advice along the way.

Many people provided valuable feedback and input throughout the entire process, but especially Aida Escriva-Sammer, Tom White, Alejandro Abdelnur, Amina Abdulla, Patrick Angeles, Paul Battaglia, Will Chase, Yanpei Chen, Eli Collins, Joe Crobak, Doug Cutting, Joey Echeverria, Sameer Farooqui, Andrew Ferguson, Brad Hedlund, Linden Hillenbrand, Patrick Hunt, Matt Jacobs, Amandeep Khurana, Aaron Kimball, Hal Lee, Justin Lintz, Todd Lipcon, Cameron Martin, Chad Metcalf, Meg McRoberts, Aaron T. Myers, Kay Ousterhout, Greg Rahn, Henry Robinson, Mark Roddy, Jonathan Seidman, Ed Sexton, Loren Siebert, Sunil Sitaula, Ben Spivey, Dan Spiewak, Omer Trajman, Kathleen Ting, Erik-Jan van Baaren, Vinithra Varadharajan, Patrick Wendell, Tom Wheeler, Ian Wrigley, Nezih Yigitbasi, and Philip Zeyliger. To those whom I may have omitted from this list, please forgive me.

The folks at O'Reilly have been amazing, especially Courtney Nash, Mike Loukides, Maria Stallone, Arlette Labat, and Meghan Blanchette.

Jaime Caban, Victor Nee, Travis Melo, Andrew Bayer, Liz Pennell, and Michael Demetria provided additional administrative, technical, and contract support.

Finally, a special thank you to Kathy Sammer for her unwavering support, and for teaching me to do *exactly* what others say you cannot.

Portions of this book have been reproduced or derived from software and documentation available under the Apache Software License, version 2 (*http://www.apache.org/licenses/LICENSE-2.0*).

## CHAPTER 1

Introduction

Over the past few years, there has been a fundamental shift in data storage, management, and processing. Companies are storing more data from more sources in more formats than ever before. This isn't just about being a "data packrat" but rather building products, features, and intelligence predicated on knowing more about the world (where the world can be users, searches, machine logs, or whatever is relevant to an organization). Organizations are finding new ways to use data that was previously believed to be of little value, or far too expensive to retain, to better serve their constituents. Sourcing and storing data is one half of the equation. Processing that data to produce *information* is fundamental to the daily operations of every modern business.

Data storage and processing isn't a new problem, though. Fraud detection in commerce and finance, anomaly detection in operational systems, demographic analysis in advertising, and many other applications have had to deal with these issues for decades. What has happened is that the volume, velocity, and variety of this data has changed, and in some cases, rather dramatically. This makes sense, as many algorithms benefit from access to more data. Take, for instance, the problem of recommending products to a visitor of an ecommerce website. You could simply show each visitor a rotating list of products they could buy, hoping that one would appeal to them. It's not exactly an informed decision, but it's a start. The question is what do you need to improve the chance of showing the right person the right product? Maybe it makes sense to show them what you think they like, based on what they've previously looked at. For some products, it's useful to know what they already own. Customers who already bought a specific brand of laptop computer from you may be interested in compatible accessories and upgrades.[1] One of the most common techniques is to cluster users by similar behavior (such as purchase patterns) and recommend products purchased by "similar" users. No matter the solution, all of the algorithms behind these options require data

---

1. I once worked on a data-driven marketing project for a company that sold beauty products. Using purchase transactions of all customers over a long period of time, the company was able to predict when a customer would run out of a given product after purchasing it. As it turned out, simply offering them the same thing about a week before they ran out resulted in a (very) noticeable lift in sales.

and generally improve in quality with more of it. Knowing more about a problem space generally leads to better decisions (or algorithm efficacy), which in turn leads to happier users, more money, reduced fraud, healthier people, safer conditions, or whatever the desired result might be.

Apache Hadoop is a platform that provides pragmatic, cost-effective, scalable infrastructure for building many of the types of applications described earlier. Made up of a distributed filesystem called the Hadoop Distributed Filesystem (HDFS) and a computation layer that implements a processing paradigm called MapReduce, Hadoop is an open source, batch data processing system for enormous amounts of data. We live in a flawed world, and Hadoop is designed to survive in it by not only tolerating hardware and software failures, but also treating them as first-class conditions that happen regularly. Hadoop uses a cluster of plain old commodity servers with no specialized hardware or network infrastructure to form a single, logical, storage and compute platform, or *cluster*, that can be shared by multiple individuals or groups. Computation in Hadoop MapReduce is performed in parallel, automatically, with a simple abstraction for developers that obviates complex synchronization and network programming. Unlike many other distributed data processing systems, Hadoop runs the user-provided processing logic on the machine where the data lives rather than dragging the data across the network; a huge win for performance.

For those interested in the history, Hadoop was modeled after two papers produced by Google, one of the many companies to have these kinds of data-intensive processing problems. The first, presented in 2003, describes a pragmatic, scalable, distributed filesystem optimized for storing enormous datasets, called the Google Filesystem (*http://research.google.com/archive/gfs.html*), or *GFS*. In addition to simple storage, GFS was built to support large-scale, data-intensive, distributed processing applications. The following year, another paper, titled "MapReduce: Simplified Data Processing on Large Clusters (*http://research.google.com/archive/mapreduce.html*)," was presented, defining a programming model and accompanying framework that provided automatic parallelization, fault tolerance, and the scale to process hundreds of terabytes of data in a single job over thousands of machines. When paired, these two systems could be used to build large data processing clusters on relatively inexpensive, commodity machines. These papers directly inspired the development of HDFS and Hadoop MapReduce, respectively.

Interest and investment in Hadoop has led to an entire ecosystem of related software both open source and commercial. Within the Apache Software Foundation alone, projects that explicitly make use of, or integrate with, Hadoop are springing up regularly. Some of these projects make authoring MapReduce jobs easier and more accessible, while others focus on getting data in and out of HDFS, simplify operations, enable deployment in cloud environments, and so on. Here is a sampling of the more popular projects with which you should familiarize yourself:

Apache Hive (http://hive.apache.org)

Hive creates a relational database–style abstraction that allows developers to write a dialect of SQL, which in turn is executed as one or more MapReduce jobs on the cluster. Developers, analysts, and existing third-party packages already know and speak SQL (Hive's dialect of SQL is called HiveQL and implements only a subset of any of the common standards). Hive takes advantage of this and provides a quick way to reduce the learning curve to adopting Hadoop and writing MapReduce jobs. For this reason, Hive is by far one of the most popular Hadoop ecosystem projects.

Hive works by defining a table-like schema over an *existing* set of files in HDFS and handling the gory details of extracting records from those files when a query is run. The data on disk is never actually changed, just parsed at query time. HiveQL statements are interpreted and an execution plan of prebuilt map and reduce classes is assembled to perform the MapReduce equivalent of the SQL statement.

Apache Pig (http://pig.apache.org)

Like Hive, Apache Pig was created to simplify the authoring of MapReduce jobs, obviating the need to write Java code. Instead, users write data processing jobs in a high-level scripting language from which Pig builds an execution plan and executes a series of MapReduce jobs to do the heavy lifting. In cases where Pig doesn't support a necessary function, developers can extend its set of built-in operations by writing user-defined functions in Java (Hive supports similar functionality as well). If you know Perl, Python, Ruby, JavaScript, or even shell script, you can learn Pig's syntax in the morning and be running MapReduce jobs by lunchtime.

Apache Sqoop (http://sqoop.apache.org)

Not only does Hadoop not want to replace your database, it wants to be friends with it. Exchanging data with relational databases is one of the most popular integration points with Apache Hadoop. Sqoop, short for "SQL to Hadoop," performs bidirectional data transfer between Hadoop and almost any database with a JDBC driver. Using MapReduce, Sqoop performs these operations in parallel with no need to write code.

For even greater performance, Sqoop supports database-specific plug-ins that use native features of the RDBMS rather than incurring the overhead of JDBC. Many of these connectors are open source, while others are free or available from commercial vendors at a cost. Today, Sqoop includes native connectors (called *direct* support) for MySQL and PostgreSQL. Free connectors exist for Teradata, Netezza, SQL Server, and Oracle (from Quest Software), and are available for download from their respective company websites.

Apache Flume (http://flume.apache.org)

Apache Flume is a streaming data collection and aggregation system designed to transport massive volumes of data into systems such as Hadoop. It supports native connectivity and support for writing directly to HDFS, and simplifies reliable, streaming data delivery from a variety of sources including RPC services, log4j appenders, syslog, and even the output from OS commands. Data can be routed, load-balanced, replicated to multiple destinations, and aggregated from thousands of hosts by a tier of agents.

Apache Oozie (http://incubator.apache.org/oozie/)
It's not uncommon for large production clusters to run many coordinated Map-Reduce jobs in a workfow. Apache Oozie is a workflow engine and scheduler built specifically for large-scale job orchestration on a Hadoop cluster. Workflows can be triggered by time or events such as data arriving in a directory, and job failure handling logic can be implemented so that policies are adhered to. Oozie presents a REST service for programmatic management of workflows and status retrieval.

Apache Whirr (http://whirr.apache.org)
Apache Whirr was developed to simplify the creation and deployment of ephemeral clusters in cloud environments such as Amazon's AWS. Run as a command-line tool either locally or within the cloud, Whirr can spin up instances, deploy Hadoop, configure the software, and tear it down on demand. Under the hood, Whirr uses the powerful jclouds (*http://www.jclouds.org/*) library so that it is cloud provider–neutral. The developers have put in the work to make Whirr support both Amazon EC2 and Rackspace Cloud. In addition to Hadoop, Whirr understands how to provision Apache Cassandra, Apache ZooKeeper, Apache HBase, ElasticSearch, Voldemort, and Apache Hama.

Apache HBase (http://hbase.apache.org)
Apache HBase is a low-latency, distributed (nonrelational) database built on top of HDFS. Modeled after Google's Bigtable (*http://research.google.com/archive/bigt able.html*), HBase presents a flexible data model with scale-out properties and a very simple API. Data in HBase is stored in a semi-columnar format partitioned by rows into *regions*. It's not uncommon for a single table in HBase to be well into the hundreds of terabytes or in some cases petabytes. Over the past few years, HBase has gained a massive following based on some very public deployments such as Facebook's Messages platform (*http://www.facebook.com/note.php?note_id= 454991608919*). Today, HBase is used to serve huge amounts of data to real-time systems in major production deployments.

Apache ZooKeeper (http://zookeeper.apache.org)
A true workhorse, Apache ZooKeeper is a distributed, consensus-based coordination system used to support distributed applications. Distributed applications that require leader election, locking, group membership, service location, and configuration services can use ZooKeeper rather than reimplement the complex coordination and error handling that comes with these functions. In fact, many projects within the Hadoop ecosystem use ZooKeeper for exactly this purpose (most notably, HBase).

Apache HCatalog (http://incubator.apache.org/hcatalog/)
A relatively new entry, Apache HCatalog is a service that provides shared schema and data access abstraction services to applications with the ecosystem. The

long-term goal of HCatalog is to enable interoperability between tools such as Apache Hive and Pig so that they can share dataset metadata information.

The Hadoop ecosystem is exploding into the commercial world as well. Vendors such as Oracle, SAS, MicroStrategy, Tableau, Informatica, Microsoft, Pentaho, Talend, HP, Dell, and dozens of others have all developed integration or support for Hadoop within one or more of their products. Hadoop is fast becoming (or, as an increasingly growing group would believe, already has become) the de facto standard for truly large-scale data processing in the data center.

If you're reading this book, you may be a developer with some exposure to Hadoop looking to learn more about managing the system in a production environment. Alternatively, it could be that you're an application or system administrator tasked with owning the current or planned production cluster. Those in the latter camp may be rolling their eyes at the prospect of dealing with yet another system. That's fair, and we won't spend a ton of time talking about writing applications, APIs, and other pesky code problems. There are other fantastic books on those topics, especially *Hadoop: The Definitive Guide* (*http://shop.oreilly.com/product/0636920021773.do*) by Tom White (O'Reilly). Administrators do, however, play an absolutely critical role in planning, installing, configuring, maintaining, and monitoring Hadoop clusters. Hadoop is a comparatively low-level system, leaning heavily on the host operating system for many features, and it works best when developers and administrators collaborate regularly. What you do impacts how things work.

It's an extremely exciting time to get into Apache Hadoop. The so-called *big data* space is all the rage, sure, but more importantly, Hadoop is growing and changing at a staggering rate. Each new version—and there have been a few big ones in the past year or two—brings another truckload of features for both developers and administrators alike. You could say that Hadoop is experiencing software puberty; thanks to its rapid growth and adoption, it's also a little awkward at times. You'll find, throughout this book, that there are significant changes between even minor versions. It's a lot to keep up with, admittedly, but don't let it overwhelm you. Where necessary, the differences are called out, and a section in Chapter 4 is devoted to walking you through the most commonly encountered versions.

This book is intended to be a pragmatic guide to running Hadoop in production. Those who have some familiarity with Hadoop may already know alternative methods for installation or have differing thoughts on how to properly tune the number of map slots based on CPU utilization.[2] That's expected and more than fine. The goal is not to enumerate all possible scenarios, but rather to call out what works, as demonstrated in critical deployments.

Chapters 2 and 3 provide the necessary background, describing what HDFS and MapReduce are, why they exist, and at a high level, how they work. Chapter 4 walks you

---

2. We also briefly cover the flux capacitor and discuss the burn rate of energon cubes during combat.

through the process of planning for an Hadoop deployment including hardware selection, basic resource planning, operating system selection and configuration, Hadoop distribution and version selection, and network concerns for Hadoop clusters. If you are looking for the meat and potatoes, Chapter 5 is where it's at, with configuration and setup information, including a listing of the most critical properties, organized by topic. Those that have strong security requirements or want to understand identity, access, and authorization within Hadoop will want to pay particular attention to Chapter 6. Chapter 7 explains the nuts and bolts of sharing a single large cluster across multiple groups and why this is beneficial while still adhering to service-level agreements by managing and allocating resources accordingly. Once everything is up and running, Chapter 8 acts as a run book for the most common operations and tasks. Chapter 9 is the rainy day chapter, covering the theory and practice of troubleshooting complex distributed systems such as Hadoop, including some real-world war stories. In an attempt to minimize those rainy days, Chapter 10 is all about how to effectively monitor your Hadoop cluster. Finally, Chapter 11 provides some basic tools and techniques for backing up Hadoop and dealing with catastrophic failure.

## CHAPTER 2

HDFS

Goals and Motivation

The first half of Apache Hadoop is a filesystem called the *Hadoop Distributed Filesystem* or simply HDFS. HDFS was built to support high throughput, streaming reads and writes of extremely large files. Traditional large storage area networks (SANs) and network attached storage (NAS) offer centralized, low-latency access to either a block device or a filesystem on the order of terabytes in size. These systems are fantastic as the backing store for relational databases, content delivery systems, and similar types of data storage needs because they can support full-featured POSIX semantics, scale to meet the size requirements of these systems, and offer low-latency access to data. Imagine for a second, though, hundreds or thousands of machines all waking up at the same time and pulling hundreds of terabytes of data from a centralized storage system at once. This is where traditional storage doesn't necessarily scale.

By creating a system composed of independent machines, each with its own I/O subsystem, disks, RAM, network interfaces, and CPUs, and relaxing (and sometimes removing) some of the POSIX requirements, it is possible to build a system optimized, in both performance and cost, for the specific type of workload we're interested in. There are a number of specific goals for HDFS:

- Store millions of large files, each greater than tens of gigabytes, and filesystem sizes reaching tens of petabytes.

- Use a *scale-out* model based on inexpensive commodity servers with internal JBOD ("Just a bunch of disks") rather than RAID to achieve large-scale storage. Accomplish availability and high throughput through application-level replication of data.

- Optimize for large, streaming reads and writes rather than low-latency access to many small files. Batch performance is more important than interactive response times.

- Gracefully deal with component failures of machines and disks.
- Support the functionality and scale requirements of MapReduce processing. See Chapter 3 for details.

While it is true that HDFS can be used independently of MapReduce to store large datasets, it truly shines when they're used together. MapReduce, for instance, takes advantage of how the data in HDFS is split on ingestion into blocks and pushes computation to the machine where blocks can be read locally.

Design

HDFS, in many ways, follows traditional filesystem design. Files are stored as opaque blocks and metadata exists that keeps track of the filename to block mapping, directory tree structure, permissions, and so forth. This is similar to common Linux filesystems such as ext3. So what makes HDFS different?

Traditional filesystems are implemented as kernel modules (in Linux, at least) and together with userland tools, can be mounted and made available to end users. HDFS is what's called a *userspace* filesystem. This is a fancy way of saying that the filesystem code runs outside the kernel as OS processes and by extension, is not registered with or exposed via the Linux VFS layer. While this is much simpler, more flexible, and arguably safer to implement, it means that you don't mount HDFS as you would ext3, for instance, and that it requires applications to be explicitly built for it.

In addition to being a userspace filesystem, HDFS is a distributed filesystem. Distributed filesystems are used to overcome the limits of what an individual disk or machine is capable of supporting. Each machine in a cluster stores a subset of the data that makes up the complete filesystem with the idea being that, as we need to store more block data, we simply add more machines, each with multiple disks. Filesystem metadata is stored on a centralized server, acting as a directory of block data and providing a global picture of the filesystem's state.

Another major difference between HDFS and other filesystems is its block size. It is common that general purpose filesystems use a 4 KB or 8 KB block size for data. Hadoop, on the other hand, uses the significantly larger block size of 64 MB by default. In fact, cluster administrators usually raise this to 128 MB, 256 MB, or even as high as 1 GB. Increasing the block size means data will be written in larger contiguous chunks on disk, which in turn means data can be written and read in larger sequential operations. This minimizes drive seek operations—one of the slowest operations a mechanical disk can perform—and results in better performance when doing large streaming I/O operations.

Rather than rely on specialized storage subsystem data protection, HDFS replicates each block to multiple machines in the cluster. By default, each block in a file is replicated three times. Because files in HDFS are *write once*, once a replica is written, it is not possible for it to change. This obviates the need for complex reasoning about the consistency between replicas and as a result, applications can read any of the available replicas when accessing a file. Having multiple replicas means multiple machine failures are easily tolerated, but there are also more opportunities to read data from a machine closest to an application on the network. HDFS actively tracks and manages the number of available replicas of a block as well. Should the number of copies of a block drop below the configured replication factor, the filesystem automatically makes a new copy from one of the remaining replicas. Throughout this book, we'll frequently use the term *replica* to mean a copy of an HDFS block.

Applications, of course, don't want to worry about blocks, metadata, disks, sectors, and other low-level details. Instead, developers want to perform I/O operations using higher level abstractions such as files and streams. HDFS presents the filesystem to developers as a high-level, POSIX-like API with familiar operations and concepts.

Daemons

There are three daemons that make up a standard HDFS cluster, each of which serves a distinct role, shown in Table 2-1.

Table 2-1. HDFS daemons

Daemon	# per cluster	Purpose
Namenode	1	Stores filesystem metadata, stores file to block map, and provides a global picture of the filesystem
Secondary namenode	1	Performs internal namenode transaction log checkpointing
Datanode	Many	Stores block data (file contents)

Blocks are nothing more than chunks of a file, binary blobs of data. In HDFS, the daemon responsible for storing and retrieving block data is called the *datanode* (DN). The datanode has direct local access to one or more disks—commonly called *data disks* —in a server on which it's permitted to store block data. In production systems, these disks are usually reserved exclusively for Hadoop. Storage can be added to a cluster by adding more datanodes with additional disk capacity, or even adding disks to existing datanodes.

One of the most striking aspects of HDFS is that it is designed in such a way that it doesn't require RAID storage for its block data. This keeps with the commodity hardware design goal and reduces cost as clusters grow in size. Rather than rely on a RAID controller for data safety, block data is simply written to multiple machines. This fulfills the safety concern at the cost of raw storage consumed; however, there's a performance aspect to this as well. Having multiple copies of each block on separate machines means that not only are we protected against data loss if a machine disappears, but during processing, any copy of this data can be used. By having more than one option, the scheduler that decides where to perform processing has a better chance of being able to find a machine with available compute resources *and* a copy of the data. This is covered in greater detail in Chapter 3.

The lack of RAID can be controversial. In fact, many believe RAID simply makes disks faster, akin to a magic go-fast turbo button. This, however, is not always the case. A very large number of independently spinning disks performing huge sequential I/O operations with independent I/O queues can actually outperform RAID *in the specific use case of Hadoop workloads.* Typically, datanodes have a large number of independent disks, each of which stores full blocks. For an expanded discussion of this and related topics, see "Blades, SANs, and Virtualization" on page 52.

While datanodes are responsible for storing block data, the *namenode (NN)* is the daemon that stores the filesystem metadata and maintains a complete picture of the filesystem. Clients connect to the namenode to perform filesystem operations; although, as we'll see later, block data is streamed to and from datanodes directly, so bandwidth is not limited by a single node. Datanodes regularly report their status to the namenode in a heartbeat. This means that, at any given time, the namenode has a complete view of all datanodes in the cluster, their current health, and what blocks they have available. See Figure 2-1 for an example of HDFS architecture.

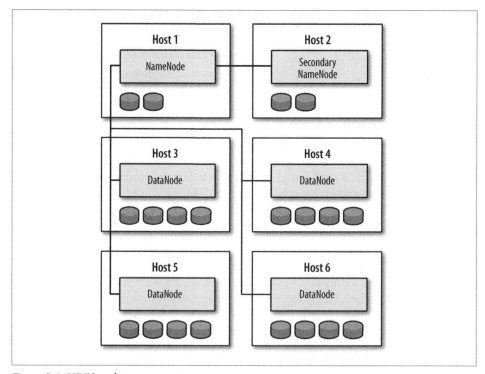

Figure 2-1. HDFS architecture overview

When a datanode initially starts up, as well as every hour thereafter, it sends what's called a *block report* to the namenode. The block report is simply a list of all blocks the datanode currently has on its disks and allows the namenode to keep track of any changes. This is also necessary because, while the file to block mapping on the namenode is stored on disk, the locations of the blocks are not written to disk. This may seem counterintuitive at first, but it means a change in IP address or hostname of any of the datanodes does not impact the underlying storage of the filesystem metadata. Another nice side effect of this is that, should a datanode experience failure of a motherboard, administrators can simply remove its hard drives, place them into a new chassis, and start up the new machine. As far as the namenode is concerned, the blocks have simply moved to a new datanode. The downside is that, when initially starting a cluster (or restarting it, for that matter), the namenode must wait to receive block reports from all datanodes to know all blocks are present.

The namenode filesystem metadata is served entirely from RAM for fast lookup and retrieval, and thus places a cap on how much metadata the namenode can handle. A rough estimate is that the metadata for 1 million blocks occupies roughly 1 GB of heap (more on this in "Hardware Selection" on page 45). We'll see later how you can overcome this limitation, even if it is encountered only at a very high scale (thousands of nodes).

Finally, the third HDFS process is called the *secondary namenode* and performs some internal housekeeping for the namenode. Despite its name, the secondary namenode is not a backup for the namenode and performs a completely different function.

 The secondary namenode may have the worst name for a process in the history of computing. It has tricked many new to Hadoop into believing that, should the evil robot apocalypse occur, their cluster will continue to function when their namenode becomes sentient and walks out of the data center. Sadly, this isn't true. We'll explore the true function of the secondary namenode in just a bit, but for now, remember what it is not; that's just as important as what it is.

Reading and Writing Data

Clients can read and write to HDFS using various tools and APIs (see "Access and Integration" on page 20), but all of them follow the same process. The client always, at some level, uses a Hadoop library that is aware of HDFS and its semantics. This library encapsulates most of the gory details related to communicating with the namenode and datanodes when necessary, as well as dealing with the numerous failure cases that can occur when working with a distributed filesystem.

The Read Path

First, let's walk through the logic of performing an HDFS read operation. For this, we'll assume there's a file */user/esammer/foo.txt* already in HDFS. In addition to using Hadoop's client library—usually a Java JAR file—each client must also have a copy of the cluster configuration data that specifies the location of the namenode (see Chapter 5). As shown in Figure 2-2, the client begins by contacting the namenode, indicating which file it would like to read. The client identity is first validated—either by trusting the client and allowing it to specify a username or by using a strong authentication mechanism such as Kerberos (see Chapter 6)—and then checked against the owner and permissions of the file. If the file exists and the user has access to it, the namenode responds to the client with the first *block ID* and the list of datanodes on which a copy of the block can be found, sorted by their distance to the client. Distance to the client is measured according to Hadoop's rack topology—configuration data that indicates which hosts are located in which racks. (More on rack topology configuration is available in "Rack Topology" on page 130.)

 If the namenode is unavailable for some reason—because of a problem with either the namenode itself or the network, for example—clients will receive timeouts or exceptions (as appropriate) and will be unable to proceed.

With the block IDs and datanode hostnames, the client can now contact the most appropriate datanode directly and read the block data it needs. This process repeats until all blocks in the file have been read or the client closes the file stream.

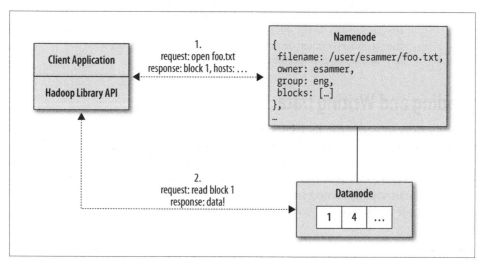

Figure 2-2. The HDFS read path

It is also possible that while reading from a datanode, the process or host on which it runs, dies. Rather than give up, the library will automatically attempt to read another replica of the data from another datanode. If all replicas are unavailable, the read operation fails and the client receives an exception. Another corner case that can occur is that the information returned by the namenode about block locations can be outdated by the time the client attempts to contact a datanode, in which case either a retry will occur if there are other replicas or the read will fail. While rare, these kinds of corner cases make troubleshooting a large distributed system such as Hadoop so complex. See Chapter 9 for a tour of what can go wrong and how to diagnose the problem.

The Write Path

Writing files to HDFS is a bit more complicated than performing reads. We'll consider the simplest case where a client is creating a new file. Remember that clients need not actually implement this logic; this is simply an overview of how data is written to the cluster by the underlying Hadoop library. Application developers use (mostly) familiar APIs to open files, write to a stream, and close them similarly to how they would with traditional local files.

Initially, a client makes a request to open a named file for write using the Hadoop FileSystem APIs. A request is sent to the namenode to create the file metadata if the user has the necessary permissions to do so. The metadata entry for the new file is made; however, it initially has no associated blocks. A response to the client indicates the open request was successful and that it may now begin writing data. At the API level, a standard Java stream object is returned, although the implementation is HDFS-specific. As the client writes data to the stream it is split into packets (not to be confused with TCP packets or HDFS blocks), which are queued in memory. A separate thread in the client consumes packets from this queue and, as necessary, contacts the namenode requesting a set of datanodes to which replicas of the next block should be written. The client then makes a direct connection to the first datanode in the list, which makes a connection to the second, which connects to the third. This forms the *replication pipeline* to be used for this block of data, as shown in Figure 2-3. Data packets are then streamed to the first datanode, which writes the data to disk, and to the next datanode in the pipeline, which writes to its disk, and so on. Each datanode in the replication pipeline acknowledges each packet as it's successfully written. The client application maintains a list of packets for which acknowledgments have not yet been received and when it receives a response, it knows the data has been written to all nodes in the pipeline. This process of writing packets to the pipeline continues until the block size is reached, at which point the client goes back to the namenode for the next set of datanodes to write to. Ultimately, the client indicates it's finished sending data by closing the stream, which flushes any remaining packets out to disk and updates the namenode to indicate the file is now complete.

Of course, things are not always this simple, and failures can occur. The most common type of failure is that a datanode in the replication pipeline fails to write data for one

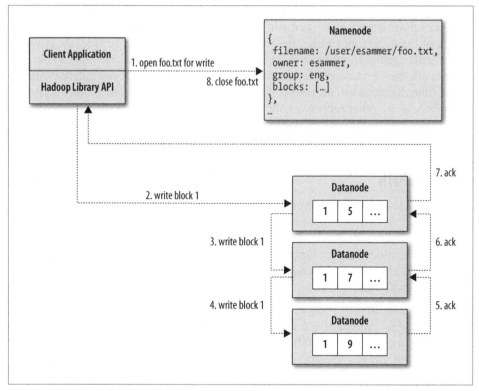

Figure 2-3. The HDFS write path

reason or another—a disk dies or a datanode fails completely, for instance. When this happens, the pipeline is immediately closed and all packets that had been sent since the last acknowledgment are pushed back into the queue to be written so that any datanodes past the failed node in the pipeline will receive the data. The current block is given a new ID on the remaining healthy datanodes. This is done so that, should the failed datanode return, the abandoned block will appear to not belong to any file and be discarded automatically. A new replication pipeline containing the remaining datanodes is opened and the write resumes. At this point, things are mostly back to normal and the write operation continues until the file is closed. The namenode will notice that one of the blocks in the file is under-replicated and will arrange for a new replica to be created asynchronously. A client can recover from multiple failed datanodes provided at least a minimum number of replicas are written (by default, this is one).

Managing Filesystem Metadata

The namenode stores its filesystem metadata on local filesystem disks in a few different files, the two most important of which are *fsimage* and *edits*. Just like a database would, *fsimage* contains a complete snapshot of the filesystem metadata whereas *edits* contains only incremental modifications made to the metadata. A common practice for high-throughput data stores, use of a *write ahead log* (WAL) such as the *edits* file reduces I/O operations to sequential, append-only operations (in the context of the namenode, since it serves directly from RAM), which avoids costly seek operations and yields better overall performance. Upon namenode startup, the *fsimage* file is loaded into RAM and any changes in the *edits* file are replayed, bringing the in-memory view of the filesystem up to date.

In more recent versions of Hadoop (specifically, Apache Hadoop 2.0 and CDH4; more on the different versions of Hadoop in "Picking a Distribution and Version of Hadoop" on page 41), the underlying metadata storage was updated to be more resilient to corruption and to support namenode high availability. Conceptually, metadata storage is similar, although transactions are no longer stored in a single *edits* file. Instead, the namenode periodically rolls the *edits* file (closes one file and opens a new file), numbering them by transaction ID. It's also possible for the namenode to now retain old copies of both *fsimage* and *edits* to better support the ability to roll back in time. Most of these changes won't impact you, although it helps to understand the purpose of the files on disk. That being said, you should never make direct changes to these files unless you *really* know what you are doing. The rest of this book will simply refer to these files using their base names, *fsimage* and *edits*, to refer generally to their function.

Recall from earlier that the namenode writes changes only to its write ahead log, *edits*. Over time, the *edits* file grows and grows and as with any log-based system such as this, would take a long time to replay in the event of server failure. Similar to a relational database, the *edits* file needs to be periodically applied to the *fsimage* file. The problem is that the namenode may not have the available resources—CPU or RAM—to do this while continuing to provide service to the cluster. This is where the *secondary namenode* comes in.

The exact interaction that occurs between the namenode and the secondary namenode (shown in Figure 2-4) is as follows:[1]

1. The secondary namenode instructs the namenode to roll its *edits* file and begin writing to *edits.new*.

2. The secondary namenode copies the namenode's *fsimage* and *edits* files to its local checkpoint directory.

3. The secondary namenode loads *fsimage*, replays *edits* on top of it, and writes a new, compacted *fsimage* file to disk.

4. The secondary namenode sends the new *fsimage* file to the namenode, which adopts it.

5. The namenode renames *edits.new* to *edits*.

---

1. This process is slightly different for Apache Hadoop 2.0 and CDH4, but it is conceptually the equivalent.

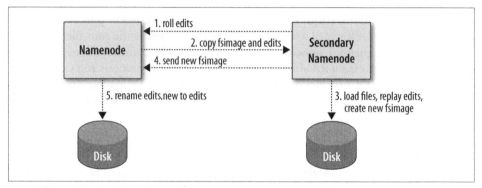

Figure 2-4. Metadata checkpoint process

This process occurs every hour (by default) *or* whenever the namenode's *edits* file reaches 64 MB (also the default). There isn't usually a good reason to modify this, although we'll explore that later. Newer versions of Hadoop use a defined number of transactions rather than file size to determine when to perform a checkpoint.

Namenode High Availability

As administrators responsible for the health and service of large-scale systems, the notion of a single point of failure should make us a bit uneasy (or worse). Unfortunately, for a long time the HDFS namenode was exactly that: a single point of failure. Recently, the Hadoop community as a whole has invested heavily in making the namenode highly available, opening Hadoop to additional mission-critical deployments.

Namenode high availability (or *HA*) is deployed as an active/passive pair of namenodes. The *edits* write ahead log needs to be available to both namenodes, and therefore is stored on a shared storage device. Currently, an NFS filer is required as the shared storage, although there are plans to remove this dependency.[2] As the active namenode writes to the *edits* log, the standby namenode is constantly replaying transactions to ensure it is up to date and ready to take over in the case of failure. Datanodes are also aware of both namenodes in an HA configuration and send block reports to both servers.

A high-availability pair of namenodes can be configured for manual or automatic failover. In the default manual failover mode, a command must be sent to effect a state transition from one namenode to the other. When configured for automatic failover, each namenode runs an additional process called a *failover controller* that monitors the health of the process and coordinates state transitions. Just as in other HA systems, there are two primary types of failover: graceful failover, initiated by an administrator, and nongraceful failover, which is the result of a detected fault in the active process. In either case, it's impossible to truly know if a namenode has relinquished active status

---

2. See Apache JIRA HDFS-3077 (*https://issues.apache.org/jira/browse/HDFS-3077*).

or if it's simply inaccessible from the standby. If both processes were allowed to continue running, they could both write to the shared state and corrupt the filesystem metadata. This is commonly called a *split brain* scenario. For this reason, the system can use a series of increasingly drastic techniques to ensure the failed node (which could still think it's active) is actually stopped. This can start with something as simple as asking it to stop via RPC, but can end with the mother of all fencing techniques: STONITH, or "shoot the other node in the head." STONITH can be implemented by issuing a reboot via IPMI (*http://www.intel.com/design/servers/ipmi/*), or even by programmatically cutting power to a machine for a short period of time if data center power distribution units (PDUs) support such functionality. Most administrators who want high availability will also want to configure automatic failover as well. See Figure 2-5 for an example of automatic failover.

When running with high availability, the standby namenode takes over the role of the secondary namenode, described earlier. In other words, there is no separate secondary namenode process in an HA cluster, only a pair of namenode processes. Those that already run Hadoop clusters that have a dedicated machine on which they run the secondary namenode process can repurpose that machine to be a second namenode in most cases. The various configuration options for high availability are covered, in detail, in "Namenode High Availability" on page 100.

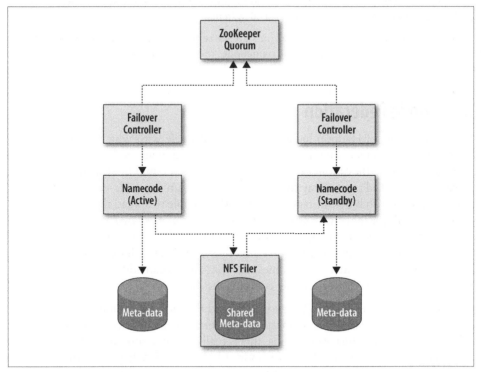

Figure 2-5. A highly available namenode pair with automatic failover

At the time of this writing, namenode high availability (sometimes abbreviated NN HA) is available in Apache Hadoop 2.0.0 and CDH4.

Why Not Use an XYZ HA Package?

Users familiar with packages such as the Linux-HA project (*http://www.linux-ha.org/wiki/Main_Page*) sometimes ask why they can't simply write some scripts and manage the HDFS namenode HA issue that way. These tools, after all, support health checks, in and out of band communication, and fencing plug-ins already. Unfortunately, HA is a tougher nut to crack than simply killing a process and starting a new one elsewhere.

The real challenge with implementing a highly available namenode stems from the fact that datanode block reports are not written to disk. In other words, even if one were to set up a namenode with one of these systems, write the proper health checks, detect a failure, initiate a state transition (failover), and activate the standby, it still wouldn't know where to find any of the blocks and wouldn't be able to service HDFS clients. Additionally, the datanodes—probably now viewing the namenode via a virtual IP (VIP)—would not realize a transition had occurred and wouldn't know to send a new block report to bring the new namenode up to speed on the state of the cluster. As we saw earlier, receiving and processing block reports from hundreds or thousands of machines is actually the part of cluster startup that takes time; on the order of tens of minutes or more. This type of interruption is still far outside of the acceptable service-level agreement for many mission-critical systems.

Systems such as Linux-HA work well for stateless services such as static content serving, but for a stateful system such as the namenode, they're insufficient.

Namenode Federation

Large-scale users of Hadoop have had another obstacle with which to contend: the limit of how much metadata the namenode can store in memory. In order to scale the namenode beyond the amount of physical memory that could be stuffed into a single server, there needed to be a way to move from a scale-up to a scale-out approach. Just like we've seen with block storage in HDFS, it's possible to spread the filesystem metadata over multiple machines. This technique is called *namespace federation* and refers to assembling one logical namespace from a number of autonomous systems. An example of a federated namespace is the Linux filesystem: many devices can be mounted at various points to form a single namespace that clients can address without concern for which underlying device actually contains the data.

Namenode federation (Figure 2-6) works around the memory limitation of the namenode by allowing the filesystem namespace to be broken up into slices and spread across multiple namenodes. Just as it sounds, this is really just like running a number of separate namenodes, each of which is responsible for a different part of the directory structure. The one major way in which namenode federation is different from running several discreet clusters is that each datanode stores blocks for multiple namenodes.

More precisely, each datanode has a *block pool* for each namespace. While blocks from different pools are stored on the same disks (there is no physical separation), they are logically exclusive. Each datanode sends heartbeats and block reports to each namenode.

Clients often do not want to have to worry about multiple namenodes, so a special client API implementation called ViewFS can be used that maps slices of the filesystem to the proper namenode. This is, conceptually, almost identical to the Linux */etc/ fstab* file, except that rather than mapping paths to physical devices, ViewFS maps paths to HDFS namenodes. For instance, we can configure ViewFS to look at namenode1 for path */logs* and namenode2 for path */hbase*. Federation also allows us to use namespace partitioning to control the availability and fault tolerance of different slices of the filesystem. In our previous example, */hbase* could be on a namenode that requires extremely high uptime while maybe */logs* is used only by batch operations in MapReduce.

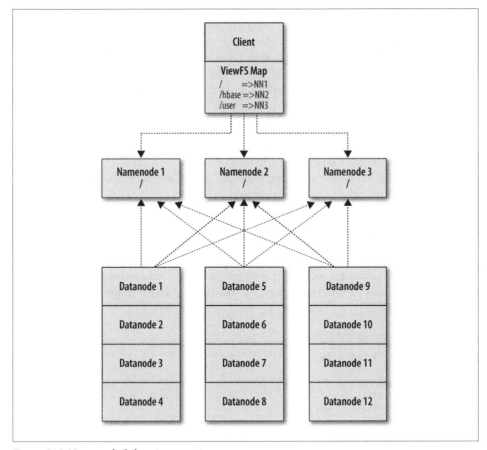

Figure 2-6. Namenode federation overview

Lastly, it's important to note that HA and federation are orthogonal features. That is, it is possible to enable them independently of each other, as they speak to two different problems. This means a namespace can be partitioned and some of those partitions (or all) may be served by an HA pair of namenodes.

Access and Integration

The sole native method of access to HDFS is its Java API. All other access methods are built on top of this API and by definition, can expose only as much functionality as it permits. In an effort to ease adoption and development of applications, the HDFS API is simple and familiar to developers, piggybacking on concepts such as Java's I/O streams. The API does differ where necessary in order to provide the features and guarantees it advertises, but most of these are obvious or documented.

In order to access HDFS, clients—applications that are written against the API—must have a copy of configuration data that tells them where the namenode is running. This is analogous to an Oracle client application requiring the *tnsnames.ora* file. Each application must also have access to the Hadoop library JAR file. Again, this is the equivalent of a database client application's dependence on a JDBC driver JAR. Clients can be on the same physical machines as any of the Hadoop daemons, or they can be separate from the cluster proper. MapReduce tasks and HBase Region Servers, for example, access HDFS as any other normal client would. They just happen to be running on the same physical machines where HDFS stores its block data.

It's important to realize that, as a consequence of the direct client to datanode communication, network access between clients and all cluster nodes' relevant ports must be unfettered. This has implications on network design, security, and bandwidth that are covered in "Network Design" on page 66.

Command-Line Tools

Hadoop comes with a number of command-line tools that enable basic filesystem operations. Like all Hadoop tools, HDFS commands are subcommands of the hadoop command-line utility. Running hadoop fs will display basic usage information, as shown in Example 2-1.

Example 2-1. hadoop fs help information

```
[esammer@hadoop01 ~]$ hadoop fs
Usage: java FsShell
           [-ls <path>]
           [-lsr <path>]
           [-df [<path>]]
           [-du <path>]
           [-dus <path>]
           [-count[-q] <path>]
           [-mv <src> <dst>]
```

```
[-cp <src> <dst>]
[-rm [-skipTrash] <path>]
[-rmr [-skipTrash] <path>]
[-expunge]
[-put <localsrc> ... <dst>]
[-copyFromLocal <localsrc> ... <dst>]
[-moveFromLocal <localsrc> ... <dst>]
[-get [-ignoreCrc] [-crc] <src> <localdst>]
[-getmerge <src> <localdst> [addnl]]
[-cat <src>]
[-text <src>]
[-copyToLocal [-ignoreCrc] [-crc] <src> <localdst>]
[-moveToLocal [-crc] <src> <localdst>]
[-mkdir <path>]
[-setrep [-R] [-w] <rep> <path/file>]
[-touchz <path>]
[-test -[ezd] <path>]
[-stat [format] <path>]
[-tail [-f] <file>]
[-chmod [-R] <MODE[,MODE]... | OCTALMODE> PATH...]
[-chown [-R] [OWNER][:[GROUP]] PATH...]
[-chgrp [-R] GROUP PATH...]
[-help [cmd]]
```

Most of these commands will be immediately obvious to an administrator with basic shell experience. The major difference is that, because HDFS is a user space filesystem, there's no concept of a current working directory. All paths are either absolute (recommended) or relative to the user's home directory *within HDFS*.[3] An absolute path can be of the form */logs/2012/01/25/*, or it can include the full URL to specify the location of the namenode, such as *hdfs://mynamenode.mycompany.com:8020/logs/2012/01/25/*. If the full URL syntax is not used, the value is taken from the `fs.default.name` parameter in the *core-site.xml* configuration file (see Example 2-2).

Example 2-2. Listing files and directories in HDFS

```
[esammer@hadoop01 ~]$ hadoop fs -ls /user/esammer
Found 4 items
drwx------   - esammer supergroup          0 2012-01-11 15:06 /user/esammer/.staging
-rw-r--r--   3 esammer supergroup   27888890 2012-01-10 13:41 /user/esammer/data.txt
drwxr-xr-x   - esammer supergroup          0 2012-01-11 13:08 /user/esammer/teragen
drwxr-xr-x   - esammer supergroup          0 2012-01-11 15:06 /user/esammer/terasort
```

To prove to ourselves that the HDFS namespace is entirely separate from the host OS, we can attempt to list the same path using the standard `ls` command (see Example 2-3).

Example 2-3. Attempting to list an HDFS path on the OS

```
esammer@hadoop01 ~]$ ls /user/esammer
ls: /user/esammer: No such file or directory
```

---

3. User home directories in HDFS are located in */user/<username>* by default.

In many ways, HDFS is more like a remote filesystem than a local OS filesystem. The act of copying files to or from HDFS is more like SCP or FTP than working with an NFS mounted filesystem, for example. Files are uploaded using either -put or the synonym -copyFromLocal and are downloaded with -get or -copyToLocal. As a convenience, the -moveFromLocal and -moveToLocal commands will copy a file from or to HDFS, respectively, and then remove the source file (see Example 2-4).

Example 2-4. Copying files to and from HDFS

```
[esammer@hadoop01 ~]$ hadoop fs -ls /user/esammer/
Found 2 items
drwx------   - esammer supergroup          0 2012-01-11 15:06 /user/esammer/.staging
-rw-r--r--   3 esammer supergroup   27888890 2012-01-10 13:41 /user/esammer/data.txt
[esammer@hadoop01 ~]$ hadoop fs -put /etc/passwd /user/esammer/
[esammer@hadoop01 ~]$ hadoop fs -ls /user/esammer/
Found 3 items
drwx------   - esammer supergroup          0 2012-01-11 15:06 /user/esammer/.staging
-rw-r--r--   3 esammer supergroup   27888890 2012-01-10 13:41 /user/esammer/data.txt
-rw-r--r--   3 esammer supergroup       2216 2012-01-25 21:07 /user/esammer/passwd
esammer@hadoop01 ~]$ ls -al passwd
ls: passwd: No such file or directory
[esammer@hadoop01 ~]$ hadoop fs -get /user/esammer/passwd ./
[esammer@hadoop01 ~]$ ls -al passwd
-rw-rw-r--+ 1 esammer esammer 2216 Jan 25 21:17 passwd
[esammer@hadoop01 ~]$ hadoop fs -rm /user/esammer/passwd
Deleted hdfs://hadoop01.sf.cloudera.com/user/esammer/passwd
```

Also unique to HDFS is the ability to set the replication factor of a file. This can be done by using the -setrep command, which takes a replication factor and an optional flag (-R) to indicate it should operate recursively (see Example 2-5).

Example 2-5. Changing the replication factor on files in HDFS

Can't change this on Argo.

```
[esammer@hadoop01 ~]$ hadoop fs -setrep 5 -R /user/esammer/tmp/
Replication 5 set: hdfs://hadoop01.sf.cloudera.com/user/esammer/tmp/a
Replication 5 set: hdfs://hadoop01.sf.cloudera.com/user/esammer/tmp/b
[esammer@hadoop01 ~]$ hadoop fsck /user/esammer/tmp -files -blocks -locations
FSCK started by esammer from /10.1.1.160 for path /user/esammer/tmp at
    Wed Jan 25 21:57:39 PST 2012
/user/esammer/tmp <dir>
/user/esammer/tmp/a 27888890 bytes, 1 block(s):  OK
0. blk_2989979708465864046_2985473 len=27888890 repl=5 [10.1.1.162:50010,
    10.1.1.161:50010, 10.1.1.163:50010, 10.1.1.165:50010, 10.1.1.164:50010]

/user/esammer/tmp/b 27888890 bytes, 1 block(s):  OK
0. blk_-771344189932970151_2985474 len=27888890 repl=5 [10.1.1.164:50010,
    10.1.1.163:50010, 10.1.1.161:50010, 10.1.1.162:50010, 10.1.1.165:50010]
```

In Example 2-5, we've changed the replication factor of files *a* and *b* in the *tmp* directory to 5. Next, the fsck, which is covered in "Checking Filesystem Integrity with fsck" on page 198, is used to inspect file health but has the nice side effect of displaying block location information for each file. Here, the five replicas of each block are spread over five different datanodes in the cluster, as expected. You may notice that only files have a block list. Directories in HDFS are purely metadata entries and have no block data.

FUSE

Filesystem In Userspace, or *FUSE (http://fuse.sourceforge.net/)*, is a system that allows developers to implement mountable filesystems in user space. That is, development of a kernel module is not required. This is not only simpler to work with because developers can use standard libraries in a familiar environment, but it is also safer because developer bugs can't necessarily cause kernel panics.

Both Apache Hadoop and CDH come with support for FUSE HDFS which, as you may have guessed, allows you to mount the Hadoop distributed filesystem as you would any other device. This allows legacy applications and systems to continue to read and write files to a regular directory on a Linux server that is backed by HDFS. While this is useful, it's not a panacea. All of the properties of HDFS are still present: no in-place modification of files, comparatively high latency, poor random access performance, optimization for large streaming operations, and huge scale. To be absolutely clear, FUSE does *not* make HDFS a POSIX-compliant filesystem. It is only a compatibility layer that can expose HDFS to applications that perform only basic file operations.

REST Support

Over the past few years, Representational State Transfer (REST) has become an increasingly popular way to interact with services in a language-agnostic way. Hadoop's native APIs are all Java-based, which presents a problem for non-Java clients. Applications have the option of shelling out and using the `hadoop fs` command, but that's inefficient and error-prone (not to mention aesthetically displeasing). Starting with Apache Hadoop 1.0.0 and CDH4, WebHDFS, a RESTful API to HDFS, is now a standard part of the software. WebHDFS makes use of the already embedded web server in each Hadoop HDFS daemon to run a set of REST APIs that mimic that of the Java `FileSystem` API, including read and write methods. Full authentication, including Kerberos SPNEGO, is supported by WebHDFS. See Example 2-6 for a sample invocation of the WebHDFS equivalent of the `hadoop fs -ls /hbase` command.

Example 2-6. Using a WebHDFS REST call to list a directory

```
[esammer@hadoop01 ~]$ curl http://hadoop01:50070/webhdfs/v1/hbase/?op=liststatus
{"FileStatuses":{"FileStatus":[
{"accessTime":0,"blockSize":0,"group":"hbase","length":0,"modificationTime":
    1342560095961,"owner":"hbase","pathSuffix":"-ROOT-","permission":"755",
    "replication":0,"type":"DIRECTORY"},
{"accessTime":0,"blockSize":0,"group":"hbase","length":0,"modificationTime":
    1342560094415,"owner":"hbase","pathSuffix":".META.","permission":"755",
    "replication":0,"type":"DIRECTORY"},
{"accessTime":0,"blockSize":0,"group":"hbase","length":0,"modificationTime":
```

```
      1342561404890,"owner":"hbase","pathSuffix":".logs","permission":"755",
      "replication":0,"type":"DIRECTORY"},
    {"accessTime":0,"blockSize":0,"group":"hbase","length":0,"modificationTime":
      1342561406399,"owner":"hbase","pathSuffix":".oldlogs","permission":"755",
      "replication":0,"type":"DIRECTORY"},
    {"accessTime":1342560093866,"blockSize":67108864,"group":"hbase","length":38,
      "modificationTime":1342560093866,"owner":"hbase","pathSuffix":"hbase.id",
      "permission":"644","replication":3,"type":"FILE"},
    {"accessTime":1342560093684,"blockSize":67108864,"group":"hbase","length":3,
      "modificationTime":1342560093684,"owner":"hbase","pathSuffix":"hbase.version",
      "permission":"644","replication":3,"type":"FILE"}
    ]}}
```

Around the same time, a standalone RESTful HDFS proxy service was created, called HttpFS. While at first glance, both WebHDFS and HttpFS solve the same problem—in fact, HttpFS is 100% API-compatible with WebHDFS—they address two separate architectual problems. By using the embedded web server in each daemon, WebHDFS clients must be able to communicate with each node of the cluster, just like native Java clients. HttpFS primarily exists to solve this problem and instead acts as a gateway service that can span network segments. Clients require only connectivity to the HttpFS daemon, which in turn performs all communication with the HDFS cluster using the standard Java APIs. The upside to HttpFS is that it minimizes the footprint required to communicate with the cluster, but at the cost of total scale and capacity because all data between clients and HDFS must now travel through a single node. Of course, it is perfectly fine to run multiple HttpFS proxies to overcome this problem. Further, because both WebHDFS and HttpFS are fully API-compatible, developers writing client applications need to concern themselves with these details. The decision can be one based exclusively on the required data throughput and network design and security requirements.

## CHAPTER 3

MapReduce

MapReduce refers to two distinct things: the programming model (covered here) and the specific implementation of the framework (covered later in "Introducing Hadoop MapReduce" on page 33). Designed to simplify the development of large-scale, distributed, fault-tolerant data processing applications, MapReduce is foremost a way of writing applications. In MapReduce, developers write *jobs* that consist primarily of a *map function* and a *reduce function*, and the framework handles the gory details of parallelizing the work, scheduling parts of the job on worker machines, monitoring for and recovering from failures, and so forth. Developers are shielded from having to implement complex and repetitive code and instead, focus on algorithms and business logic. User-provided code is invoked by the framework rather than the other way around. This is much like Java application servers that invoke servlets upon receiving an HTTP request; the container is responsible for setup and teardown as well as providing a runtime environment for user-supplied code. Similarly, as servlet authors need not implement the low-level details of socket I/O, event handling loops, and complex thread coordination, MapReduce developers program to a well-defined, simple interface and the "container" does the heavy lifting.

The idea of MapReduce was defined in a paper written by two Google engineers in 2004, titled "MapReduce: Simplified Data Processing on Large Clusters" (J. Dean, S. Ghemawat). The paper describes both the programming model and (parts of) Google's specific implementation of the framework. Hadoop MapReduce is an open source implementation of the model described in this paper and tracks the implementation closely.

Specifically developed to deal with large-scale workloads, MapReduce provides the following features:

Simplicity of development
> MapReduce is dead simple for developers: no socket programming, no threading or fancy synchronization logic, no management of retries, no special techniques to deal with enormous amounts of data. Developers use functional programming concepts to build data processing applications that operate on one record at a time.

Map functions operate on these records and produce intermediate key-value pairs. The reduce function then operates on the intermediate key-value pairs, processing all values that have the same key together and outputting the result. These primitives can be used to implement filtering, projection, grouping, aggregation, and other common data processing functions.

Scale

Since tasks do not communicate with one another explicitly and do not share state, they can execute in parallel and on separate machines. Additional machines can be added to the cluster and applications immediately take advantage of the additional hardware with no change at all. MapReduce is designed to be a *share nothing* system.

Automatic parallelization and distribution of work

Developers focus on the map and reduce functions that process individual records (where "record" is an abstract concept—it could be a line of a file or a row from a relational database) in a dataset. The storage of the dataset is not prescribed by MapReduce, although it is extremely common, as we'll see later, that files on a distributed filesystem are an excellent pairing. The framework is responsible for splitting a MapReduce job into tasks. Tasks are then executed on *worker nodes* or (less pleasantly) *slaves*.

Fault tolerance

Failure is not an exception; it's the norm. MapReduce treats failure as a first-class citizen and supports reexecution of failed tasks on healthy worker nodes in the cluster. Should a worker node fail, all tasks are assumed to be lost, in which case they are simply rescheduled elsewhere. The unit of work is always the task, and it either completes successfully or it fails completely.

In MapReduce, users write a *client application* that submits one or more *jobs* that contain user-supplied map and reduce code and a job configuration file to a cluster of machines. The job contains a *map* function and a *reduce* function, along with *job configuration* information that controls various aspects of its execution. The framework handles breaking the job into *tasks*, scheduling tasks to run on machines, monitoring each task's health, and performing any necessary retries of failed tasks. A job processes an input dataset specified by the user and usually outputs one as well. Commonly, the input and output datasets are one or more files on a distributed filesystem. This is one of the ways in which Hadoop MapReduce and HDFS work together, but we'll get into that later.

The Stages of MapReduce

A MapReduce job is made up of four distinct stages, executed in order: client job submission, map task execution, shuffle and sort, and reduce task execution. Client applications can really be any type of application the developer desires, from command-line tools to services. The MapReduce framework provides a set of APIs for submitting jobs and interacting with the cluster. The job itself is made up of code written by a developer against the MapReduce APIs and the configuration which specifies things such as the input and output datasets.

As described earlier, the client application submits a job to the cluster using the framework APIs. A master process, called the *jobtracker* in Hadoop MapReduce, is responsible for accepting these submissions (more on the role of the jobtracker later). Job submission occurs over the network, so clients may be running on one of the cluster nodes or not; it doesn't matter. The framework gets to decide how to split the input dataset into chunks, or *input splits*, of data that can be processed in parallel. In Hadoop MapReduce, the component that does this is called an *input format*, and Hadoop comes with a small library of them for common file formats. We're not going to get too deep into the APIs of input formats or even MapReduce in this book. For that, check out *Hadoop: The Definitive Guide* by Tom White (O'Reilly).

In order to better illustrate how MapReduce works, we'll use a simple application log processing example where we count all events of each severity within a window of time. If you're allergic to writing or reading code, don't worry. We'll use just enough pseudocode for you to get the idea. Let's assume we have 100 GB of logs in a directory in HDFS. A sample of log records might look something like this:

```
2012-02-13 00:23:54-0800 [INFO - com.company.app1.Main] Application started!
2012-02-13 00:32:02-0800 [WARN - com.company.app1.Main] Something hinky↵
    is going down...
2012-02-13 00:32:19-0800 [INFO - com.company.app1.Main] False alarm. No worries.
...
2012-02-13 09:00:00-0800 [DEBUG - com.company.app1.Main] coffee units remaining:zero↵
    - triggering coffee time.
2012-02-13 09:00:00-0800 [INFO - com.company.app1.Main] Good morning. It's↵
    coffee time.
```

For each input split, a *map task* is created that runs the user-supplied map function on each record in the split. Map tasks are executed in parallel. This means each chunk of the input dataset is being processed at the same time by various machines that make up the cluster. It's fine if there are more map tasks to execute than the cluster can handle. They're simply queued and executed in whatever order the framework deems best. The map function takes a *key-value pair* as input and produces zero or more intermediate key-value pairs.

The input format is responsible for turning each record into its key-value pair representation. For now, trust that one of the built-in input formats will turn each line of the file into a value with the byte offset into the file provided as the key. Getting back to our example, we want to write a map function that will filter records for those within a specific timeframe, and then count all events of each severity. The map phase is where we'll perform the filtering. We'll output the severity and the number 1 for each record that we see with that severity.

```
function map(key, value) {
    // Example key: 12345 - the byte offset in the file (not really interesting).
```

```
// Example value: 2012-02-13 00:23:54-0800 [INFO - com.company.app1.Main]↵
//   Application started!

// Do the nasty record parsing to get dateTime, severity,
// className, and message.
(dateTime, severity, className, message) = parseRecord(value);

// If the date is today...
if (dateTime.date() == '2012-02-13') {
  // Emit the severity and the number 1 to say we saw one of these records.
  emit(severity, 1);
}
}
```

Notice how we used an if statement to filter the data by date so that we got only the records we wanted. It's just as easy to output multiple records in a loop. A map function can do just about whatever it wants with each record. Reducers, as we'll see later, operate on the intermediate key-value data we output from the mapper.

Given the sample records earlier, our intermediate data would look as follows:

```
DEBUG, 1
INFO, 1
INFO, 1
INFO, 1
WARN, 1
```

A few interesting things are happening here. First, we see that the key INFO repeats, which makes sense because our sample contained three INFO records that would have matched the date 2012-02-13. It's perfectly legal to output the same key or value multiple times. The other notable effect is that the output records are not in the order we would expect. In the original data, the first record was an INFO record, followed by WARN, but that's clearly not the case here. This is because the framework sorts the output of each map task by its key. Just like outputting the value 1 for each record, the rationale behind sorting the data will become clear in a moment.

Further, each key is assigned to a *partition* using a component called the *partitioner*. In Hadoop MapReduce, the default partitioner implementation is a hash partitioner that takes a hash of the key, modulo the number of configured reducers in the job, to get a partition number. Because the hash implementation used by Hadoop ensures the hash of the key INFO is always the same on all machines, all INFO records are guaranteed to be placed in the same partition. The intermediate data isn't physically partitioned, only logically so. For all intents and purposes, you can picture a partition number next to each record; it would be the same for all records with the same key. See Figure 3-1 for a high-level overview of the execution of the map phase.

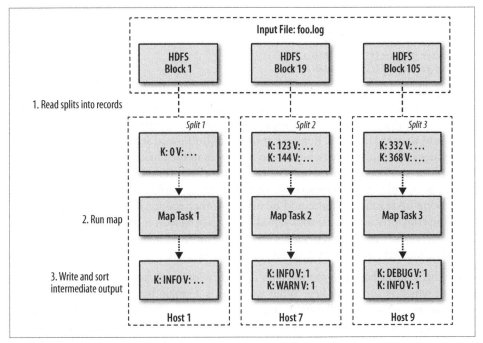

Figure 3-1. Map execution phase

Ultimately, we want to run the user's reduce function on the intermediate output data. A number of guarantees, however, are made to the developer with respect to the reducers that need to be fulfilled.

- If a reducer sees a key, it will see all values for that key. For example, if a reducer receives the INFO key, it will always receive the three number 1 values.
- A key will be processed by exactly one reducer. This makes sense given the preceding requirement.
- Each reducer will see keys in sorted order.

The next phase of processing, called the *shuffle and sort*, is responsible for enforcing these guarantees. The shuffle and sort phase is actually performed by the reduce tasks before they run the user's reduce function. When started, each reducer is assigned one of the partitions on which it should work. First, they copy the intermediate key-value data from each worker for their assigned partition. It's possible that tens of thousands of map tasks have run on various machines throughout the cluster, each having output key-value pairs for each partition. The reducer assigned partition 1, for example, would need to fetch each piece of its partition data from potentially every other worker in the cluster. A logical view of the intermediate data across all machines in the cluster might look like this:

```
worker 1, partition 2, DEBUG, 1
worker 1, partition 1, INFO, 1
worker 2, partition 1, INFO, 1
worker 2, partition 1, INFO 1
worker 3, partition 2, WARN, 1
```

Copying the intermediate data across the network can take a fair amount of time, depending on how much data there is. To minimize the total runtime of the job, the framework is permitted to begin copying intermediate data from completed map tasks as soon as they are finished. Remember that the shuffle and sort is being performed by the reduce tasks, each of which takes up resources in the cluster. We want to start the copy phase soon enough that most of the intermediate data is copied before the final map task completes, but not so soon that the data is copied leaving the reduce tasks idly taking up resources that could be used by other reduce tasks. Knowing when to start the copy process can be tricky, and it's largely based on the available bandwidth of the network. See `mapred.reduce.slowstart.completed.maps` on page 129 for information about how to configure when the copy is started.

Once the reducer has received its data, it is left with many small bits of its partition, each of which is sorted by key. What we want is a single list of key-value pairs, still sorted by key, so we have all values for each key together. The easiest way to accomplish this is by performing a *merge sort* of the data. A merge sort takes a number of sorted items and merges them together to form a fully sorted list using a minimal amount of memory. With the partition data now combined into a complete sorted list, the user's reducer code can now be executed:

```
# Logical data input to the reducer assigned partition 1:
INFO, [ 1, 1, 1 ]

# Logical data input to the reducer assigned partition 2:
DEBUG, [ 1 ]
WARN, [ 1 ]
```

The reducer code in our example is hopefully clear at this point:

```
function reduce(key, iterator<values>) {
  // Initialize a total event count.
  totalEvents = 0;

  // For each value (a number one)...
  foreach (value in values) {
    // Add the number one to the total.
    totalEvents += value;
  }

  // Emit the severity (the key) and the total events we saw.
  // Example key: INFO
  // Example value: 3
  emit(key, totalEvents);
}
```

Each reducer produces a separate output file, usually in HDFS (see Figure 3-2). Separate files are written so that reducers do not have to coordinate access to a shared file. This greatly reduces complexity and lets each reducer run at whatever speed it can. The format of the file depends on the _output format_ specified by the author of the MapReduce job in the job configuration. Unless the job does something special (and most don't) each reducer output file is named _part-<XXXXX>_, where _<XXXXX>_ is the number of the reduce task within the job, starting from zero. Sample reducer output for our example job would look as follows:

```
# Reducer for partition 1:
INFO, 3

# Reducer for partition 2:
DEBUG, 1
WARN, 1
```

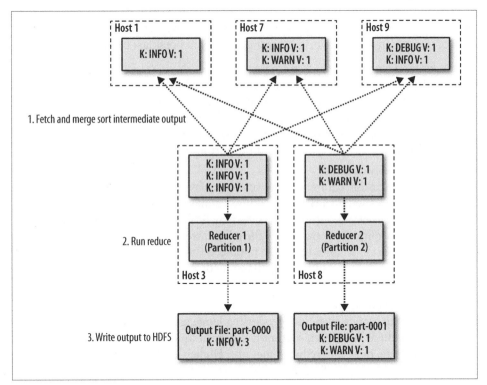

Figure 3-2. _Shuffle and sort, and reduce phases_

For those that are familiar with SQL and relational databases, we could view the logs as a table with the schema:

```
CREATE TABLE logs (
  EVENT_DATE DATE,
  SEVERITY  VARCHAR(8),
```

```
       SOURCE    VARCHAR(128),
       MESSAGE   VARCHAR(1024)
    )
```

We would, of course, have to parse the data to get it into a table with this schema, but that's beside the point. (In fact, the ability to deal with semi-structured data as well as act as a data processing engine are two of Hadoop's biggest benefits.) To produce the same output, we would use the following SQL statement. In the interest of readability, we're ignoring the fact that this doesn't yield identically formatted output; the data is the same.

```
SELECT SEVERITY,COUNT(*)
  FROM logs GROUP BY SEVERITY
  WHERE EVENT_DATE = '2012-02-13'
  GROUP BY SEVERITY
  ORDER BY SEVERITY
```

As exciting as all of this is, MapReduce is not a silver bullet. It is just as important to know how MapReduce works and what it's good for, as it is to understand why Map-Reduce is not going to end world hunger or serve you breakfast in bed.

MapReduce is a batch data processing system

The design of MapReduce assumes that jobs will run on the order of minutes, if not hours. It is optimized for full table scan style operations. Consequently, it underwhelms when attempting to mimic low-latency, random access patterns found in traditional online transaction processing (OLTP) systems. MapReduce is not a relational database killer, nor does it purport to be.

MapReduce is overly simplistic

One of its greatest features is also one of its biggest drawbacks: MapReduce is simple. In cases where a developer knows something special about the data and wants to make certain optimizations, he may find the model limiting. This usually manifests as complaints that, while the job is faster in terms of wall clock time, it's far less efficient in MapReduce than in other systems. This can be very true. Some have said MapReduce is like a sledgehammer driving a nail; in some cases, it's more like a wrecking ball.

MapReduce is too low-level

Compared to higher-level data processing languages (notably SQL), MapReduce seems extremely low-level. Certainly for basic query-like functionality, no one wants to write, map, and reduce functions. Higher-level languages built atop Map-Reduce exist to simplify life, and unless you truly need the ability to touch terabytes (or more) of raw data, it can be overkill.

Not all algorithms can be parallelized

There are entire classes of problems that cannot easily be parallelized. The act of training a model in machine learning, for instance, cannot be parallelized for many types of models. This is true for many algorithms where there is shared state or dependent variables that must be maintained and updated centrally. Sometimes it's possible to structure problems that are traditionally solved using shared state differently such that they can be fit into the MapReduce model, but at the cost of efficiency (shortest path-finding algorithms in graph processing are excellent examples of this). Other times, while this is possible, it may not be ideal for a host of reasons. Knowing how to identify these kinds of problems and create alternative solutions is far beyond the scope of this book and an art in its own right. This is the same problem as the "mythical man month," but is most succinctly expressed by stating, "If one woman can have a baby in nine months, nine women should be able to have a baby in one month," which, in case it wasn't clear, is decidedly false.

Introducing Hadoop MapReduce

Hadoop MapReduce is a specific implementation of the MapReduce programming model, and the computation component of the Apache Hadoop project. The combination of HDFS and MapReduce is incredibly powerful, in much the same way that Google's GFS and MapReduce complement each other. Hadoop MapReduce is inherently aware of HDFS and can use the namenode during the scheduling of tasks to decide the best placement of map tasks with respect to machines where there is a local copy of the data. This avoids a significant amount of network overhead during processing, as workers do not need to copy data over the network to access it, and it removes one of the primary bottlenecks when processing huge amounts of data.

Hadoop MapReduce is similar to traditional distributed computing systems in that there is a framework and there is the user's application or job. A master node coordinates cluster resources while workers simply do what they're told, which in this case is to run a map or reduce task on behalf of a user. Client applications written against the Hadoop APIs can submit jobs either synchronously and block for the result, or asynchronously and poll the master for job status. Cluster daemons are long-lived while user tasks are executed in ephemeral child processes. Although executing a separate process incurs the overhead of launching a separate JVM, it isolates the framework from untrusted user code that could—and in many cases does—fail in destructive ways. Since MapReduce is specifically targeting batch processing tasks, the additional overhead, while undesirable, is not necessarily a showstopper.

One of the ingredients in the secret sauce of MapReduce is the notion of *data locality*, by which we mean the ability to execute computation on the same machine where the data being processed is stored. Many traditional high-performance computing (HPC) systems have a similar master/worker model, but computation is generally distinct from data storage. In the classic HPC model, data is usually stored on a large shared centralized storage system such as a SAN or NAS. When a job executes, workers fetch the data from the central storage system, process it, and write the result back to the storage device. The problem is that this can lead to a storm effect when there are a large number of workers attempting to fetch the same data at the same time and, for large datasets, quickly causes bandwidth contention. MapReduce flips this model on its head. Instead of using a central storage system, a distributed filesystem is used where each worker is usually[1] both a storage node as well as a compute node. Blocks that make up files are distributed to nodes when they are initially written and when computation is performed, the user-supplied code is executed on the machine where the block can be pushed to the machine where the block is stored locally. Remember that HDFS stores multiple replicas of each block. This is not just for data availability in the face of failures, but also to increase the chance that a machine with a copy of the data has available capacity to run a task.

Daemons

There are two major daemons in Hadoop MapReduce: the *jobtracker* and the *tasktracker*.

Jobtracker

The jobtracker is the master process, responsible for accepting job submissions from clients, scheduling tasks to run on worker nodes, and providing administrative functions such as worker health and task progress monitoring to the cluster. There is one jobtracker per MapReduce cluster and it usually runs on reliable hardware since a failure of the master will result in the failure of all running jobs. Clients and tasktrackers (see "Tasktracker" on page 35) communicate with the jobtracker by way of remote procedure calls (RPC).

Just like the relationship between datanodes and the namenode in HDFS, tasktrackers inform the jobtracker as to their current health and status by way of regular heartbeats. Each heartbeat contains the total number of map and reduce *task slots* available (see "Tasktracker" on page 35), the number occupied, and detailed information about any currently executing tasks. After a configurable period of no heartbeats, a tasktracker is assumed dead. The jobtracker uses a thread pool to process heartbeats and client requests in parallel.

When a job is submitted, information about each task that makes up the job is stored in memory. This task information updates with each tasktracker heartbeat while the tasks are running, providing a near real-time view of task progress and health. After the job completes, this information is retained for a configurable window of time or until a specified number of jobs have been executed. On an active cluster where many jobs, each with many tasks, are running, this information can consume a considerable amount of RAM. It's difficult to estimate memory consumption without knowing how big each job will be (measured by the number of tasks it contains) or how many jobs

---

1. While it's possible to separate them, this rarely makes sense because you lose the data locality features of Hadoop MapReduce. Those that wish to run *only* Apache HBase, on the other hand, very commonly run just the HDFS daemons along with their HBase counterparts.

will run within a given timeframe. For this reason, monitoring jobtracker memory utilization is absolutely critical.

The jobtracker provides an administrative web interface that, while a charming flashback to web (anti-)design circa 1995, is incredibly information-rich and useful. As tasktrackers all must report in to the jobtracker, a complete view of the available cluster resources is available via the administrative interface. Each job that is submitted has a job-level view that offers links to the job's configuration, as well as data about progress, the number of tasks, various metrics, and task-level logs. If you are to be responsible for a production Hadoop cluster, you will find yourself checking this interface constantly throughout the day.

The act of deciding which tasks of a job should be executed on which worker nodes is referred to as *task scheduling*. This is not scheduling in the way that the cron daemon executes jobs at given times, but instead is more like the way the OS kernel schedules process CPU time. Much like CPU time sharing, tasks in a MapReduce cluster share worker node resources, or space, but instead of context switching—that is, pausing the execution of a task to give another task time to run—when a task executes, it executes completely. Understanding task scheduling—and by extension, resource allocation and sharing—is so important that an entire chapter (Chapter 7) is dedicated to the subject.

Tasktracker

The second daemon, the tasktracker, accepts task assignments from the jobtracker, instantiates the user code, executes those tasks locally, and reports progress back to the jobtracker periodically. There is always a single tasktracker on each worker node. Both tasktrackers and datanodes run on the same machines, which makes each node both a compute node and a storage node, respectively. Each tasktracker is configured with a specific number of map and reduce *task slots* that indicate how many of each type of task it is capable of executing in parallel. A task slot is exactly what it sounds like; it is an allocation of available resources on a worker node to which a task may be assigned, in which case it is executed. A tasktracker executes some number of map tasks and reduce tasks in parallel, so there is concurrency both within a worker where many tasks run, and at the cluster level where many workers exist. Map and reduce slots are configured separately because they consume resources differently. It is common that tasktrackers allow more map tasks than reduce tasks to execute in parallel for reasons described in "MapReduce" on page 120. You may have picked up on the idea that deciding the number of map and reduce task slots is extremely important to making full use of the worker node hardware, and you would be correct.

Upon receiving a task assignment from the jobtracker, the tasktracker executes an *attempt* of the task in a separate process. The distinction between a task and a task attempt is important: a task is the logical unit of work, while a task attempt is a specific, physical instance of that task being executed. Since an attempt may fail, it is possible that a task has multiple attempts, although it's common for tasks to succeed on their first attempt when everything is in proper working order. As this implies, each task in a job will always have at least one attempt, assuming the job wasn't administratively killed. Communication between the task attempt (usually called the *child*, or *child process*) and the tasktracker is maintained via an RPC connection over the loopback interface called the *umbilical protocol*. The task attempt itself is a small application that acts as the container in which the user's map or reduce code executes. As soon as the task completes, the child exits and the slot becomes available for assignment.

The tasktracker uses a list of user-specified directories (each of which is assumed to be on a separate physical device) to hold the intermediate map output and reducer input during job execution. This is required because this data is usually too large to fit exclusively in memory for large jobs or when many jobs are running in parallel.

Tasktrackers, like the jobtracker, also have an embedded web server and user interface. It's rare, however, that administrators access this interface directly since it's unusual to know the machine you need to look at without first referencing the jobtracker interface, which already provides links to the tasktracker interface for the necessary information.

When It All Goes Wrong

Rather than panic when things go wrong, MapReduce is designed to treat failures as common and has very well-defined semantics for dealing with the inevitable. With tens, hundreds, or even thousands of machines making up a Hadoop cluster, machines—and especially hard disks—fail at a significant rate. It's not uncommon to find that approximately 2% to 5% of the nodes in a large Hadoop cluster have some kind of fault, meaning they are operating either suboptimally or simply not at all. In addition to faulty servers, there can sometimes be errant user MapReduce jobs, network failures, and even errors in the data.

Child task failures

It's common for child tasks to fail for a variety of reasons: incorrect or poorly implemented user code, unexpected data problems, temporary machine failures, and administrative intervention are a few of the more common causes. A child task is considered to be failed when one of three things happens:

- It throws an uncaught exception.
- It exits with a nonzero exit code.
- It fails to report progress to the tasktracker for a configurable amount of time.

When a failure is detected by the tasktracker, it is reported to the jobtracker in the next heartbeat. The jobtracker, in turn, notes the failure and if additional attempts are permitted (the default limit is four attempts), reschedules the task to run. The task may be run either on the same machine or on another machine in the cluster, depending on available capacity. Should multiple tasks from the *same job* fail on the same tasktracker repeatedly, the tasktracker is added to a job-level blacklist that prevents any other tasks from the same job from executing on the tasktracker in question. If multiple tasks from *different jobs* repeatedly fail on a specific tasktracker, the tasktracker in question is added to a global blacklist for 24 hours, which prevents any tasks from being scheduled on that tasktracker.

Tasktracker/worker node failures

The next obvious failure condition is the loss of the tasktracker daemon or the entire worker node. The jobtracker, after a configurable amount of time with no heartbeats, will consider the tasktracker dead along with any tasks it was assigned. Tasks are rescheduled and will execute on another tasktracker; the client application is completely shielded from the internal failure and as far as it's concerned, the job appears to simply slow down for some time while tasks are retried.

Jobtracker failures

The loss of the jobtracker is more severe in Hadoop MapReduce. Should the jobtracker (meaning either the process or the machine on which it runs) fail, its internal state about currently executing jobs is lost. Even if it immediately recovers, all running tasks will eventually fail. This effectively means the jobtracker is a single point of failure (SPOF) for the MapReduce layer—a current limitation of Hadoop MapReduce.

HDFS failures

For jobs whose input or output dataset is on HDFS, it's possible that HDFS could experience a failure. This is the equivalent of the filesystem used by a relational database experiencing a failure while the database is running. In other words, it's bad. If a datanode process fails, any task that is currently reading from or writing to it will follow the HDFS error handling described in Chapter 2. Unless all datanodes containing a block fail during a read, or the namenode cannot find any datanodes on which to place a block during a write, this is a recoverable case and the task will complete. When the namenode fails, tasks will fail the next time they try to make contact with it. The framework will retry these tasks, but if the namenode doesn't return, all attempts will be exhausted and the job will eventually fail. Additionally, if the namenode isn't available, new jobs cannot be submitted to the cluster since job artifacts (such as the JAR file containing the user's code) cannot be written to HDFS, nor can input splits be calculated.

YARN

Hadoop MapReduce is not without its flaws. The team at Yahoo! ran into a number of scalability limitations that were difficult to overcome given Hadoop's existing architecture and design. In large-scale deployments such as Yahoo!'s "Hammer" cluster—a single, 4,000-plus node Hadoop cluster that powers various systems—the team found that the resource requirements on a single jobtracker were just too great. Further, operational issues such as dealing with upgrades and the single point of failure of the jobtracker were painful. *YARN* (or "Yet Another Resource Negotiator") was created to address these issues.

Rather than have a single daemon that tracks and assigns resources such as CPU and memory and handles MapReduce-specific job tracking, these functions are separated into two parts. The resource management aspect of the jobtracker is run as a new daemon called the *resource manager*,; a separate daemon responsible for creating and allocating resources to multiple *applications*. Each application is an individual MapReduce job, but rather than have a single jobtracker, each job now has its own jobtracker-equivalent called an *application master* that runs on one of the workers of the cluster. This is very different from having a centralized jobtracker in that the application master of one job is now completely isolated from that of any other. This means that if some catastrophic failure were to occur within the jobtracker, other jobs are unaffected. Further, because the jobtracker is now dedicated to a specific job, multiple jobtrackers can be running on the cluster at once. Taken one step further, each jobtracker can be a different version of the software, which enables simple rolling upgrades and multiversion support. When an application completes, its application master, such as the jobtracker, and other resources are returned to the cluster. As a result, there's no central jobtracker daemon in YARN.

Worker nodes in YARN also run a new daemon called the *node manager* in place of the traditional tasktracker. While the tasktracker expressly handled MapReduce-specific functionality such as launching and managing tasks, the node manager is more generic. Instead, the node manager launches any type of process, dictated by the application, in an *application container*. For instance, in the case of a MapReduce application, the node manager manages both the application master (the jobtracker) as well as individual map and reduce tasks.

With the ability to run arbitrary applications, each with its own application master, it's even possible to write non-MapReduce applications that run on YARN. Not entirely an accident, YARN provides a compute-model-agnostic resource management framework for any type of distributed computing framework. Members of the Hadoop community have already started to look at alternative processing systems that can be built on top of YARN for specific problem domains such as graph processing and more traditional HPC systems such as MPI.

The flexibility of YARN is enticing, but it's still a new system. At the time of this writing, YARN is still considered alpha-level software and is not intended for production use. Initially introduced in the Apache Hadoop 2.0 branch, YARN hasn't yet been battle-tested in large clusters. Unfortunately, while the Apache Hadoop 2.0 lineage includes highly desirable HDFS features such as high availability, the old-style jobtracker and tasktracker daemons (now referred to as MapReduce version one, or MRv1) have been removed in favor of YARN. This creates a potential conflict for Apache Hadoop users that want these features with the tried and true MRv1 daemons. CDH4, however, includes the HDFS features as well as both MRv1 and YARN. For more information on Hadoop distributions, versions, and features, see "Picking a Distribution and Version of Hadoop" on page 41. Since YARN is not yet stable, and the goal of this book is to provide pragmatic operational advice, the remainder of the content will focus exclusively on the MRv1 daemons and their configuration.

## CHAPTER 4

Planning a Hadoop Cluster

Picking a Distribution and Version of Hadoop

One of the first tasks to take on when planning an Hadoop deployment is selecting the distribution and version of Hadoop that is most appropriate given the features and stability required. This process requires input from those that will eventually use the cluster: developers, analysts, and possibly other systems such as business intelligence applications. This isn't dissimilar from selecting a relational database based on what is required by downstream applications. For instance, some relational databases support extensions to SQL for advanced analytics, while other support features such as table partitioning in order to scale large tables or improve query performance.

Hadoop is, as previously mentioned, an Apache Software Foundation (ASF) project. This means it's available directly from Apache in both source and binary formats. It's extremely common though for people to use more than just core Hadoop. While Hadoop is absolutely critical—after all, it provides not just the distributed file-system, but also the MapReduce processing framework—many users view it as the core of a larger system. In this sense, Hadoop is analogous to an operating system kernel, giving us the core functionality upon which we build higher-level systems and tools. Many of these related libraries, tools, languages, and systems are also open source projects available from the ASF.

There is an inherent complexity in assembling these projects or components into a cohesive system. Because Hadoop is a distributed system, tools and libraries that access it must be wire- and API-compatible. Going back to the relational database analogy, this isn't a new set of problems, but it's something of which administrators must be aware during the planning and deployment phases.

Apache Hadoop

The Apache Software Foundation is where all Apache Hadoop development happens. Administrators can download Hadoop directly from the project website at *http://ha doop.apache.org*. Historically, Apache Hadoop has produced infrequent releases, although starting with version 1.0, this has changed, with releases coming more frequently. All code produced by the ASF is Apache-licensed.

Apache Hadoop is distributed as tarballs containing both source and binary artifacts. Starting around version 1.0, support for building RPM and Debian packages was added to the build system, and later releases provide these artifacts for download.

Cloudera's Distribution Including Apache Hadoop

Cloudera, a company that provides support, consulting, and management tools for Hadoop, also has a distribution of software called Cloudera's Distribution Including Apache Hadoop, or just CDH. Just as with the ASF version, this is 100% open source software available under the Apache Software License and is free for both personal and commercial use. Just as many open source software companies do for other systems, Cloudera starts with a stable Apache Hadoop release, puts it on a steady release cadence, backports critical fixes, provides packages for a number of different operating systems, and has a commercial-grade QA and testing process. Cloudera employs many of the Apache Hadoop committers (the people who have privileges to commit code to the Apache source repositories) who work on Hadoop full-time.

Since many users deploy many of the projects related to Apache Hadoop, Cloudera includes these projects in CDH as well and guarantees compatibility between components. CDH currently includes Apache Hadoop, Apache HBase, Apache Hive, Apache Pig, Apache Sqoop, Apache Flume, Apache ZooKeeper, Apache Oozie, Apache Mahout, and Hue. A complete list of components included in CDH is available at *http://www.cloudera.com/hadoop-details/*.

Major versions of CDH are released yearly with patches released quarterly. At the time of this writing, the most recent major release of CDH is CDH4, which is based on Apache Hadoop 2.0.0. It includes the major HDFS improvements such as namenode high availability, as well as also a forward port of the battle-tested MRv1 daemons (in addition to the alpha version of YARN) so as to be production-ready.

CDH is available as tarballs, RedHat Enterprise Linux 5 and 6 RPMs, SuSE Enterprise Linux RPMs, and Debian Deb packages. Additionally, Yum, Zypper, and Apt repositories are provided for their respective systems to ease installation.

Versions and Features

Hadoop has seen significant interest over the past few years. This has led to a proportional uptick in features and bug fixes. Some of these features were so significant or had such a sweeping impact that they were developed on branches. As you might expect, this in turn led to a somewhat dizzying array of releases and parallel lines of development.

Here is a whirlwind tour of the various lines of development and their status. This information is also depicted visually in Figure 4-1.

0.20.0–0.20.2

The 0.20 branch of Hadoop is extremely stable and has seen quite a bit of production burn-in. This branch has been one of the longest-lived branches in Hadoop's history since being at Apache, with the first release appearing in April 2009. CDH2 and CDH3 are both based off of this branch, albeit with many features and bug fixes from 0.21, 0.22, and 1.0 back-ported.

0.20-append

One of the features missing from 0.20 was support for file appends in HDFS. Apache HBase relies on the ability to sync its write ahead log, (such as force file contents to disk) which under the hood, uses the same basic functionality as file append. Append was considered a potentially destabilizing feature and many disagreed on the implementation, so it was relegated to a branch. This branch was called 0.20-append. No official release was ever made from the 0.20-append branch.

0.20-security

Yahoo!, one of the major contributors to Apache Hadoop, invested in adding full Kerberos support to core Hadoop. It later contributed this work back to Hadoop in the form of the 0.20-security branch, a version of Hadoop 0.20 with Kerberos authentication support. This branch would later be released as the 0.20.20X releases.

0.20.203–0.20.205

There was a strong desire within the community to produce an official release of Hadoop that included the 0.20-security work. The 0.20.20X releases contained not only security features from 0.20-security, but also bug fixes and improvements on the 0.20 line of development. Generally, it no longer makes sense to deploy these releases as they're superseded by 1.0.0.

0.21.0

The 0.21 branch was cut from Hadoop trunk and released in August 2010. This was considered a developer preview or alpha quality release to highlight some of the features that were currently in development at the time. Despite the warning from the Hadoop developers, a small number of users deployed the 0.21 release anyway. This release does not include security, but does have append.

0.22.0

Hold on, because this is where the story gets weird. In December 2011, the Hadoop community released version 0.22, which was based on trunk, like 0.21 was. This release includes security, but only for HDFS. Also a bit strange, 0.22 was released after 0.23 with less functionality. This was due to when the 0.22 branch was cut from trunk.

0.23.0

In November 2011, version 0.23 of Hadoop was released. Also cut from trunk, 0.23 includes security, append, YARN, and HDFS federation. This release has been dubbed a developer preview or alpha-quality release. This line of development is superseded by 2.0.0.

1.0.0

In a continuing theme of confusion, version 1.0.0 of Hadoop was released from the 0.20.205 line of development. This means that 1.0.0 does not contain all of the features and fixes found in the 0.21, 0.22, and 0.23 releases. That said, it does include security.

2.0.0

In May 2012, version 2.0.0 was released from the 0.23.0 branch and like 0.23.0, is considered alpha-quality. Mainly, this is because it includes YARN and removes the traditional MRv1 jobtracker and tasktracker daemons. While YARN is API-compatible with MRv1, the underlying implementation is different enough for it to require more significant testing before being considered production-ready.

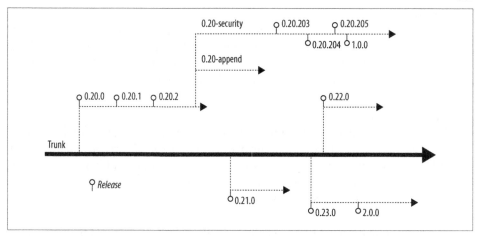

Figure 4-1. Hadoop branches and releases

What Should I Use?

The version of Hadoop you select for deployment will ultimately be driven by the feature set you require for your applications. For many, only the releases targeted for production use are an option. This narrows the field to the 0.20, 1.0, and CDH releases almost immediately. Users who want to run HBase will also require append support.

Feature	0.20	0.21	0.22	0.23	1.0	2.0	CDH 3	CDH 4
Production quality	X				X		X	X
HDFS append		X	X	X	X	X	X	X
Kerberos security		X[a]	X	X	X	X	X	X
HDFS symlinks		X	X	X		X		X
YARN (MRv2)				X		X		X
MRv1 daemons[b]	X	X	X		X		X	X
Namenode federation				X		X		X
Namenode HA				X		X		X

a. Support for Kerberos-enabled HDFS only.
b. All versions include support for the MRv1 APIs.

Hardware Selection

When planning an Hadoop cluster, picking the right hardware is critical. No one likes the idea of buying 10, 50, or 500 machines just to find out she needs more RAM or disk. Hadoop is not unlike traditional data storage or processing systems in that the proper ratio of CPU to memory to disk is heavily influenced by the workload. There are, of course, some guidelines and a reasonable base configuration, but some knowledge of the intended workload will greatly increase the likelihood of optimum utilization of the hardware.

As you probably already know, one of the major advantages of Hadoop is its ability to run on so-called *commodity hardware*. This isn't just a function of cost, although that certainly plays a large role. One example of this is Hadoop's preference for JBOD[1] and how its I/O patterns fit this model explicitly. This isn't to say production Hadoop clusters commonly run on $1,000 machines—your expectations of what is meant by commodity may need adjustment—but rather that you won't need to break the bank by purchasing top-end servers.

Hadoop hardware comes in two distinct classes: masters and workers. Master nodes are typically more robust to hardware failure and run critical cluster services. Loss of a master almost certainly means some kind of service disruption. On the other hand, worker nodes are expected to fail regularly. This directly impacts the type of hardware as well as the amount of money spent on these two classes of hardware. It is common that administrators, in an effort to reduce the proliferation of hardware profiles in the data center, will select a single hardware profile for all masters and a single profile for all workers. Those with deep pockets may find it even easier to purchase a single

1. Just a bunch of disks; a disk configuration where individual disks are accessed directly by the operating system without the need for RAID.

Hadoop node profile and simply ignore wasted disk on the masters, for example. There's no single correct answer. Factors such as hardware availability, corporate standards, cost, utilization standards, and deployment profile are beyond the scope of this book. That being said, exercise good judgment and common sense and realize that strict adherence to existing standards may negate many of the benefits of Hadoop.

 The distinction between a node and the service assigned to said node is important. When talking about machines, there are masters and workers. These designations reflect the class of hardware. Separately, there are the five core Hadoop services: namenode, secondary namenode, datanode, jobtracker, and tasktracker, each a separate daemon. Services are run on nodes of the cluster. Worker services such as the datanode and tasktracker always run together. In smaller clusters, it sometimes makes sense to run the master services—the namenode, secondary namenode, and jobtracker—together. As the cluster grows, these services are separated and dedicated hardware for each is provisioned. When you hear "master," the next question is always "what process?" "Slave," or "worker," will always mean the datanode and tasktracker pair.

Master Hardware Selection

For master nodes—the machines that run one or more of the namenode, jobtracker, and secondary namenode—redundancy is the name of the game. Each of these machines serves a critical function the cluster can't live without.[2] While proponents of Hadoop beat the commodity hardware drum, this is the place where people spend more money and spring for the higher-end features. Dual power supplies, bonded network interface cards (NICs), and sometimes even RAID 10 in the case of the namenode storage device, are not uncommon to find in the wild. In general, master processes tend to be RAM-hungry but low on disk space consumption. The namenode and jobtracker are also rather adept at producing logs on an active cluster, so plenty of space should be reserved on the disk or partition on which logs will be stored.

The operating system device for master nodes should be highly available. This usually means RAID-1 (a mirrored pair of disks). Since the OS does not consume a significant amount of space, RAID-10 or RAID-5 would be overkill and lead to unusable capacity. Most of the real work is done on the data devices, while the OS device usually only has to contend with logfiles in */var/log*.

Small clusters—clusters with fewer than 20 worker nodes—do not require much for master nodes in terms of hardware. A solid baseline hardware profile for a cluster of this size is a dual quad-core 2.6 Ghz CPU, 24 GB of DDR3 RAM, dual 1 Gb Ethernet NICs, a SAS drive controller, and at least two SATA II drives in a JBOD configuration

2. ...or at least not for long.

in addition to the host OS device. Clusters of up to 300 nodes fall into the mid-size category and usually benefit from an additional 24 GB of RAM for a total of 48 GB. Master nodes in large clusters should have a total of 96 GB of RAM. Remember that these are baseline numbers meant to give you a place from which to start.

Namenode considerations

The namenode is absolutely critical to a Hadoop cluster and usually receives special treatment. There are three things a healthy namenode absolutely requires in order to function properly: RAM, modest but dedicated disk, and to be left alone! As we covered previously, the namenode serves all of its metadata directly from RAM. This has the obvious implication that all metadata must fit in physical memory. The exact amount of RAM required depends on how much metadata there is to maintain. Remember that the metadata contains the filename, permissions, owner and group data, list of blocks that make up each file, and current known location of each replica of each block. As you'd expect, this adds up.

There are subtleties to the namenode metadata that you might not otherwise think much about. One instance of this is that the length of filenames actually starts to matter at scale; the longer the filename, the more bytes it occupies in memory. More dubious, though, is the *small files problem*. Each file is made up of one or more blocks and has associated metadata. The more files the namenode needs to track, the more metadata it maintains, and the more memory it requires as a result. As a base rule of thumb, the namenode consumes roughly 1 GB for every 1 million blocks. Again, this is a guideline and can easily be invalidated by the extremes.

Namenode disk requirements are modest in terms of storage. Since all metadata must fit in memory, by definition, it can't take roughly more than that on disk. Either way, the amount of disk this really requires is minimal—less than 1 TB.

While namenode space requirements are minimal, reliability is paramount. When provisioning, there are two options for namenode device management: use the namenode's ability to write data to multiple JBOD devices, or write to a RAID device. No matter what, a copy of the data should always be written to an NFS (or similar) mounted volume in addition to whichever local disk configuration is selected. This NFS mount is the final hope for recovery when the local disks catch fire or when some equally unappealing, apocalyptic event occurs.[3] The storage configuration selected for production usage is usually dictated by the decision to purchase homogeneous hardware versus specially configured machines to support the master daemons. There's no single correct answer and as mentioned earlier, what works for you depends on a great many factors.

---

3. Almost certainly, and without fail, a human will be the demise of your namenode should you not heed the warning to leave it alone.

Secondary namenode hardware

The secondary namenode is almost always identical to the namenode. Not only does it require the same amount of RAM and disk, but when absolutely everything goes wrong, it winds up being the replacement hardware for the namenode. Future versions of Hadoop (which should be available by the time you read this) will support a highly available namenode (HA NN) which will use a pair of identical machines. When running a cluster with an HA namenode, the standby or inactive namenode instance performs the checkpoint work the secondary namenode normally does.

Jobtracker hardware

Similar to the namenode and secondary namenode, the jobtracker is also memory-hungry, although for a different reason. In order to provide job and task level-status, counters, and progress quickly, the jobtracker keeps metadata information about the last 100 (by default) jobs executed on the cluster in RAM. This, of course, can build up very quickly and for jobs with many tasks, can cause the jobtracker's JVM heap to balloon in size. There are parameters that allow an administrator to control what information is retained in memory and for how long, but it's a trade-off; job details that are purged from the jobtracker's memory no longer appear in its web UI.

Due to the way job data is retained in memory, jobtracker memory requirements can grow independent of cluster size. Small clusters that handle many jobs, or jobs with many tasks, may require more RAM than expected. Unlike the namenode, this isn't as easy to predict because the variation in the number of tasks from job to job can be much greater than the metadata in the namenode, from file to file.

Worker Hardware Selection

When sizing worker machines for Hadoop, there are a few points to consider. Given that each worker node in a cluster is responsible for both storage and computation, we need to ensure not only that there is enough storage capacity, but also that we have the CPU and memory to process that data. One of the core tenets of Hadoop is to enable access to all data, so it doesn't make much sense to provision machines in such a way that prohibits processing. On the other hand, it's important to consider the type of applications the cluster is designed to support. It's easy to imagine use cases where the cluster's primary function is long-term storage of extremely large datasets with infrequent processing. In these cases, an administrator may choose to deviate from the balanced CPU to memory to disk configuration to optimize for storage-dense configurations.

Starting from the desired storage or processing capacity and working backward is a technique that works well for sizing machines. Consider the case where a system ingests new data at a rate of 1 TB per day. We know Hadoop will replicate this data three times by default, which means the hardware needs to accommodate 3 TB of new data every day! Each machine also needs additional disk capacity to store temporary data during processing with MapReduce. A ballpark estimate is that 20-30% of the machine's raw disk capacity needs to be reserved for temporary data. If we had machines with 12 × 2 TB disks, that leaves only 18 TB of space to store HDFS data, or six days' worth of data.

The same exercise can be applied to CPU and memory, although in this case, the focus is how much a machine can do in parallel rather than how much data it can store. Let's take a hypothetical case where an hourly data processing job is responsible for processing data that has been ingested. If this job were to process 1/24th of the aforementioned 1 TB of data, each execution of the job would need to process around 42 GB of data. Commonly, data doesn't arrive with such an even distribution throughout the day, so there must be enough capacity to be able to handle times of the day when more data is generated. This also addresses only a single job whereas production clusters generally support many concurrent jobs.

In the context of Hadoop, controlling concurrent task processing means controlling throughput with the obvious caveat of having the available processing capacity. Each worker node in the cluster executes a predetermined number of map and reduce tasks simultaneously. A cluster administrator configures the number of these *slots*, and Hadoop's task scheduler—a function of the jobtracker—assigns tasks that need to execute to available slots. Each one of these slots can be thought of as a compute unit consuming some amount of CPU, memory, and disk I/O resources, depending on the task being performed. A number of cluster-wide default settings dictate how much memory, for instance, each slot is allowed to consume. Since Hadoop forks a separate JVM for each task, the overhead of the JVM itself needs to be considered as well. This means each machine must be able to tolerate the sum total resources of all slots being occupied by tasks at once.

Typically, each task needs between 2 GB and 4 GB of memory, depending on the task being performed. A machine with 48 GB of memory, some of which we need to reserve for the host OS and the Hadoop daemons themselves, will support between 10 and 20 tasks. Of course, each task needs CPU time. Now there is the question of how much CPU each task requires versus the amount of RAM it consumes. Worse, we haven't yet considered the disk or network I/O required to execute each task. Balancing the resource consumption of tasks is one of the most difficult tasks of a cluster administrator. Later, we'll explore the various configuration parameters available to control resource consumption between jobs and tasks.

If all of this is just too nuanced, Table 4-1 has some basic hardware configurations to start with. Note that these tend to change rapidly given the rate at which new hardware is introduced, so use your best judgment when purchasing anything.

Table 4-1. Typical worker node hardware configurations

Midline configuration (all around, deep storage, 1 Gb Ethernet)	
CPU	2 × 6 core 2.9 Ghz/15 MB cache
Memory	64 GB DDR3-1600 ECC
Disk controller	SAS 6 Gb/s
Disks	12 × 3 TB LFF SATA II 7200 RPM
Network controller	2 × 1 Gb Ethernet
Notes	CPU features such as Intel's Hyper-Threading and QPI are desirable. Allocate memory to take advantage of triple- or quad-channel memory configurations.
High end configuration (high memory, spindle dense, 10 Gb Ethernet)	
CPU	2 × 6 core 2.9 Ghz/15 MB cache
Memory	96 GB DDR3-1600 ECC
Disk controller	2 × SAS 6 Gb/s
Disks	24 × 1 TB SFF Nearline/MDL SAS 7200 RPM
Network controller	1 × 10 Gb Ethernet
Notes	Same as the midline configuration

Cluster Sizing

Once the hardware for the worker nodes has been selected, the next obvious question is how many of those machines are required to complete a workload. The complexity of sizing a cluster comes from knowing—or more commonly, not knowing—the specifics of such a workload: its CPU, memory, storage, disk I/O, or frequency of execution requirements. Worse, it's common to see a single cluster support many diverse types of jobs with conflicting resource requirements. Much like a traditional relational database, a cluster can be built and optimized for a specific usage pattern or a combination of diverse workloads, in which case some efficiency may be sacrificed.

There are a few ways to decide how many machines are required for a Hadoop deployment. The first, and most common, is sizing the cluster based on the amount of storage required. Many clusters are driven by high data ingest rates; the more data coming into the system, the more machines required. It so happens that as machines are added to the cluster, we get compute resources in addition to the storage capacity. Given the earlier example of 1 TB of new data every day, a growth plan can be built that maps out how many machines are required to store the total amount of data. It usually makes sense to project growth for a few possible scenarios. For instance, Table 4-2 shows a typical plan for flat growth, 5% monthly growth, and 10% monthly growth. (See Figure 4-2.)

Table 4-2. Sample cluster growth plan based on storage

Average daily ingest rate	1 TB	
Replication factor	3 (copies of each block)	
Daily raw consumption	3 TB	Ingest × replication
Node raw storage	24 TB	12 × 2 TB SATA II HDD
MapReduce temp space reserve	25%	For intermediate MapReduce data
Node-usable raw storage	18 TB	Node raw storage − MapReduce reserve
1 year (flat growth)	61 nodes[a]	Ingest × replication × 365 / node raw storage
1 year (5% growth per month[b])	81 nodes[a]	
1 year (10% growth per month)	109 nodes[a]	

[a] Rounded to the nearest whole machine.

[b] To simplify, we treat the result of the daily ingest multiplied by 365, divided by 12, as one month. Growth is compounded each month.

In Table 4-2, we assume 12 × 2 TB hard drives per node, but we could have just as easily used half the number of drives per node and doubled the number of machines. This is how we can adjust the ratio of resources such as the number of CPU cores to hard drive spindles. This leads to the realization that we could purchase machines that are half as powerful and simply buy twice as many. The trade-off, though, is that doing so would require significantly more power, cooling, rack space, and network port density. For these reasons, it's usually preferable to purchase reasonably dense machines without falling outside the normal boundaries of what is considered commodity hardware.

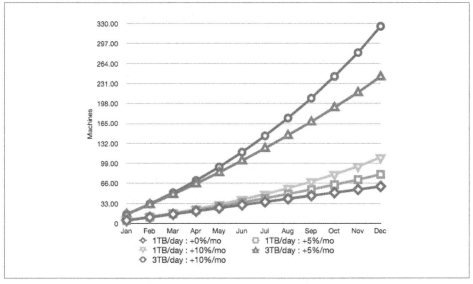

Figure 4-2. Cluster size growth projection for various scenarios (18 TB usable/node)

Projecting cluster size based on the completion time of specific jobs is less common, but still makes sense in certain circumstances. This tends to be more complicated and requires significantly more information than projections based solely on data size. Calculating the number of machines required to complete a job necessitates knowing, roughly, the amount of CPU, memory, and disk I/O used while performing a previous invocation of the same job.

There's a clear chicken and egg problem; a job must be run with a subset of the data in order to understand how many machines are required to run the job at scale. An interesting property of MapReduce jobs is that map tasks are almost always uniform in execution. If a single map task takes one minute to execute and consumes some amount of user and system CPU time, some amount of RAM and some amount of I/O, 100 map tasks will simply take 100 times the resources. Reduce tasks, on the other hand, don't have this property. The number of reducers is defined by the developer rather than being based on the size of the data, so it's possible to create a situation where the job bottlenecks on the number of reducers or an uneven distribution of data between the reducers. The latter problem is referred to as *reducer skew* and is covered in greater detail in Chapter 9.

Blades, SANs, and Virtualization

The large-scale data storage and processing industry moves in cycles. In the past, administrators have purchased large beefy "scale-up" machines with the goal of stuffing as much CPU, RAM, and disk into a single machine as possible. At some point, we collectively realized this was difficult and expensive. For many data center services, we moved to running "pizza boxes" and building in the notion of failure as a first-class concept. A few years later, we were confronted with another problem: many machines in the data center were drastically underutilized and the sheer number of machines was difficult to manage. This was the dawn of the great virtualization rush. Machines were consolidated onto a smaller number of beefy boxes, reducing power and improving utilization. Local disk was eschewed in favor of large storage area networks (SANs) and network attached storage (NAS) because virtual machines could now run on any physical machine in the data center. Now along comes Hadoop and everything you read says commodity, scale-out, share-nothing hardware, but what about the existing investment in blades, shared storage systems, and virtualized infrastructure?

Hadoop, generally speaking, does not benefit from virtualization. Some of the reasons concern the techniques used in modern virtualization, while others have more to do with the common practices that exist in virtualized environments. Virtualization works by running a hypervisor either in a host OS or directly on bare metal, replacing the host OS entirely. Virtual machines (VMs) can then be deployed within a hypervisor and have access to whatever hardware resources are allocated to them by the hypervisor. Historically, virtualization has hurt I/O performance-sensitive applications such as Hadoop rather significantly because guest OSes are unaware of one another as they perform I/O scheduling operations and, as a result, can cause excessive drive seek operations. Many virtualization vendors are aware of this and are working toward more intelligent hypervisors, but ultimately, it's still slower than being directly on bare metal. For all the reasons you would not run a high-performance relational database in a VM, you should not run Hadoop in a VM.

Those new to Hadoop from the high-performance computing (HPC) space may look to use blade systems in their clusters. It is true that the density and power consumption properties of blade systems are appealing; however, the shared infrastructure between blades is generally undesirable. Blade enclosures commonly share I/O planes and network connectivity, and the blades themselves usually have little to no local storage. This is because these systems are built for compute-intensive workloads where comparatively little I/O is done. For those workloads, blade systems may be cost-effective and have a distinct advantage, but for Hadoop, they struggle to keep up.

In "Worker Hardware Selection" on page 48, we talked about how Hadoop prefers JBOD disk configurations. For many years—and for many systems—RAID has been dominant. There's nothing inherently wrong with RAID; it's fast, it's proven, and it scales for certain types of applications. Hadoop uses disk differently. MapReduce is all about processing massive datasets, in parallel, in large sequential I/O access patterns. Imagine a machine with a single RAID-5 stripe with a stripe size of 64 KB running 10 simultaneous map tasks. Each task is going to read a 128 MB sequential block of data from disk in a series of read operations. Each read operation will be of some unknown length, dependent on the records being read and the format of the data. The problem is that even though these 10 tasks are attempting to perform sequential reads, because all I/O requests are issued to the same underlying device, the end result of interleaved reads will look like random reads, drastically reducing throughput. Contrast this with the same scenario but with 12 individual devices, each of which contains only complete 128 MB blocks. Now as I/O requests are issued by the kernel to the underlying device, it is almost certainly in the same position it was since the last read and no seek is performed. While it's true that two map tasks could still contend for a block on a single device, the probability of that being so is significantly reduced.

Another potential pain point with RAID comes from the variation in drive rotation speed among multiple drives. Even within the same lot of drives from the same manufacturer, large variance in rotation speed can occur. In RAID, since all blocks are spread over all spindles, all operations are limited to the speed of the slowest device. In a JBOD configuration, each disk is free to spin independently and consequently, variance is less of an issue.

This brings us to shared storage systems such as SANs and NAS. Again, these systems are built with specific workloads in mind, but for Hadoop, they fall short. Keep in mind that in many ways, Hadoop was created to obviate these kinds of systems. Many of these systems put a large number of fast disks behind one or two controllers with a lot of cache. Hosts are connected to the storage system either via a SAN switch or directly, depending on the configuration. The storage system is usually drastically oversubscribed; there are many more machines connected to the disks than can possibly perform

I/O at once. Even with multiple controllers and multiple HBAs per host, only a small number of machines can perform concurrent I/O. On top of the oversubscription of the controller, these systems commonly configure disks in RAID groups, which means all the problems mentioned earlier are an issue as well. This is counterintuitive in that many administrators think of SANs as being extremely fast and in many ways, scalable.

Hadoop was specifically designed to run on a large number of completely standalone commodity systems. Attempting to shoehorn it back into traditional enterprise storage and virtualization systems only results in significantly higher cost for reduced performance. Some percentage of readers will build clusters out of these components and they will work, but they will not be optimal. Exotic deployments of Hadoop usually end in exotic results, and not in a good way. You have been sufficiently warned.

Operating System Selection and Preparation

While most of Hadoop is written in Java, enough native code and Linux-isms are in its surrounding infrastructure to make Linux the only production-quality option today. A significant number of production clusters run on RedHat Enterprise Linux or its freely available sister, CentOS. Ubuntu, SuSE Enterprise Linux, and Debian deployments also exist in production and work perfectly well. Your choice of operating system may be influenced by administration tools, hardware support, or commercial software support; the best choice is usually to minimize the variables and reduce risk by picking the distribution with which you're most comfortable.

Preparing the OS for Hadoop requires a number of steps, and repeating them on a large number of machines is both time-consuming and error-prone. For this reason, it is strongly advised that a software configuration management system be used. Puppet and Chef are two open source tools that fit the bill. Extolling the virtues of these tools is beyond the scope of what can be accomplished in this section, but there's a breadth of documentation for both to get you going. No matter what, find a configuration management suite that makes sense to you and get familiar with it. It will save you hours (or more) of tinkering and debugging down the road.

Deployment Layout

Hadoop uses a number of directories on the host filesystem. It's important to understand what each location is for and what the growth patterns are. Some directories, for instance, are used for long-term block storage of HDFS data, and others contain temporary data while MapReduce jobs are running. Each of these directories has different security requirements as well. Later, in Chapter 5, we'll see exactly how to configure each of these locations, but for now, it's enough to understand that they exist.

Hadoop home

> This is the directory in which the Hadoop software is installed. Despite the name, it is commonly not installed in a user's home directory. This directory can be made to be read only when configured correctly and usually lives in */usr/local*, */opt*, or */usr* when Hadoop is installed via packages.

Datanode data directories

> One or more of these directories are used by the datanode to store HDFS block data. The datanode assumes that each directory provided is a separate physical device with independent spindles and round-robin blocks between disks. These directories occupy the vast majority of disk space and act as the long-term storage for data, and they are often put on the same devices as the tasktracker MapReduce local directories.

Namenode directories

> One or more of these directories are used by the namenode to store filesystem metadata. The namenode assumes that each directory provided is a separate physical device and replicates all writes to each device synchronously to ensure data availability in the event of disk failure. These directories will all require the same amount of space and generally do not use more than 100 GB. One of these directories is usually an NFS mount, so data is written off the physical machine.

MapReduce local directories

> One or more directories used by the tasktracker to store temporary data during a MapReduce job. More spindles usually means better performance as MapReduce tasks interfere with one another to a lesser degree. These directories store a moderate amount, depending on what the MapReduce job is doing, and are often put on the same devices as the datanode data directories.

Hadoop log directory

> This is a common directory used by all daemons to store log data as well as job- and task-level data. It's normal for Hadoop to generate log data proportional to cluster usage; more MapReduce jobs means more logs.

Hadoop pid directory

> This is a directory used by all daemons to store pid files. This data is very small and doesn't grow.

Hadoop temp directory

> Hadoop uses a temp directory for small, short-lived files it sometimes needs to create. The temp directory is most notably used on the machines from which Map-Reduce jobs are submitted and contains a copy of the JAR file that ultimately gets sent to the jobtracker. This is */tmp/hadoop-<${user.name}>* by default and many administrators leave it there.

Software

Hadoop has few external software package requirements. The most critical piece of software required is the Java Development Kit (JDK). Internally, Hadoop uses many of the features introduced with Java 6, such as generics and concurrency utilities. Hadoop has surfaced bugs in every JDK on which it has been tested. To date, the Oracle (formally Sun Microsystems) HotSpot JVM is, by far, the best performing, most stable implementation available for Hadoop. That being said, the HotSpot VM has proven to be a moving target from patch to patch. Patch versions 24, 26, and 31 have been thoroughly tested and work well for production. The Hadoop community keeps a list of tested JVMs at *http://wiki.apache.org/hadoop/HadoopJavaVersions* where users can post their experiences with various Java VMs and versions.

All machines in the cluster should run the exact same version of Java, down to the patch level. Use of a 64-bit architecture and JDK is strongly encouraged because of the larger heap sizes required by the namenode and jobtracker. To install the JDK, follow the instructions for your OS at *http://www.oracle.com/technetwork/java/javase/index -137561.html*.

 If you choose to install Hadoop using Cloudera's RPM packages, you will need to install Java using the Oracle RPM as well. This is because the CDH packages have a dependency on the Oracle RPM.

Beyond the JDK, there are a number of system services that will simplify the life of an administrator. This is less about Hadoop specifically and applies to general system maintenance, monitoring, and administration.

cron

> Every system needs a functioning cron daemon to drive scheduled tasks. Cleaning up temporary files, compressing old logs, and running configuration management processes are a few examples of common cluster maintenance jobs.

ntp

> The ability to correlate events on a cluster is necessary to diagnose and fix problems. One of the common gotchas is to forget to synchronize clocks between machines. Pick a node in the cluster—usually one of the master nodes—and make it a local NTP server for all other nodes. Details on configuring NTP properly are available at *http://www.ntp.org/*.

ssh

> Hadoop itself does not rely on SSH,[4] although it is incredibly useful for administration and debugging. Depending on the environment, developers may also have direct access to machines to view logs.

---

4. Some of the supporting shell scripts do use ssh to start and stop services on the cluster.

postfix/sendmail

While nothing in Hadoop sends email, it is sometimes useful to have an MTA that supports outbound email only. This is useful for automated tasks running from cron to be able to notify administrators of exceptional circumstances. Both postfix and sendmail are fine for this purpose.

rsync

One of the most underrated tools, rsync allows administrators to copy files efficiently locally and between hosts. If you're not already familiar with rsync, learn it.

Hostnames, DNS, and Identification

Let's just get this out of the way: when it comes to host identification, discovery, and the treatment of hostnames, Hadoop is complicated and extremely picky. This topic is responsible for a fair number of cries for support on the mailing lists and almost certainly an equal amount of lost sleep on the part of many who are new to Hadoop.

But before we get into the list of things that can go wrong, let's first talk about how Hadoop actually discovers and identifies hosts. As we discussed previously, Hadoop worker processes such as the tasktracker and datanodes heartbeat into the jobtracker and namenode (respectively) every few seconds. The first time this occurs, Hadoop learns about the worker's existence. Part of this heartbeat includes the identity of the machine, either by hostname or by IP address. This identifier—again, either the hostname *or* the IP address—is how Hadoop will refer to this machine. This means that when an HDFS client, for instance, asks the namenode to open a file, the namenode will return this identifier to the client as the proper way in which to contact the worker. The exact implications of this are far-reaching; both the client and the worker now must be able to directly communicate, but the client must also be able to resolve the hostname and communicate with the worker using the identifier *as it was reported to the namenode*. But what name does the datanode report to the namenode? That's the real question.

When the datanode starts up, it follows a rather convoluted process to discover the name of the machine. There are a few different configuration parameters that can affect the final decision. These parameters are covered in Chapter 5, but in its default configuration the datanode executes the following series of steps:

1. Get the hostname of the machine, as returned by Java's InetAddress.getLocal Host().
2. Canonicalize the hostname by calling InetAddress#getCanonicalHostName().
3. Set this name internally and send it to either the namenode or the jobtracker.

This seems simple enough. The only real question is what getLocalHost() and getCa nonicalHostName() do, under the hood. Unfortunately, this turns out to be platform-specific and sensitive to the environment in a few ways. On Linux, with the HotSpot JVM, getLocalHost() uses the POSIX, gethostname() which in Linux, uses the uname() syscall. This has absolutely no relationship to DNS or /etc/hosts, although the name it returns is usually similar or even identical. The command hostname, for instance, exclusively uses gethostname() and sethostname() whereas host and dig use gethostbyname() and gethostbyaddr(). The former is how you interact with the hostname as the kernel sees it, while the latter follows the normal Linux name resolution path.

The implementation of getLocalHost() on Linux gets the hostname of the machine and then immediately calls gethostbyname(). As a result, if the hostname doesn't resolve to an IP address, expect issues. Normally, this isn't a concern because there's usually at least an entry in /etc/hosts as a result of the initial OS installation. Oddly enough, on Mac OS X, if the hostname doesn't resolve, it still returns the hostname and the IP address active on the preferred network interface.

The second half of the equation is the implementation of getCanonicalHostName(), which has an interesting quirk. Hostname canonicalization is the process of finding the complete, official, hostname according to the resolution system, in this case, the host's resolver library. In lay terms, this usually means finding the fully qualified hostname. Since getLocalHost() returns a nonqualified hostname—hadoop01 on our example cluster—there's some work to be done. According to the OpenJDK source code (which may, in fact, differ from the Oracle HotSpot VM in subtle ways), getCanonicalHostName() calls the internal method InetAddress.getHostFromNameService(), which gets the hostname by address via the OS resolver. What it does next is the quirk; it gets all IP addresses for the given hostname, and checks to make sure the original IP address appears in the list. If this fails for any reason, including a SecurityManager implementation that disallows resolution, the original IP address is returned as the canonical name.

Using a simple Java[5] program, let's examine our test cluster to see all of this in action (see Example 4-1).

Example 4-1. Java utility to display hostname information

```
import java.net.InetAddress;
import java.net.UnknownHostException;

public class dns {

  public static void main(String[] args) throws UnknownHostException {
    InetAddress addr = InetAddress.getLocalHost();

    System.out.println(
      String.format(
        "IP:%s hostname:%s canonicalName:%s",
        addr.getHostAddress(),       // The "default" IP address
        addr.getHostName(),          // The hostname (from gethostname())
        addr.getCanonicalHostName()  // The canonicalized hostname (from resolver)
```

---

5. This code can be compiled and run using javac dns.java followed by java dns.

```
    )
  );
}

}
```

```
esammer@hadoop01 ~]$ hostname
hadoop01
[esammer@hadoop01 ~]$ java dns
IP:10.1.1.160 hostname:hadoop01 canonicalName:hadoop01.sf.cloudera.com
```

We can see that the hostname of the machine becomes fully qualified, as we expected. If we change the hostname of the machine to something that doesn't resolve, things fail.

```
[esammer@hadoop01 ~]$ sudo hostname bananas
[sudo] password for esammer:
[esammer@hadoop01 ~]$ hostname
bananas
[esammer@hadoop01 ~]$ java dns
Exception in thread "main" java.net.UnknownHostException: bananas: bananas
        at java.net.InetAddress.getLocalHost(InetAddress.java:1354)
        at dns.main(dns.java:7)
```

Adding an entry to */etc/hosts* for bananas fixes the problem, but the canonical name is the same.

```
[esammer@hadoop01 ~]$ cat /etc/hosts
127.0.0.1               localhost.localdomain localhost

10.1.1.160 hadoop01.sf.cloudera.com hadoop01 bananas
10.1.1.161 hadoop02.sf.cloudera.com hadoop02
# Other hosts...
[esammer@hadoop01 ~]$ java dns
IP:10.1.1.160 hostname:bananas canonicalName:hadoop01.sf.cloudera.com
```

Moving bananas to the "canonical name" position in the *hosts* file changes the result.[6]

```
[esammer@hadoop01 ~]$ java dns
IP:10.1.1.160 hostname:bananas canonicalName:bananas
[esammer@hadoop01 ~]$ cat /etc/hosts
127.0.0.1               localhost.localdomain localhost

10.1.1.160 bananas hadoop01.sf.cloudera.com hadoop01
10.1.1.161 hadoop02.sf.cloudera.com hadoop02
# Other hosts...
```

This is all well and good, but what could really go wrong? After all, hostnames are just hostnames. Unfortunately, it's not that simple. There are a few pathological cases where seemingly benign (and worse, common) configuration leads to very unexpected results.

One of the most common issues is that the machine believes its name to be 127.0.01. Worse, some versions of CentOS and RHEL configure things this way by default! This is extremely dangerous because datanodes communicate to the namenode that they're

---

6. See man 5 hosts for details on the difference between fields two and three in the *hosts* file.

alive and well, but they report their IP address to be 127.0.0.1 or localhost, which, in turn, is given to clients attempting to read or write data to the cluster. The clients are told to write to the datanode at 127.0.0.1—in other words, themselves—and they constantly fail. This goes down as one of the worst configuration mistakes that can occur because neither traditional monitoring tools nor the untrained administrator will notice this until it's far too late. Even then, it still may not be clear why the machine reports itself this way.

```
[esammer@hadoop01 ~]$ cat /etc/hosts
127.0.0.1                    localhost.localdomain localhost bananas

10.1.1.160 hadoop01.sf.cloudera.com hadoop01
10.1.1.161 hadoop02.sf.cloudera.com hadoop02
# Other hosts...
[esammer@hadoop01 ~]$ java dns
IP:127.0.0.1 hostname:bananas canonicalName:localhost.localdomain
```

Users, Groups, and Privileges

Hadoop is, in many ways, an arbitrary code execution engine. Users submit code in the form of MapReduce jobs to the cluster, which is instantiated and executed on worker nodes within the cluster. To mitigate obvious attack vectors and protect potentially sensitive data, it's advisable to run HDFS daemons as one user and MapReduce daemons as another. MapReduce jobs, in turn, execute either as the same user as the tasktracker daemon or as the user that submitted the job (see Table 4-3). The latter option is only available when a cluster is operating in so-called *secure mode*.

Table 4-3. Hadoop daemon users

Process	User
Namenode	hdfs
Secondary namenode	hdfs
Datanode	hdfs
Jobtracker	mapred
Tasktracker	mapred
Child tasks	mapred [a]

[a] In secure mode, the user that submitted the job.

Historically, it was common to run all daemons as a single user, usually named hadoop. This was prior to support for secure operation being a first class deployment mode and suffered from potential data exposure issues. For example, if a MapReduce task is running as user hadoop, that process can simply open raw blocks on the worker's Linux filesystem, bypassing all application-level authorization checks. By running child tasks as user mapred the standard filesystem access controls can be used to restrict direct access to datanode block data. For more information about user identity, authentication, and authorization in MapReduce see Chapter 6.

By default, the CDH Hadoop RPM and Deb packages will create these users if they don't already exist, and the init scripts will start the daemons as the correct users. Users of Apache Hadoop can write similar scripts or use an external system to ensure daemons are started as the correct users.

Each Hadoop daemon consumes various system resources, as you can guess. Linux supports, via Pluggable Authentication Modules (PAM) system, the ability to control resources such as file descriptors and virtual memory at the user level. These resource limits are defined in */etc/security/limits.conf* or as fragment files in the */etc/security/limits.d* directory, and affect all new logins. The format of the file isn't hard to understand, as shown in Example 4-2.

Example 4-2. Sample limits.conf for Hadoop

```
# Allow users hdfs, mapred, and hbase to open 32k files. The
# type '-' means both soft and hard limits.
#
# See 'man 5 limits.conf' for details.

# user type    resource  value

hdfs    -      nofile    32768
mapred  -      nofile    32768
hbase   -      nofile    32768
```

Each daemon uses different reserved areas of the local filesystem to store various types of data, as shown in Table 4-4. Chapter 5 covers how to define the directories used by each daemon.

Table 4-4. Hadoop directories and permissions

Daemon	Sample path(s)	Configuration parameter	Owner:Group	Permissions
Namenode	*/data/1/dfs/nn,/data/2/dfs/nn,/data/3/dfs/nn*	dfs.name.dir	hdfs:hadoop	0700
Secondary namenode	*/data/1/dfs/snn*	fs.check point.dir	hdfs:hadoop	0700
Datanode	*/data/1/dfs/dn,/data/2/dfs/dn,/data/3/dfs/dn,/data/4/dfs/dn*	dfs.data node.dir	hdfs:hadoop	0700
Tasktracker	*/data/1/mapred/local,/data/2/mapred/local,/data/3/mapred/local,/data/4/mapred/local*	mapred.local.dir	mapred:hadoop	0770

Daemon	Sample path(s)	Configuration parameter	Owner:Group	Permissions
Jobtracker	/data/1/mapred/local	`mapred.local.dir`	`mapred:hadoop`	0700
All	/var/log/hadoop	`$HADOOP_LOG_DIR`	`root:hadoop`	0775 [a]
	/tmp/hadoop-user.name	`hadoop.tmp.dir`	`root:root`	1777

[a] Optionally 0770 in highly restricted environments.

These directories should be created with the proper permissions prior to deploying Hadoop. Users of Puppet or Chef usually create a Hadoop manifest or recipe, respectively, that ensures proper directory creation during host provisioning. Note that incorrect permissions or ownership of directories can result in daemons that don't start, ignored devices, or accidental exposure of sensitive data. When operating in secure mode, some of the daemons validate permissions on critical directories and will refuse to start if the environment is incorrectly configured.

Kernel Tuning

There are a few kernel parameters that are of special interest when deploying Hadoop. Since production Hadoop clusters always have dedicated hardware, it makes sense to tune the OS based on what we know about how Hadoop works. Kernel parameters should be configured in /etc/sysctl.conf so that settings survive reboots.

vm.swappiness

The kernel parameter vm.swappiness controls the kernel's tendency to swap application data from memory to disk, in contrast to discarding filesystem cache. The valid range for vm.swappiness is 0 to 100 where higher values indicate that the kernel should be more aggressive in swapping application data to disk, and lower values defer this behavior, instead forcing filesystem buffers to be discarded. Swapping Hadoop daemon data to disk can cause operations to timeout and potentially fail if the disk is performing other I/O operations. This is especially dangerous for HBase as Region Servers must maintain communication with ZooKeeper lest they be marked as failed. To avoid this, vm.swappiness should be set to 0 (zero) to instruct the kernel to never swap application data, if there is an option. Most Linux distributions ship with vm.swappiness set to 60 or even as high as 80.

vm.overcommit_memory

Processes commonly allocate memory by calling the function malloc(). The kernel decides if enough RAM is available and either grants or denies the allocation request.

Linux (and a few other Unix variants) support the ability to overcommit memory; that is, to permit more memory to be allocated than is available in physical RAM plus swap. This is scary, but sometimes it is necessary since applications commonly allocate memory for "worst case" scenarios but never use it.

There are three possible settings for vm.overcommit_memory.

0 (zero)
> Check if enough memory is available and, if so, allow the allocation. If there isn't enough memory, deny the request and return an error to the application.

1 (one)
> Permit memory allocation in excess of physical RAM plus swap, as defined by vm.overcommit_ratio. The vm.overcommit_ratio parameter is a percentage added to the amount of RAM when deciding how much the kernel can overcommit. For instance, a vm.overcommit_ratio of 50 and 1 GB of RAM would mean the kernel would permit up to 1.5 GB, plus swap, of memory to be allocated before a request failed.

2 (two)
> The kernel's equivalent of "all bets are off," a setting of 2 tells the kernel to always return success to an application's request for memory. This is absolutely as weird and scary as it sounds.

When a process forks, or calls the fork() function, its entire page table is cloned. In other words, the child process has a complete copy of the parent's memory space, which requires, as you'd expect, twice the amount of RAM. If that child's intention is to immediately call exec() (which replaces one process with another) the act of cloning the parent's memory is a waste of time. Because this pattern is so common, the vfork() function was created, which unlike fork(), does not clone the parent memory, instead blocking it until the child either calls exec() or exits. The problem is that the HotSpot JVM developers implemented Java's fork operation using fork() rather than vfork().

So why does this matter to Hadoop? Hadoop Streaming—a library that allows MapReduce jobs to be written in any language that can read from standard in and write to standard out—works by forking the user's code as a child process and piping data through it. This means that not only do we need to account for the memory the Java child task uses, but also that when it forks, for a moment in time before it execs, it uses twice the amount of memory we'd expect it to. For this reason, it is sometimes necessary to set vm.overcommit_memory to the value 1 (one) and adjust vm.overcommit_ratio accordingly.

Disk Configuration

Disk configuration and performance is extremely important to Hadoop. Since many kinds of MapReduce jobs are I/O-bound, an underperforming or poorly configured disk can drastically reduce overall job performance. Datanodes store block data on top of a traditional filesystem rather than on raw devices. This means all of the attributes of the filesystem affect HDFS and MapReduce, for better or worse.

Choosing a Filesystem

Today Hadoop primarily runs on Linux: as a result we'll focus on common Linux filesystems. To be sure, Hadoop can run on more exotic filesystems such as those from commercial vendors, but this usually isn't cost-effective. Remember that Hadoop is designed to be not only low-cost, but also modest in its requirements on the hosts on which it runs. By far, the most common filesystems used in production clusters are ext3, ext4, and xfs.

As an aside, the Linux Logical Volume Manager (LVM) should never be used for Hadoop data disks. Unfortunately, this is the default for CentOS and RHEL when using automatic disk allocation during installation. There is obviously a performance hit when going through an additional layer such as LVM between the filesystem and the device, but worse is the fact that LVM allows one to concatenate devices into larger devices. If you're not careful during installation, you may find that all of your data disks have been combined into a single large device without any protection against loss of a single disk. The dead giveaway that you've been bitten by this unfortunate configuration mishap is that your device name shows up as */dev/vg** or something other than */dev/sd**.

 The commands given here will format disks. Formatting a disk is a destructive operation and *will* destroy any existing data on the disk. Do not format a disk that contains data you need!

ext3

The third extended filesystem, or ext3, is an enhanced version of ext2. The most notable feature of ext3 is support for journaling, which records changes in a journal or log prior to modifying the actual data structures that make up the filesystem. Ext3 has been included in Linux since kernel version 2.4.15 and has significant production burn-in. It supports files up to 2 TB and a max filesystem size of 16 TB when configured with a 4 KB block size. Note that the maximum filesystem size is less of a concern with Hadoop because data is written across many machines and many disks in the cluster. Multiple journal levels are supported, although ordered mode, where the journal records metadata changes only, is the most common. If you're not sure what filesystem to use, or you're extremely risk-averse, ext3 is for you.

When formatting devices for ext3, the following options are worth specifying:

```
mkfs -t ext3 -j -m 1 -O sparse_super,dir_index /dev/sdXN
```

The option `-t ext3` simply tells `mkfs` to create an ext3 filesystem while `-j` enables the journal. The `-m1` option is a hidden gem and sets the percentage of reserved blocks for the superuser to 1% rather than 5%. Since no root processes should be touching data disks, this leaves us with an extra 4% of usable disk space. With 2 TB disks, that's up to 82 GB! Additional options to the filesystem are specified by the `-O` option. Admittedly, the two options shown—`sparse_super`, which creates fewer super-block backups, and `dir_index`, which uses b-tree indexes for directory trees for faster lookup of files in large directories—are almost certainly the defaults on your Linux distro of choice. Of course, */dev/sdXN* specifies the device to format, where *X* is the drive and *N* is the partition number.

ext4

Ext4 is the successor to ext3; it was released as of Linux 2.6.28 and contains some desirable improvements. Specifically, ext4 is extent-based, which improves sequential performance by storing contiguous blocks together in a larger unit of storage. This is especially interesting for Hadoop, which is primarily interested in reading and writing data in larger blocks. Another feature of ext4 is journal checksum calculation; a feature that improves data recoverability in the case of failure during a write. Newer Linux distributions such as RedHat Enterprise Linux 6 (RHEL6) will use ext4 as the default filesystem unless configured otherwise.

All of this sounds great, but ext4 has a major drawback: burn-in time. Only now is ext4 starting to see significant deployment in production systems. This can be disconcerting to those that are risk-averse. The following format command is similar to that of ext3, except we add the `extent` argument to the `-O` option to enable the use of extent-based allocation:

```
mkfs -t ext4 -m 1 -O dir_index,extent,sparse_super /dev/sdXN
```

xfs

XFS, a filesystem created by SGI, has a number of unique features. Like ext3 and ext4, it's a journaling filesystem, but the way data is organized on disk is very different. Similar to ext4, allocation is extent-based, but its extents are within allocation groups, each of which is responsible for maintaining its own inode table and space. This model allows concurrent operations in a way that ext3 and 4 cannot, because multiple processes can modify data in each allocation group without conflict. Its support for high concurrency makes xfs very appealing for systems such as relational databases that perform many parallel, but short-lived, operations.

```
mkfs -t xfs /dev/sdXN
```

There are no critical options to creating xfs filesystems for Hadoop.

Mount Options

After filesystems have been formatted, the next step is to add an entry for each newly formatted filesystem to the system's /etc/fstab file, as shown in Example 4-3. The reason this somewhat mundane task is called out is because there's an important optimization to be had: disabling file access time. Most filesystems support the notion of keeping track of the access time of both files and directories. For desktops, this is a useful feature; it's easy to figure out what files you've most recently viewed as well as modified. This feature isn't particularly useful in the context of Hadoop. Users of HDFS are, in many cases, unaware of the block boundaries of files, so the fact that block two of file *foo* was accessed last week is of little value. The real problem with maintaining access time (or atime as it's commonly called) is that every time a file is read, the metadata needs to be updated. That is, for each read, there's also a mandatory write. This is relatively expensive at scale and can negatively impact the overall performance of Hadoop, or any other system, really. When mounting data partitions, it's best to disable both file atime and directory atime.

Example 4-3. Sample /etc/fstab file

```
LABEL=/           /          ext3     noatime,nodiratime      1 1
LABEL=/data/1     /data/1    ext3     noatime,nodiratime      1 2
LABEL=/data/2     /data/2    ext3     noatime,nodiratime      1 2
LABEL=/data/3     /data/3    ext3     noatime,nodiratime      1 2
LABEL=/data/4     /data/4    ext3     noatime,nodiratime      1 2
tmpfs             /dev/shm   tmpfs    defaults            0 0
devpts            /dev/pts   devpts   gid=5,mode=620      0 0
sysfs             /sys       sysfs    defaults            0 0
proc              /proc      proc     defaults            0 0
LABEL=SWAP-sda2   swap       swap     defaults            0 0
```

Network Design

Network design and architecture is a complex, nuanced topic on which many books have been written. This is absolutely not meant to be a substitute for a complete understanding of such a deep subject. Instead, the goal is to highlight what elements of network design are crucial from the perspective of Hadoop deployment and performance.

The following sections assume you're already familiar with basic networking concepts such as the OSI model (*http://en.wikipedia.org/wiki/OSI_model*), Ethernet standards such as 1- (*1GbE*) and 10-gigabit (*10GbE*), and the associated media types. Cursory knowledge of advanced topics such as routing theory (*http://en.wikipedia.org/wiki/Routing*) and at least one protocol such as IS-IS (*http://en.wikipedia.org/wiki/IS-IS*), OSPF (*http://en.wikipedia.org/wiki/OSPF*), or BGP (*http://en.wikipedia.org/wiki/BGP*) is helpful in getting the most out of "Spine fabric" on page 72. In the interest of simplicity, we don't cover bonded hosts or switch redundancy where it's obviously desirable. This isn't because it's not important, but because how you accomplish that tends to get into switch-specific features and vendor-supported options.

Network Usage in Hadoop: A Review

Hadoop was developed to exist and thrive in real-world network topologies. It doesn't require any specialized hardware, nor does it employ exotic network protocols. It will run equally well in both flat Layer 2 networks or routed Layer 3 environments. While it does attempt to minimize the movement of data around the network when running MapReduce jobs, there are times when both HDFS and MapReduce generate considerable traffic. Rack topology information is used to make reasonable decisions about data block placement and to assist in task scheduling, but it helps to understand the traffic profiles exhibited by the software when planning your cluster network.

HDFS

In Chapter 2, we covered the nuts and bolts of how HDFS works and why. Taking a step back and looking at the system from the perspective of the network, there are three primary forms of traffic: cluster housekeeping traffic such as datanode block reports and heartbeats to the namenode, client metadata operations with the namenode, and block data transfer. Basic heartbeats and administrative commands are infrequent and only transfer small amounts of data in remote procedure calls. Only in extremely large cluster deployments—on the order of thousands of machines—does this traffic even become noticeable.

Most administrators will instead focus on dealing with the rate of data being read from, or written to, HDFS by client applications. Remember, when clients that execute on a datanode where the block data is stored perform read operations, the data is read from the local device, and when writing data, they write the first replica to the local device. This reduces a significant amount of network data transfer. Clients that do not run on a datanode or that read more than a single block of data will cause data to be transferred across the network. Of course, with a traditional NAS device, for instance, all data moves across the network, so anything HDFS can do to mitigate this is already an improvement, but it's nothing to scoff at. In fact, writing data from a noncollocated client causes the data to be passed over the network three times, two of which pass over the core switch in a traditional tree network topology. This replication traffic moves in an *East/West* pattern rather than the more common client/server-oriented *North/South*. Significant East/West traffic is one of the ways Hadoop is different from many other traditional systems.

Beyond normal client interaction with HDFS, failures can also generate quite a bit of traffic. Much simpler to visualize, consider what happens when a datanode that contains 24 TB of block data fails. The resultant replication traffic matches the amount of data contained on the datanode when it failed.

MapReduce

It's no surprise that the MapReduce cluster membership and heartbeat infrastructure matches that of HDFS. Tasktrackers regularly heartbeat small bits of information to the jobtracker to indicate they're alive. Again, this isn't a source of pain for most administrators, save for the extreme scale cases. Client applications also do not communicate directly with tasktrackers, instead performing most operations against the jobtracker and HDFS. During job submission, the jobtracker communicates with the namenode, but also in the form of small RPC requests. The true bear of MapReduce is the tasktracker traffic during the shuffle phase of a MapReduce job.

As map tasks begin to complete and reducers are started, each reducer must fetch the map output data for its partition from each tasktracker. Performed by HTTP, this results in a full mesh of communication; each reducer (usually) must copy some amount of data from every other tasktracker in the cluster. Additionally, each reducer is permitted a certain number of concurrent fetches. This shuffle phase accounts for a rather significant amount of East/West traffic within the cluster, although it varies in size from job to job. A data processing job, for example, that transforms every record in a dataset will typically transform records in map tasks in parallel. The result of this tends to be a different record of roughly equal size that must be shuffled, passed through the reduce phase, and written back out to HDFS in its new form. A job that transforms an input dataset of 1 million 100 KB records (roughly 95 GB) to a dataset of one million 82 KB records (around 78 GB) will shuffle at least 78 GB over the network for that job alone, not to mention the output from the reduce phase that will be replicated when written to HDFS.

Remember that active clusters run many jobs at once and typically must continue to take in new data being written to HDFS by ingestion infrastructure. In case it's not clear, that's a lot of data.

1 Gb versus 10 Gb Networks

Frequently, when discussing Hadoop networking, users will ask if they should deploy 1 Gb or 10 Gb network infrastructure. Hadoop does not require one or the other; however, it can benefit from the additional bandwidth and lower latency of 10 Gb connectivity. So the question really becomes one of whether the benefits outweigh the cost. It's hard to truly evaluate cost without additional context. Vendor selection, network size, media, and phase of the moon all seem to be part of the pricing equation. You have to consider the cost differential of the switches, the host adapters (as 10 GbE LAN on motherboard is still not yet pervasive), optics, and even cabling, to decide if 10 Gb networking is feasible. On the other hand, plenty of organizations have simply made the jump and declared that all new infrastructure must be 10 Gb, which is also fine. Estimates, at the time of publication, are that a typical 10 Gb top of rack switch is roughly three times more expensive than its 1 Gb counterpart, port for port.

Those that primarily run ETL-style or other high input to output data ratio MapReduce jobs may prefer the additional bandwidth of a 10 Gb network. Analytic MapReduce jobs—those that primarily count or aggregate numbers—perform far less network data transfer during the shuffle phase, and may not benefit at all from such an investment. For space- or power-constrained environments, some choose to purchase slightly beefier hosts with more storage that, in turn, require greater network bandwidth in order to take full advantage of the hardware. The latency advantages of 10 Gb may also benefit those that wish to run HBase to serve low-latency, interactive applications. Finally, if you find yourself considering bonding more than two 1 Gb interfaces, you should almost certainly look to 10 Gb as, at that point, the port-for-port cost starts to become equivalent.

Typical Network Topologies

It's impossible to fully describe all possible network topologies here. Instead, we focus on two: a common tree, and a spine/leaf fabric that is gaining popularity for applications with strong East/West traffic patterns.

Traditional tree

By far, the *N*-tiered tree network (see Figure 4-3) is the predominant architecture deployed in data centers today. A tree may have multiple *tiers*, each of which brings together (or aggregates) the branches of another tier. Hosts are connected to leaf or *access* switches in a tree, which are then connected via one or more uplinks to the next tier. The number of tiers required to build a network depends on the total number of hosts that need to be supported. Using a switch with 48 1GbE and four 10GbE port

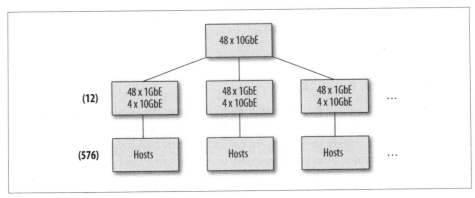

Figure 4-3. Two-tier tree network, 576 hosts

switches as an access switch, and a 48-port 10GbE switch as a *distribution* switch, it's possible to support up to 576 hosts (because each access switch uses 4-ports of the 48-port distribution switch).

Notice that the sum of the four 10GbE uplinks from each distribution switch can't actually support the full bandwidth of the 48 1GbE ports. This is referred to as *oversubscription* of the bandwidth. In simpler terms, it's not possible for all 48 hosts to communicate at the full, advertised rate of the port to which they are connected. Oversubscription is commonly expressed as a ratio of the amount of desired bandwidth required versus bandwidth available. In our example, the 48 1GbE ports can theoretically carry 48 Gb of traffic, but the four 10GbE ports only support 40 Gb. Dividing the desired bandwidth (48) by the available bandwidth (40) yields an oversubscription ratio of 1.2:1. It's very common for some amount of oversubscription to occur at the uplink of one tier to the next in a tree. This is one of the primary reasons why Hadoop tries to keep network activity confined to a single rack, or switch, really.

What happens, though, when we run out of ports at the distribution switch? At some point, it becomes either cost-prohibitive or simply impossible to buy switches with more ports. In a tree, the answer is to add another tier of aggregation. The problem with this is that each time you add a tier, you increase the number of switches between some nodes and others. Worse, the amount of oversubscription is compounded with each tier in the tree. Consider what happens if we extend our tree network from earlier beyond 576 hosts. To increase our port density any further we must create a third tier (see Figure 4-4). The problem now becomes the oversubscription between tiers two and three. With 576 Gb of traffic at each tier two switch, we won't be able to maintain the 1.2:1 oversubscription rate; that would require roughly 48 10GbE or 12 40GbE uplink ports per distribution switch. With each tier that is added, oversubscription worsens, and creates wildly different bandwidth availability between branches of the tree. As we've seen, Hadoop does its best to reduce interswitch communication during some operations, but others cannot be avoided, leading to frequent, and sometimes severe, contention at these oversubscribed choke points in the network. Ultimately, most network administrators come to the conclusion that a modular chassis switch that supports high port density is the answer to this problem. Beefy modular switches such as the Cisco Nexus 7000 series (*http://www.cisco.com/en/US/products/ps9402/in dex.html*) are not unusual to find in large tree networks supporting Hadoop clusters, but they can be expensive and can simply push the problem out until you run out of ports again. For large clusters, this is not always sufficient.

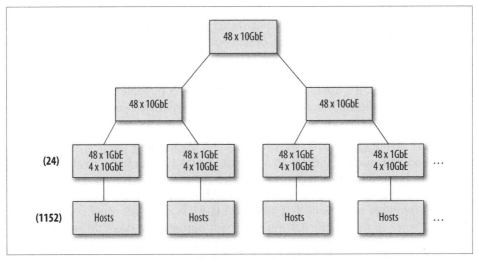

Figure 4-4. Three-tier tree network, 1,152 hosts (oversubscribed)

If we look instead at the North/South traffic support, a tree makes a lot of sense. Traffic enters via the root of the tree and is, by definition, limited to the capacity of the root itself. This traffic never traverses more than one branch and is far simpler to handle as a result.

It's worth noting that cluster data ingress and egress should be nearest to the root of a tree network. This prevents branch monopolization and unbalanced traffic patterns that negatively impact some portions of the network and not others. Placing the border of the cluster at the cluster's core switch makes this traffic equidistant to all nodes in the tree and amortizes the bandwidth cost over all branches equally.

A tree network works for small and midsize networks that fit within two tiers with minimal oversubscription. Typical access switches for a 1GbE network tend to be 48 ports with four 10GbE uplinks to a distribution layer. The distribution switch size depends on how many nodes need to be supported, but 48-port 10GbE switches are common. If you are tacking Hadoop onto an existing tree, bring the cluster's distribution layer in nearest to that of ETL, process orchestration, database, or other systems with which you plan to exchange data. Do not, under any circumstances, place low-latency services on the cluster distribution switch. Hadoop tends to monopolize shared resources such as buffers, and can (and will) create problems for other hosts.

Spine fabric

Over the past few years, general purpose virtualized infrastructure and large-scale data processing clusters have grown in popularity. These types of systems have very different traffic patterns from traditional systems in that they both require significantly greater East/West bandwidth. We've already discussed Hadoop's traffic patterns, but in many ways it's similar to that of a virtualized environment. In a true virtualized environment, applications relinquish explicit control over physical placement in exchange for flexibility and dynamism. Implicitly, this means that two applications that may need high-bandwidth communication with each other could be placed on arbitrary hosts, and by extension, switches, in the network. While it's true that some virtualization systems support the notion of locality groups that attempt to place related virtual machines "near" one another, it's usually not guaranteed, nor is it possible to ensure you're not placed next to another high-traffic application. A new type of network design is required to support this new breed of systems.

Enter the scale-out *spine fabric*, seen in Figure 4-5. As its name implies, a fabric looks more like a tightly weaved mesh with as close to equal distance between any two hosts as possible. Hosts are connected to leaf switches, just as in the tree topology; however, each leaf has one or more uplinks to every switch in the second tier, called the spine. A routing protocol such as IS-IS, OSPF, or EIGRP is run with *equal cost multipath* (ECMP) routes so that traffic has multiple path options and takes the shortest path between two hosts. If each leaf has an uplink to each spine switch, every host (that isn't on the same leaf) is always exactly three hops away. This equidistant, uniform bandwidth configuration is perfect for applications with strong East/West traffic patterns. Using the same example as earlier, converting our two distribution switches to a spine, it's possible to support 24-leaf switches or 1,152 hosts at the same 1.2:1 oversubscription rate.

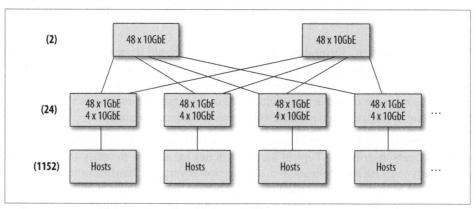

Figure 4-5. Two-switch spine fabric, 1,152 hosts

In a fabric, it's not uncommon to use more and more ports on each leaf to support a wider spine for greater port density. To give you an idea of how this scales, four

48-port 10GbE spine switches will support forty-eight 48-port 1GbE leaf switches at the same 1.2:1 oversubscription rate for a total of 2,304 1GbE ports, as shown in Figure 4-6. That's not a typo. Each leaf switch has one uplink to each of the four spine switches with 48 1GbE ports for host connectivity. It's safe to reduce the number of uplinks from leaf to spine because ECMP routing says we can simply take a different path to the same place; the bandwidth isn't gone, just spread out. Scaling out further is possible by increasing the number of spine switches and uplinks per leaf. For leaf switches with only four 10GbE ports things get a little complicated, but it's possible to buy switches with two 40GbE QSFP+ ports to overcome this. Using a breakout cable, it's possible to use each 40GbE QSFP+ port as four 10GbE ports for up to eight uplinks. Beyond eight spine switches (which, by the way, is 96 leaf switches or 4,608 1GbE ports), it's usually necessary to go to 10GbE leaf switches to support additional uplinks. We then start taking away ports for hosts on each leaf and using them for uplinks, but it still allows larger and larger networks. Some Hadoop community members have written, at length, about the port density, bandwidth, cost, and power concerns when building large-scale fabrics; Brad Hedlund has an amazing blog (*http://bradhedlund .com/*) where he regularly talks about building large-scale networks for Hadoop and OpenStack deployments.

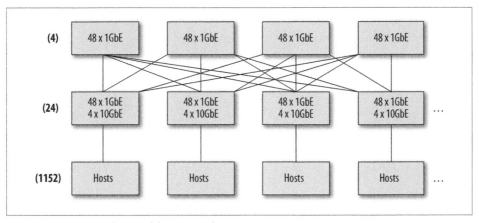

Figure 4-6. Four-switch spine fabric, 2,304 hosts

Cluster access in a spine fabric can be placed on a dedicated leaf. Since all leaves have equidistant access to all others via the spine, bandwidth is not sacrificed. Also note-worthy is that the spine fabric implicitly supports redundancy because of the use of ECMP routing. It's possible to lose up $N - 1$ spine switches where N is the number of uplinks per leaf, although bandwidth is obviously reduced with each loss as well.

## CHAPTER 5

Installation and Configuration

Installing Hadoop

Once you've prepped the environment, selected the version and distribution of Hadoop, and decided which daemons will run where, you're ready to install Hadoop. The act of installing Hadoop is relatively simple once the machines have been properly prepared. There are almost endless ways of installing Hadoop. The goal here, though, is to define some best practices for deployment to avoid the most common mistakes and pain points.

In all deployment scenarios, there are a few common tasks. Hadoop is always downloaded and installed in a select location on the filesystem. For tarball-based installs, this leaves quite a bit of flexibility but also an equal amount of ambiguity. Tarball installs are also complicated because the administrator needs to perform extra steps to create system users, relocate log and pid file directories, set permissions appropriately, and so forth. If you're not sure which method of install to perform, start with RPM or Deb packages. It will save you from making common mistakes and keep you in line with best practices developed by the Hadoop community over time.

Do I Need Root Access to Install Hadoop?

Sometimes, due to organizational boundaries or security restrictions, administrators responsible for deploying Hadoop do not have Linux root user privileges. While Hadoop itself does not necessarily require root privileges, installation—at least according to best practices—does require that some actions be performed as a superuser. Whether one can get away without requiring root access depends on the method of deployment, the features of Hadoop that are to be enabled, and how much planning can be done beforehand. It is, however, possible to divide the tasks that require superuser privileges from those that do not. Expect that, for a production deployment, root privileges will be required during installation and for specific maintenance operations (covered later in Chapter 8).

If you truly wish to install and configure Hadoop as a nonroot user, you can follow the tarball installation process and simply change the owner to another, nonprivileged user

---

rather than root. Note that running Hadoop in secure mode *does* require root privileges for various reasons, one being because the daemons must bind to privileged ports. Be careful that in your quest to avoid root you do not inadvertently make your cluster *less* secure.

Always remember that requiring root during installation does not equate to running as root (which Hadoop does not do).

Apache Hadoop

Apache Hadoop is available for download directly from the Apache Software Foundation (ASF) at *http://hadoop.apache.org* and is available as tarballs, RPMs, and Debs. While tarball installation offers the greatest amount of flexibility, it is also the most complicated for a production deployment. Administrators with extremely specific requirements about where software is installed and how will prefer to use tarball installation. The RPM and Deb package format artifacts greatly simplify the process of installation in that files are placed in predictable locations in the filesystem according to the Filesystem Hierarchy Standard (*http://www.linuxfoundation.org/collaborate/work groups/lsb/fhs*) (FHS). To simplify things, we'll assume Apache Hadoop version 1.0.0 is being installed in the examples that follow.

Tarball installation

To install Apache Hadoop using tarballs:

1. Download Apache Hadoop.

   The Apache Software Foundation uses a mirroring system which presents a list of locations from which one may download a specific release. Unfortunately, the Apache Hadoop project site is confusing. Visiting the site reveals no obvious download links. Instead, you'll find three subprojects called Common, HDFS, and MapReduce shown as tabs along the top of the page.

   Without delving too much into the history of the project, at some point Hadoop was divided into three components: Common, HDFS, and MapReduce. The Common subproject was to contain code shared by both HDFS and MapReduce, while HDFS and MapReduce would be home to their respective components. The idea here was that Hadoop could, in theory, support other compute and storage layers. While this is true, it made development of Hadoop itself extremely difficult and ultimately there was still only a single software artifact that came out of the project that contained the cumulative source code of all three components. This artifact, for lack of a better way to do deal with the situation, is now released under the Common subproject.

   Clicking on the "Common" tab and then on the "Releases" link leads to the download page. Scrolling down, you'll find a link labeled "Download a release now." This leads to the list of mirrors with a recommended mirror based on your geographic location at the top of the page. If you'd rather simply bookmark the location for downloads without being stuck to a specific mirror, the proper URL is *http://www.apache.org/dyn/closer.cgi/hadoop/common/*. In the following examples, we use *selected-mirror* to indicate the location of the software on one of the mirror sites:

```
[esammer@hadoop01 hadoop]$ wget \
  http://selected-mirror/hadoop/core/hadoop-1.0.0/hadoop-1.0.0.tar.gz
--2012-02-04 18:29:31--  http://selected-mirror/hadoop/core/hadoop-1.0.0↵
  /hadoop-1.0.0.tar.gz
Resolving selected-mirror... a.b.c.d
Connecting to selected-mirror|a.b.c.d|:80... connected.
HTTP request sent, awaiting response... 200 OK
Length: 59468784 (57M) [application/x-gzip]
Saving to: `hadoop-1.0.0.tar.gz'

100%[====================================================>] 59,468,784  1.88M/s in 26s

2012-02-04 18:29:56 (2.21 MB/s) - `hadoop-1.0.0.tar.gz' saved [59468784/59468784]
```

2. Unpack the tarball.

```
[esammer@hadoop01 hadoop]$ tar -zxf hadoop-1.0.0.tar.gz
[esammer@hadoop01 hadoop]$ ls hadoop-1.0.0
bin          docs                       ivy           README.txt
build.xml    hadoop-ant-1.0.0.jar       ivy.xml       sbin
c++          hadoop-core-1.0.0.jar      lib           share
CHANGES.txt  hadoop-examples-1.0.0.jar  libexec       src
conf         hadoop-test-1.0.0.jar      LICENSE.txt   webapps
contrib      hadoop-tools-1.0.0.jar     NOTICE.txt
```

You'll notice that the directory includes common directories like *bin*, *sbin*, *lib*, *libexec*, *share*, as well as *conf* directory that contains configuration files. The primary jar files containing the Hadoop code are *hadoop-core-1.0.0.jar* and *hadoop-tools-1.0.0.jar*. In the *src* directory, you'll find the source code for Hadoop itself. This can be a useful reference for how Hadoop works, although it does require intermediate to advanced level Java knowledge to understand.

The version 1.0.0 lineage of Hadoop releases has a large number of group writable files in the tarball. While not critical, it is a strange decision and some administrators will want to remove this permission:

```
[esammer@hadoop01 hadoop]$ chmod -R g-w hadoop-1.0.0/
```

3. Move the unpacked directory to the proper location on the filesystem.

The proper location to install Hadoop is left entirely to the administrator when installing from a tarball. For personal testing installations, your home directory may be fine, whereas production deployments may live in */usr/local* or */opt*. If you elect to deploy Hadoop in a system directory such as */usr/local*, you'll need root privileges to move files there; */usr/local* usually has the ownership root:root with the permissions 0755. We'll use */usr/local* for now:

```
[esammer@hadoop01 hadoop]$ sudo mv hadoop-1.0.0 /usr/local/
```

If you've moved Hadoop to a system directory, don't forget to change the owner and group:

```
[esammer@hadoop01 hadoop]$ cd /usr/local/
[esammer@hadoop01 local]$ sudo chown -R root:root hadoop-1.0.0/
```

From here on out, you'll need to work as **root** to make changes within the directory.

 Make sure that the directory containing the Hadoop software is not writable by the user MapReduce tasks will execute as. If it is, it's trivial to write a MapReduce job that alters the software itself to change its behavior.

4. Relocate the *conf* directory (optional).

   Hadoop expects to find its *conf* directory in $HADOOP_HOME (which in our case is *hadoop-1.0.0*). One option is to leave the *conf* directory where it is, but that has a few notable downsides. For instance, leaving the directory where it is means that when we inevitably upgrade to a newer version of Hadoop, we now need to copy configuration files between versions. Another problem is that we may want to monitor the directory tree in which we'll install this directory with an intrusion detection system (IDS) like Tripwire. The most obvious reason to move the *conf* directory, though, is that configuration files for every other system live in */etc* and we're just used to looking there.

   The simplest way to relocate *conf* is to move the directory where you want it and create a symlink to the new location:

   ```
   [esammer@hadoop01 local]$ sudo mkdir /etc/hadoop/
   [esammer@hadoop01 local]$ cd hadoop-1.0.0
   [esammer@hadoop01 hadoop-1.0.0]$ sudo mv conf /etc/hadoop/conf-1.0.0
   [esammer@hadoop01 hadoop-1.0.0]$ ln -s /etc/hadoop/conf-1.0.0 ./conf
   ```

   Later, we'll use configuration variables in hadoop-env.sh to specify alternate locations for Hadoop's log and pid file directories.

Package installation

Starting with release 0.20.203, Apache Hadoop is also available as RPM and Debian format packages. Using packages for installation greatly simplifies the process and reduces the chance of error. The packages provided by the ASF do not specify any external dependencies and should work on any system that supports packages of that format. While simpler than producing versions of the packages for each version of each distribution of Linux, it means that package conflicts are ignored and dependencies are not automatically pulled in during installation so care must be taken to first validate the system is in a clean state prior to installation. Although there aren't distribution specific versions of packages, there are specific packages for both x86 (i386) and x86-64 (amd64) architectures; be sure to download the proper packages for your machines.

The act of installing packages on RPM or Debian based systems is trivial. For RPM based systems, administrators can use rpm directly or a higher level tool like yum. Similarly, Debian derivatives use either deb or apt-get for package installation.

We can examine the metadata included in the rpm prior to installing it. Note that even though it is possible to relocate some of the directory trees, it may break Hadoop at runtime. If you're using packages, it's strongly advised that you do not attempt to relocate files or directories after installation:

```
[esammer@hadoop01 hadoop]$ rpm -q -p hadoop-1.0.0-1.amd64.rpm --info
Name        : hadoop                    Relocations: /usr /etc/hadoop
                                                     /var/log/hadoop
                                                     /var/run/hadoop
Version     : 1.0.0                          Vendor: Apache Software Foundation
Release     : 1                          Build Date: Thu 15 Dec 2011
                                                     11:41:22 AM EST
Install Date: (not installed)           Build Host: devadm900.cc1.ygridcore.net
Group       : Development/Libraries      Source RPM: hadoop-1.0.0-1.src.rpm
Size        : 55430227                      License: Apache License, Version 2.0
Signature   : (none)
URL         : http://hadoop.apache.org/core/
Summary     : The Apache Hadoop project develops open-source software for reliable,
              scalable, distributed computing
Description :
The Apache Hadoop project develops open-source software for reliable, scalable,
distributed computing.  Hadoop includes these subprojects:

Hadoop Common: The common utilities that support the other Hadoop subprojects.
HDFS: A distributed file system that provides high throughput access to
    application data.
MapReduce: A software framework for distributed processing of large data sets on
    compute clusters.
```

As mentioned earlier, the act of installation is relatively simple when using packages:

```
[esammer@hadoop01 hadoop]$ sudo rpm -ihv hadoop-1.0.0-1.amd64.rpm
Preparing...                ########################################### [100%]
   1:hadoop                 ########################################### [100%]
```

Some of advantages of installing Hadoop using packages include:

Simplicity
   Files and directories are guaranteed to have the correct permissions.

Consistency
   Files and directories are installed according to the FHS; configuration files are in */etc/hadoop*, logs in */var/log/hadoop*, executables are in */usr/bin*, and so forth.

Integration
   It is easy to integrate an Hadoop installation with configuration management software like Chef and Puppet since Hadoop can now be installed just like other software packages.

Versioning

As newer versions of Hadoop are related, the process of upgrading the software on disk can be deferred to the package manager.

A brief check of `rpm -q hadoop -l` reveals a complete list of all files contained in the package and their install locations. The most important paths to know about are as follows:

/etc/hadoop

Hadoop's configuration files. The equivalent of the *conf* directory in the tarball.

/etc/rc.d/init.d

Standard SYSV style init scripts for each Hadoop daemon. On CentOS and RHEL, */etc/init.d* is actually a symlink to */etc/rc.d/init.d* meaning you can access these files as you would any other init script.

/usr/bin

The main `hadoop` executable as well as the `task-controller` binary (see Chapter 6 for details on `task-controller`).

/usr/include/hadoop

C++ header files for Hadoop Pipes.

/usr/lib

C libraries for Hadoop. This is where *libhdfs.so*, *libhadoop.a*, and *libhadoop-pipes.a* live, for example.

/usr/libexec

Miscellaneous files used by various libraries and scripts that come with Hadoop. These files are normally not touched by administrators.

/usr/sbin

Many of the helper shell scripts used by administrators of Hadoop are installed here such as *start-*.sh*, *stop-*.sh*, *hadoop-daemon.sh* and the recently added *hadoop-setup-*.sh* scripts.

/usr/share/doc/hadoop

License, *NOTICE*, and *README* files.

CDH

Cloudera's Distribution including Apache Hadoop (or just CDH) is an alternative to downloading Hadoop directly from the Apache Software Foundation. Starting with a given release of Hadoop, Cloudera backports critical features and bug fixes from newer versions of Apache Hadoop and in some cases, previously unreleased branches of development. All code in CDH is fully open source and available under the Apache Software License 2.0; the same license as Apache Hadoop itself. Additionally, CDH includes packages of other open source projects related to Apache Hadoop like Hive, HBase, Pig, Sqoop, Flume, and others.

Just like Apache Hadoop proper, CDH is available as tarballs as well as popular package formats like RPM and Debian packages. Reasons for choosing one format of CDH over the other are driven by the same factors outlined earlier. All releases of CDH can be downloaded directly from Cloudera at *http://www.cloudera.com/downloads*. Cloudera also provides extensive documentation on their support portal (*http://ccp.cloudera .com*) for the operating systems and installation methods they support.

Cloudera has both yum and apt-get format repositories available, which further simplifies large deployments. Users who opt to use these repositories only need to install a single package to make their machines aware of the repository and then may use yum or apt-get to install any of the packages available therein.

```
[root@hadoop01 ~]# rpm -ihv http://archive.cloudera.com/redhat/cdh/▧
   cdh3-repository-1.0-1.noarch.rpm
Retrieving http://archive.cloudera.com/redhat/cdh/cdh3-repository-1.0-1.noarch.rpm
Preparing...                ########################################### [100%]
   1:cdh3-repository        ########################################### [100%]
```

The *cdh3-repository-1.0-1.noarch.rpm* package simply installs the proper files to make yum aware of the Cloudera repository of CDH3 packages. If we were to examine the contents of the package, we'd see that it simply added a file in */etc/yum.repos.d*:

```
[root@hadoop01 ~]# rpm -q cdh3-repository -l
/etc/pki/rpm-gpg
/etc/pki/rpm-gpg/RPM-GPG-KEY-cloudera
/etc/yum.repos.d/cloudera-cdh3.repo
/usr/share/doc/cdh3-repository-1.0
/usr/share/doc/cdh3-repository-1.0/LICENSE
```

With the machine now aware of Cloudera's repository, packages can be installed using yum:

```
[root@hadoop01 ~]# yum install hadoop-0.20
Loaded plugins: fastestmirror
Loading mirror speeds from cached hostfile
 * base: mirrors.usc.edu
 * extras: mirror.cogentco.com
 * updates: mirrors.usc.edu
Setting up Install Process
Resolving Dependencies
--> Running transaction check
---> Package hadoop-0.20.noarch 0:0.20.2+923.194-1 set to be updated
--> Finished Dependency Resolution

Dependencies Resolved

================================================================================
 Package         Arch        Version              Repository          Size
================================================================================
Installing:
 hadoop-0.20     noarch      0.20.2+923.194-1     cloudera-cdh3       30 M
```

```
Transaction Summary
================================================================================
Install      1 Package(s)
Upgrade      0 Package(s)

Total download size: 30 M
Is this ok [y/N]: y
Downloading Packages:
hadoop-0.20-0.20.2+923.194-1.noarch.rpm                | 30 MB     04:29
warning: rpmts_HdrFromFdno: Header V4 DSA signature: NOKEY, key ID e8f86acd
cloudera-cdh3/gpgkey                                   | 1.7 kB    00:00
Importing GPG key 0xE8F86ACD "Yum Maintainer <webmaster@cloudera.com>" ↵
   from http://archive.cloudera.com/redhat/cdh/RPM-GPG-KEY-cloudera
Is this ok [y/N]: y
Running rpm_check_debug
Running Transaction Test
Finished Transaction Test
Transaction Test Succeeded
Running Transaction
  Installing    : hadoop-0.20                                          1/1

Installed:
  hadoop-0.20.noarch 0:0.20.2+923.194-1

Complete!
```

In CDH, some components are provided as separate packages to minimize download size and allow administrators to customize their deployment. For example, you may note that the hadoop-0.20 package is listed as being architecture agnostic (noarch), but we know Hadoop has native code. These components are available as separate RPMs and can be just as easily installed, but what packages are available? We can use `yum list available | grep cloudera-cdh3` to find all available packages from the repository.

```
[root@hadoop01 ~]# yum list available | grep cloudera-cdh3
flume.noarch                      0.9.4+25.40-1            cloudera-cdh3
flume-master.noarch               0.9.4+25.40-1            cloudera-cdh3
flume-node.noarch                 0.9.4+25.40-1            cloudera-cdh3
hadoop-0.20.noarch                0.20.2+923.194-1         cloudera-cdh3
hadoop-0.20-conf-pseudo.noarch    0.20.2+923.194-1         cloudera-cdh3
hadoop-0.20-datanode.noarch       0.20.2+923.194-1         cloudera-cdh3
hadoop-0.20-debuginfo.i386        0.20.2+923.194-1         cloudera-cdh3
hadoop-0.20-debuginfo.x86_64      0.20.2+923.194-1         cloudera-cdh3
hadoop-0.20-doc.noarch            0.20.2+923.194-1         cloudera-cdh3
hadoop-0.20-fuse.i386             0.20.2+923.194-1         cloudera-cdh3
hadoop-0.20-fuse.x86_64           0.20.2+923.194-1         cloudera-cdh3
hadoop-0.20-jobtracker.noarch     0.20.2+923.194-1         cloudera-cdh3
hadoop-0.20-libhdfs.i386          0.20.2+923.194-1         cloudera-cdh3
hadoop-0.20-libhdfs.x86_64        0.20.2+923.194-1         cloudera-cdh3
hadoop-0.20-namenode.noarch       0.20.2+923.194-1         cloudera-cdh3
hadoop-0.20-native.i386           0.20.2+923.194-1         cloudera-cdh3
hadoop-0.20-native.x86_64         0.20.2+923.194-1         cloudera-cdh3
hadoop-0.20-pipes.i386            0.20.2+923.194-1         cloudera-cdh3
hadoop-0.20-pipes.x86_64          0.20.2+923.194-1         cloudera-cdh3
```

hadoop-0.20-sbin.i386	0.20.2+923.194-1	cloudera-cdh3
hadoop-0.20-sbin.x86_64	0.20.2+923.194-1	cloudera-cdh3
hadoop-0.20-secondarynamenode.noarch	0.20.2+923.194-1	cloudera-cdh3
hadoop-0.20-source.noarch	0.20.2+923.194-1	cloudera-cdh3
hadoop-0.20-tasktracker.noarch	0.20.2+923.194-1	cloudera-cdh3
hadoop-hbase.noarch	0.90.4+49.137-1	cloudera-cdh3
hadoop-hbase-doc.noarch	0.90.4+49.137-1	cloudera-cdh3
hadoop-hbase-master.noarch	0.90.4+49.137-1	cloudera-cdh3
hadoop-hbase-regionserver.noarch	0.90.4+49.137-1	cloudera-cdh3
hadoop-hbase-thrift.noarch	0.90.4+49.137-1	cloudera-cdh3
hadoop-hive.noarch	0.7.1+42.36-2	cloudera-cdh3
hadoop-hive-metastore.noarch	0.7.1+42.36-2	cloudera-cdh3
hadoop-hive-server.noarch	0.7.1+42.36-2	cloudera-cdh3
hadoop-pig.noarch	0.8.1+28.26-1	cloudera-cdh3
hadoop-zookeeper.noarch	3.3.4+19.3-1	cloudera-cdh3
hadoop-zookeeper-server.noarch	3.3.4+19.3-1	cloudera-cdh3
hue.noarch	1.2.0.0+114.20-1	cloudera-cdh3
hue-about.noarch	1.2.0.0+114.20-1	cloudera-cdh3
hue-beeswax.noarch	1.2.0.0+114.20-1	cloudera-cdh3
hue-common.i386	1.2.0.0+114.20-1	cloudera-cdh3
hue-common.x86_64	1.2.0.0+114.20-1	cloudera-cdh3
hue-filebrowser.noarch	1.2.0.0+114.20-1	cloudera-cdh3
hue-help.noarch	1.2.0.0+114.20-1	cloudera-cdh3
hue-jobbrowser.noarch	1.2.0.0+114.20-1	cloudera-cdh3
hue-jobsub.noarch	1.2.0.0+114.20-1	cloudera-cdh3
hue-plugins.noarch	1.2.0.0+114.20-1	cloudera-cdh3
hue-proxy.noarch	1.2.0.0+114.20-1	cloudera-cdh3
hue-shell.i386	1.2.0.0+114.20-1	cloudera-cdh3
hue-shell.x86_64	1.2.0.0+114.20-1	cloudera-cdh3
hue-useradmin.noarch	1.2.0.0+114.20-1	cloudera-cdh3
mahout.noarch	0.5+9.3-1	cloudera-cdh3
oozie.noarch	2.3.2+27.12-1	cloudera-cdh3
oozie-client.noarch	2.3.2+27.12-1	cloudera-cdh3
sqoop.noarch	1.3.0+5.68-1	cloudera-cdh3
sqoop-metastore.noarch	1.3.0+5.68-1	cloudera-cdh3
whirr.noarch	0.5.0+4.8-1	cloudera-cdh3

The hadoop-0.20 packages with the debuginfo, fuse, libhdfs, native, pipes, and sbin suffixes all have both x86 as well as x86-64 architecture versions available. Specifying multilib_policy=best in */etc/yum.conf* will instruct yum to install the architecture that best matches your system. By default, multilib_policy is set to the value all which causes all architecture versions of a package to be installed. You may also notice that there are separate packages named for each daemon. These packages contain just the init scripts for their respective daemon process; all of the code is contained in the main *hadoop-0.20* package. In most cases, and when you're unsure of what daemons will run where, it's best to simply install all of the hadoop-0.20, hadoop-0.20-doc, hadoop-0.20-native, hadoop-0.20-libhdfs, hadoop-0.20-sbin, and the init script packages on all machines in the cluster.

CDH packaging looks very similar to that of Apache Hadoop's RPMs with some important differences.

Use of `alternatives`
> CDH makes heavy use of the `alternatives` system, which allows multiple alternative versions of files to be installed on the system concurrently and easily switched between. Specifically, Hadoop's *conf* directory, main executable, log directory, and even the Hadoop software itself, are all managed by alternatives and can be altered should this be desirable. Of course, this isn't something most users want to concern themselves with, and you aren't necessarily encouraged to start moving things around, but it's worth understanding where all the symlinks come from. For details on the `alternatives` system, see `man 8 alternatives` on RedHat-like systems or `man 8 update-alternatives` on Debian derivatives.

Modification of limits
> Cloudera's packages install include files in */etc/security/limits.d* that automatically add the proper `nofile` and `nproc` limits for the users hdfs and mapred.

Hadoop home location
> The Hadoop software itself is installed in */usr/lib/hadoop-0.20* (and symlinked to */usr/lib/hadoop* by way of `alternatives`) rather than */usr/share/hadoop*. Users are encouraged to use the version agnostic path for scripts and tools whenever possible. This alleviates substantial pain when migrating from one version of Hadoop to another.

It's not uncommon for large-scale Linux environments to have internal `yum` or `apt-get` repositories that are mirrors of the outside world. This reduces external network traffic but more importantly, solves the problem of having segments of the network without external Internet connectivity. If your Hadoop cluster doesn't have external connectivity and you still want to be able to take advantage of `yum` or `apt-get` features, you can mirror the Cloudera repository internally and point machines at your copy of the packages. There are a number of tutorials on the Internet describing how to configure an internal package mirror including on Cloudera's support portal (*https://ccp.cloudera.com/display/CDHDOC/Creating+a+Local+Yum+Repository*).

Configuration: An Overview

This is almost certainly the section that motivated your purchase of this book, and with good reason. As you're probably aware, the good news is that Hadoop is highly configurable. The bad news, of course, is that Hadoop is highly configurable. Developers can sneak by, tweaking only a handful of parameters, but administrators responsible for large scale, mission critical clusters aren't so lucky. A thorough understanding of at least half of the almost 300 parameters is not a luxury, but the cost of doing business. Don't let the volume of parameters, the number of configuration files, or the somewhat (shall we say) succinct documentation scare you off.

This section is organized by subsystem or component in an effort to make the information accessible. Critical parameters are highlighted and when appropriate, related or interdependent parameters are cross referenced. Further, each section below is organized such that the most generic, system wide parameters are described first, while optimizations and special cases follow later. Since the topic of securing Hadoop is so vast, an entire chapter—Chapter 6—is dedicated to the subject.

Deprecated Property Names

In Apache Hadoop 2.0 and CDH4, as a result, many of the configuration properties found in the primary XML files were renamed to better indicate what they did and the daemons they affect. Rather than force administrators to go through the painful process of updating all configuration files, the developers chose to maintain backward compatibility with the old property names. Throughout this book, we'll continue to use the old property names since many users still deploy Apache Hadoop 1.0 and CDH3 and they still work in the newer versions of the software. Clearly the writing is on the wall, however, and you should begin to familiarize yourself with the new property names as soon as possible. Thankfully, the developers were kind enough to publish a list of the deprecated properties along with their new names, available at *http://hadoop.apache .org/common/docs/r2.0.0-alpha/hadoop-project-dist/hadoop-common/DeprecatedPro perties.html*. There are cases, notably namenode high availability and federation, where the new property names *must* be used. When describing those features we use these new names, as there's no other option.

Configuration of Hadoop can be divided into four major scopes: cluster, daemon, job, and individual operation level scope. Administrators exclusively control the first two, while developers primarily deal with the latter two, although it is possible to prevent certain parameters from being overridden as we'll see later. Global, cluster level parameters control how the software itself is deployed, service identification, access controls, and integration with the OS and external systems. Some parameters vary from daemon to daemon and, most notably, between services like HDFS and MapReduce. These parameters can not be changed without restarting the daemons which they affect. As this implies, not all configuration parameters can be changed without some degree, even minor, of service interruption. Many of Hadoop's parameters can be specified at the MapReduce job level with administrators providing only default values. Developers or automated systems that submit jobs can override these values in code or from the command line, where applicable. Lastly, some parameters can be specified per operation, provided the code or context supports it. A good example of this are the `hadoop fs` commands; files, for instance, may be copied to HDFS with different replication factors or even to different clusters.

The primary method of specifying configuration parameters is a series of configuration files read by Hadoop daemons and clients. The following configuration files exist in the *conf* directory:

hadoop-env.sh

    A bourne shell fragment sourced by the Hadoop scripts, this file specifies environment variables that affect the JDK used by Hadoop, daemon JDK options, the pid file, and log file directories. Covered in "Environment Variables and Shell Scripts" on page 88.

core-site.xml
> An XML file that specifies parameters relevant to all Hadoop daemons and clients.

hdfs-site.xml
> An XML file that specifies parameters used by the HDFS daemons and clients.

mapred-site.xml
> An XML file that specifies parameters used by the MapReduce daemons and clients.

log4j.properties
> A Java property file that contains all log configuration information. Covered in "Logging Configuration" on page 90.

masters (optional)
> A newline separated list of machines that run the secondary namenode, used only by the `start-*.sh` helper scripts.

slaves (optional)
> A newline separated list of machine names that run the datanode / tasktracker pair of daemons, used only by the `start-*.sh` helper scripts.

fair-scheduler.xml (optional)
> The file used to specify the resource pools and settings for the Fair Scheduler task scheduler plugin for MapReduce.

capacity-scheduler.xml (optional)
> The name of the file used to specify the queues and settings for the Capacity Scheduler task scheduler plugin for MapReduce.

dfs.include (optional, conventional name)
> A newline separated list of machine names that are permitted to connect to the namenode.

dfs.exclude (optional, conventional name)
> A newline separated list of machine names that are not permitted to connect to the namenode.

hadoop-policy.xml
> An XML file that defines which users and / or groups are permitted to invoke specific RPC functions when communicating with Hadoop.

mapred-queue-acls.xml
> An XML file that defines which users and / or groups are permitted to submit jobs to which MapReduce job queues.

taskcontroller.cfg
> A Java property–style file that defines values used by the setuid `task-controller` MapReduce helper program used when operating in secure mode.

Many of these files are loaded by Hadoop by way of Java's `ClassLoader` (*http://docs .oracle.com/javase/6/docs/api/java/lang/ClassLoader.html*) resource loading mechanic which provides an API to load files by name from any directory in the classpath of the application. The Hadoop scripts ensure the *conf* directory is always at the head of the classpath so files can easily be located by the code. For files like *hadoop-env.sh*, *masters*, and *slaves* the supporting shell scripts use some rather complicated logic to find them; so complicated, in fact, it is covered separately in "Environment Variables and Shell Scripts" on page 88. Other files like *dfs.include*, *dfs.exclude*, *fair-scheduler.xml*, and *capacity-scheduler.xml* must be separately configured, depending on what features you choose to enable. The *taskcontroller.cfg* file is related to Hadoop security, and is discussed in "Configuring Hadoop security" on page 152.

The Hadoop XML Configuration Files

Hadoop uses a simple XML file format for its three primary configuration files *core-site.xml*, *hdfs-site.xml*, and *mapred-site.xml*. These files control the configuration of the common libraries used by Hadoop, HDFS, and MapReduce, respectively. Properties defined in each of these three files override built in default values which are contained within the main Hadoop jar file. When a MapReduce job is run, the job configuration provided by the developer can, in turn, override properties configured on the server.

The line between which properties can be overridden at runtime and which cannot is a bit fuzzy at times. For instance, a developer can (and usually should) override the number of reducers for a given MapReduce job while it never makes sense for a developer to try and specify the port on which the namenode should listen for RPC connections (not to mention it would be too late; the namenode is already running). In situations where it is possible for a developer to override a property but they should not be permitted to do so, an administrator can mark a property as *final* to prevent it from happening. When a property is marked final on the cluster but it's set by a job, the framework simply disregards the value set by the job, and allows it to continue. That is, the offending property is simply ignored. Sometimes a developer will complain that a property they set does not appear to "stick." This is usually the result of a property they're trying to set being marked final.

The format of each of these XML files (see Example 5-1) should be self explanatory.

Example 5-1. Sample Hadoop XML configuration file

```
<?xml version="1.0"?>
<configuration>

  <!-- Set 'some.property.name' to the value 'some-value'.
  <property>
    <name>some.property.name</name>
    <value>some-value</value>
  </property>
```

```
<!--
  Set 'foo.bar.baz' to the value '42' and prevent it from
  being overridden by marking it final.
-->
<property>
  <name>foo.bar.baz</name>
  <value>42</value>
  <final>true</final>
</property>

<!-- Additional property elements... -->

</configuration>
```

In the following sections, only property names and values are given in the interest of space. Each property should be defined as in Example 5-1. The file in which a given group of properties should be set is listed in the beginning of each section. When there are exceptions, the configuration file is called out next to the property name. For example, the `fs.default.name` property (`fs.default.name` (*core-site.xml*) on page 93) is an HDFS property, but must be set in *core-site.xml*.

Environment Variables and Shell Scripts

The Hadoop executable, along with many of the scripts it calls and those that call it, uses a myriad of environment variables to locate files and alter the behavior of the system. There are two types of environment variables: those that are used by the scripts to locate the software and configuration files, and those that define the environment in which the daemons and child tasks execute. Variables that affect daemon settings such as the location of the JDK and Java options used to launch daemons are necessary to the operation of Hadoop. The set of variables that alter how Hadoop locates its configuration files and even the software itself are used far less often, but are explained as well. To be absolutely clear, this is not an endorsement of making excessive use of such so called features. There are, however, exceptional circumstances when there is little other choice, and this kind of flexibility is useful. In most cases, knowledge of Hadoop's environmental intricacies is useful only to aid in troubleshooting the more clever solutions dreamt up by cluster users.

The file that controls the environment of the Hadoop daemons, including the arguments with which they're launched, the location of the JDK, and the log and pid file directories is *hadoop-env.sh*, and it's found in the standard Hadoop configuration directory. Within *hadoop-env.sh* you must properly configure the location of the JDK by setting $JAVA_HOME. It is true that the hadoop command will try and discover the location of Java if this isn't set, but you run the risk of accidentally picking up the wrong version if multiple JDKs are installed on the system. Additionally, any options that should be passed to the daemon processes can be set in the $HADOOP_*daemon*_OPTS variables where *daemon* is the name of the process. Usually, the maximum Java heap size, JMX

---

configuration options, and garbage collection tuning parameters are the most commonly passed arguments. See Example 5-2 for an example environment configuration file.

Apache Bigtop

Newer versions of Hadoop are based on a new project called Apache Bigtop. Bigtop is a *meta-project* in that it strictly deals with the build, packaging, and testing of Hadoop ecosystem projects under a single umbrella. In order to unify the behavior of functions like locating the proper JDK to use, versions of Hadoop based on Bigtop use a set of helper scripts provided by Bigtop rather than each project implementing this logic. This means some versions of Hadoop may not respect all settings in files like *hadoop-env.sh*. See the Hadoop release notes for your version for more information. More information about Apache Bigtop is available at *http://incubator.apache.org/bigtop/*.

Rarely should there be a need to set these variables within individual shell sessions. In fact, if you catch yourself thinking about setting something like $HADOOP_CONF_DIR or $HADOOP_HOME, it's probably worth taking a hard look at how the software is deployed. The hadoop command will, provided it's in your path, locate $HADOOP_HOME correctly in almost all cases. It also looks for a *conf* directory in $HADOOP_HOME as the default value of $HADOOP_CONF_DIR. Rather than redefine $HADOOP_CONF_DIR, it is usually far simpler to just symlink the *conf* directory to minimize the amount of special knowledge applications need to use the cluster.

In some cases, users may ask administrators to add jar files to $HADOOP_CLASSPATH so they may be used in MapReduce jobs. Resist this at all costs. Instead, gently encourage users to use Hadoop's Distributed Cache feature to push job dependencies to the nodes of the cluster where they are required when they submit the job. By using the Distributed Cache, you avoid adding user defined classes to the classpath of the Hadoop daemons (which is what $HADOOP_CLASSPATH actually does) and potentially destablizing the framework. Should you or your users require further motivation, remember that to alter the classes on $HADOOP_CLASSPATH, all tasktrackers must be restarted. You definitely don't want to interrupt all cluster activity every time a new version of someone's favorite Java library is released. See Example 5-2.

Example 5-2. Sample hadoop-env.sh file

```
# Set Hadoop-specific environment variables here.

# The java implementation to use.  Required.
# export JAVA_HOME=/usr/lib/j2sdk1.6-sun
JAVA_HOME=/usr/java/jdk1.6.0_31/

# Extra Java CLASSPATH elements.  Optional.
# export HADOOP_CLASSPATH="<extra_entries>:$HADOOP_CLASSPATH"
```

```
# Command specific options appended to HADOOP_OPTS when specified
export HADOOP_NAMENODE_OPTS="-Xmx8g -Dcom.sun.management.jmxremote ↵
  $HADOOP_NAMENODE_OPTS"
export HADOOP_SECONDARYNAMENODE_OPTS="-Xmx8g -Dcom.sun.management.jmxremote ↵
  $HADOOP_SECONDARYNAMENODE_OPTS"
export HADOOP_DATANODE_OPTS="-Dcom.sun.management.jmxremote $HADOOP_DATANODE_OPTS"
export HADOOP_BALANCER_OPTS="-Dcom.sun.management.jmxremote $HADOOP_BALANCER_OPTS"
export HADOOP_JOBTRACKER_OPTS="-Xmx8g -Dcom.sun.management.jmxremote ↵
  $HADOOP_JOBTRACKER_OPTS"
# export HADOOP_TASKTRACKER_OPTS=
# The following applies to multiple commands (fs, dfs, fsck, distcp etc)
# export HADOOP_CLIENT_OPTS

# Where log files are stored.  $HADOOP_HOME/logs by default.
# export HADOOP_LOG_DIR=${HADOOP_HOME}/logs

# File naming remote slave hosts.  $HADOOP_HOME/conf/slaves by default.
# export HADOOP_SLAVES=${HADOOP_HOME}/conf/slaves

# The directory where pid files are stored. /tmp by default.
# export HADOOP_PID_DIR=/var/hadoop/pids

# A string representing this instance of hadoop. $USER by default.
# export HADOOP_IDENT_STRING=$USER

# The scheduling priority for daemon processes.  See 'man nice'.
# export HADOOP_NICENESS=10
```

The Legacy of $HADOOP_HOME and $HADOOP_PREFIX

After version 0.20.205 (and subsequently 1.0), the environment variable $HADOOP_HOME was deprecated in favor of $HADOOP_PREFIX. It's unclear as to the motivation (there's no Apache JIRA that mentions the introduction of $HADOOP_PREFIX or the deprecation of $HADOOP_HOME) and has caused a noticeable amount of grumbling in the Hadoop community from cluster administrators. The speculation is that this is the result of the plan to separate the three Hadoop components - common, HDFS, and MapReduce - into separate projects, but provide a simpler method of letting each know about the location of the other without requiring three separate $HADOOP_COMPONENT_HOME variables. Of course, the result is that we're left with a single project and a single variable, just with a different name.

Logging Configuration

Almost all of Hadoop uses the Java logging package log4j (*http://logging.apache.org/log4j/*) to control log output. The main log4j configuration file is a standard Java property format file called *log4j.properties* and can be found in Hadoop's *conf* directory. This file controls the overall log levels of both the Hadoop daemons as well as MapReduce jobs that execute on the cluster.

If you're not already familiar with log4j, there are a few core concepts of which to be aware. A logger is a named channel for log events that has a specified minimum log level. The supported log levels, in order of most severe to least, are FATAL, ERROR, WARN, INFO, DEBUG, and TRACE. The minimum log level acts as a filter: log events with a log level greater than or equal to that which is specified are accepted while less severe events are simply discarded. Loggers are hierarchical; each logger has a parent logger from which it inherits its configuration information. At the top of the inheritance tree is a root logger which is a logger with no parent. As you would expect, each logger is free to override any of the parameters it so chooses. Loggers output their log events to an *appender* which is responsible to handling the event in some meaningful way. By far, the most commonly used appenders write log events to disk, but appenders for outputting log events to the console, sending data to syslog, or even to JMS exist. The final component in log4j is the *layout* which acts as a formatter for log events. One of the most powerful aspects of log4j is that the log level of each logger, its appender, and the layout are all configured via the configuration file so they may be changed at runtime.

The log4j configuration file format is a standard Java properties file (i.e. key value pairs) as mentioned earlier. What is notable is how it uses a dot separated pseudo-hierarchical naming convention to model concepts like inheritance. Log4j properties begin with the `log4j` prefix, but since the file is a properties file, administrators are free to set their own variables and reference them later: something the Hadoop *log4j.properties* file does often. Log4j has a few special properties that must be set for it to function, the most important of which is `log4j.rootLogger` which specifies the default log level and appender to be used by all loggers. Loggers can be specified by using the naming convention of `log4j.logger.`*logger-name*. Logger names are defined by the application, but are almost always the name of the Java class that is generating the log events. The hierarchical relationship of a logger is defined by dotted notation with descendants having their parent's prefix. For example, the logger `org.apache` is the parent of `org.apache.hadoop`, which is the parent of `org.apache.hadoop.hdfs` and so on. If we wanted to limit the log level of all HDFS classes (or, more accurately, loggers which were named for their respective HDFS classes) to the WARN level, we could set the property `log4j.logger.org.apache.hadoop.hdfs = WARN`. The value of a logger parameter is always a log level, a comma, and the name of one or more appenders. The comma and appender list is optional, in which case, the logger inherits the appender of its parent.

The default log4j.properties file that ships with Hadoop is complex, at a minimum. Table 5-1 contains a summary of what it all means.

Table 5-1. Hadoop log4j configuration summary

Setting	Value
hadoop.log.dir	.
hadoop.root.logger	INFO, console

Setting	Value
log4j.rootLogger	${hadoop.root.logger}, EventCounter
hadoop.security.logger	INFO, console
hadoop.mapreduce.jobsummary.logger	${hadoop.root.logger}
hadoop.security.log.file	*SecurityAuth.audit*
hadoop.mapreduce.jobsummary.log.file	*hadoop-mapreduce.jobsummary.log*

Logger name	Value
SecurityLogger	${hadoop.security.logger}
org.apache.hadoop.mapred.JobInProgress$JobSummary	${hadoop.mapreduce.jobsummary.logger}
org.apache.hadoop.hdfs.server.namenode.FSNamesystem.audit	WARN[a]
org.jets3t.service.impl.rest.httpclient.RestS3Service	ERROR

Appender	Value
console	stderr
RFA	*${hadoop.log.dir}/${hadoop.log.file}*
DRFA	*${hadoop.log.dir}/${hadoop.log.file}*
DRFAS	*${hadoop.log.dir}/${hadoop.security.log.file}*
JSA	*${hadoop.log.dir}/${hadoop.mapreduce.jobsummary.log.file}*
TLA	org.apache.hadoop.mapred.TaskLogAppender
EventCounter	org.apache.hadoop.metrics.jvm.EventCounter

[a] Since HDFS audit events are logged at the INFO level, this effectively disables auditing.

You may notice that some of the appenders listed aren't referenced by any of the loggers. This is perfectly legal (although the inverse is not) and is done to make it as simple as possible to select a different type of appender quickly. If all of this has you wondering how much of this you really need to worry about in practice, don't worry. None of these settings *need* to be changed to run Hadoop in production although you may find them to be of interest in special circumstances. If all you want to do is increase or decrease the verbosity of Hadoop *globally*, look no further than hadoop.root.logger, but be warned; too much logging can fill up disks and too little will leave you without the necessary information when debugging production problems. When in doubt, adjust the log level of individual packages (by creating a logger for the Java package of interest) rather than making global changes.

HDFS

The following properties should be set in the *hdfs-site.xml* file unless otherwise indicated. The format of *hdfs-site.xml* is explained "The Hadoop XML Configuration Files" on page 87.

Identification and Location

Configuring HDFS is relatively straight forward with only a few parameter changes required for a sound base configuration. The first set of parameters we'll examine are those that identify HDFS to clients and specify local filesystem paths used by the namenode, datanode, and secondary namenode daemons.

fs.default.name *(core-site.xml)*

> The fs.default.name parameter is a URL that specifies the default filesystem used by clients. Developers use the static get() method of the FileSystem abstract class to gain access to a specific implementation of a filesystem. The implementation returned by get() is based on the URL specified in the configuration file. By default, fs.default.name is set to file:/// which means clients access the local Linux filesystem, similar to Java's standard File class. This is sometimes used for testing or special cases, but production clusters that use HDFS will want this to instead use the form *hdfs://hostname:port* where *hostname* and *port* are the machine and port on which the namenode daemon runs and listens. This parameter serves double duty in that it also informs the namenode as to which IP and port it should bind. Datanodes heartbeat to this hostname and port as well. Although many administrators choose to specify hostnames, it is possible to instead reference machines by IP address. The commonly used port for the namenode is 8020 and, although you are free to specify any port you wish, you may find it easier to follow documentation and reference material if you don't have to constantly translate port numbers in your head.
>
> Used by: NN, DN, SNN, JT, TT, clients.

dfs.name.dir

> One of the most critical parameters, dfs.name.dir specifies a comma separated list of local directories (with no spaces) in which the namenode should store a copy of the HDFS filesystem metadata. Given the criticality of the metadata, administrators are strongly encouraged to specify two internal disks and a low latency, highly reliable, NFS mount. A complete copy of the metadata is stored in each directory; in other words, the namenode mirrors the data between directories. For this reason, the underlying disks need not be part of a RAID group, although some administrators choose to do so and forego specifying multiple directories in dfs.name.dir (although an NFS mount should still be used, no matter what). The namenode metadata is not excessively large; usually far below 1TB in size, although running out of disk space is not something you want to occur.

Idle spindle syndrome

When deploying homogeneous hardware, it's not uncommon for the machine running the namenode to have a large amount of unused disks in the system. This can also occur if the disk for `dfs.name.dir` is a large RAID-5 group. All too often, administrators are tempted to put this disk to so called good use and run a datanode on the same machine. The next obvious thought is to run a tasktracker so data can be processed locally. Now, the dedicated hardware reserved for the namenode is running spiky workloads that can impact its stability and performance. Do not fall victim to idle spindle syndrome.

As if by some cruel joke, the default value of `dfs.name.dir` is *hadoop.tmp.dir/dfs/ name* and, when coupled with `hadoop.tmp.dir`'s default of */tmp/hadoop- user.name*, lands the filesystem metadata squarely in a volatile directory. Many new to Hadoop have quickly setup Hadoop, missed setting `dfs.name.dir`, and found themselves with an unusable filesystem after rebooting the namenode because */ tmp* was cleared during boot. If there's a single parameter that should be triple-checked for correctness, it's `dfs.name.dir`.

Example value: */data/1/dfs/nn,/data/2/dfs/nn,/data/3/dfs/nn*. Used by: NN.

`dfs.data.dir`

While `dfs.name.dir` specifies the location of the namenode metadata, `dfs.data.dir` is used to indicate where datanodes should store HDFS block data. Also a comma separate list, rather than mirroring data to each directory specified, the datanode round robins blocks between disks in an attempt to allocate blocks evenly across all drives. The datanode assumes each directory specifies a separate physical device in a JBOD group. As described earlier, by JBOD, we mean each disk individually addressable by the OS, and formatted and mounted as a separate mount point. Loss of a physical disk is not critical since replicas will exist on other machines in the cluster.

Example value: */data/1/dfs/dn,/data/2/dfs/dn,/data/3/dfs/dn,/data/4/dfs/dn*. Used by: DN.

`fs.checkpoint.dir`

The `fs.checkpoint.dir` parameter specifies the comma separated list of directories used by the secondary namenode in which to store filesystem metadata during a checkpoint operation. If multiple directories are provided, the secondary namenode mirrors the data in each directory the same way the namenode does. It is rare, however, that multiple directories are given because the checkpoint data is transient and, if lost, is simply copied during the next checkpoint operation. Some administrators treat the contents of this directory as a worst case scenario location from which they can recover the namenode's metadata. It is, after all, a valid copy of the data required to restore a completely failed namenode. With that said, this shouldn't be treated as a true backup because it's possible that the secondary namenode could fail, leaving you without a backup at all.

Example value: */data/1/dfs/snn*. Used by: SNN.

`dfs.permissions.supergroup`
Within HDFS, a designated group is given special privileges equivalent to being the superuser. Users in the group specified by `dfs.permissions.supergroup` are permitted to perform any filesystem operation. More specifically, all permission checks will always return success for users in this group. By default, this is set to the group supergroup which isn't a common group in Linux so it's unlikely that users will be accidentally granted permissions they shouldn't have although administrators should change it if necessary. This privilege, just like root privileges in Linux, should never be given to users used for every day activities.

Example value: hadoop. Used by: NN, clients.

Optimization and Tuning

`io.file.buffer.size` *(core-site.xml)*
Hadoop performs file IO operations all throughout the codebase. In many of these instances, the property io.file.buffer.size is used as a general purpose buffer size. Larger buffers tend to result in more efficient data transfer, either from disk or during network operations, at the cost of increased memory consumption and latency. This property should be set to a multiple of the system page size, defined in bytes, and is 4KB by default. A value of 64KB (65536 bytes) is a good starting point.

Example value: 65536. Used by: Clients, daemons.

`dfs.balance.bandwidthPerSec`
The HDFS balancer utility looks for over or underutilized datanodes in the cluster and moves blocks between them in an effort to balance the distribution of blocks. If the balancing operation were not rate limited, it would easily monopolize the network leaving nothing for MapReduce jobs or data ingest. The `dfs.balance.band` `widthPerSec` parameter specifies how much bandwidth *each datanode* is allowed to used for balancing. The value is given in bytes which is unintuitive since network bandwidth is always described in terms of bits so double check your math!

Unfortunately, as mentioned above, this parameter is used by each datanode to control bandwidth and is read by the daemon at startup time. This prevents the value from being specified by the administrator at the time the balancer is run.

Example value: Used by: DN.

`dfs.block.size`
A common misconception is that HDFS has a block size; this isn't true. Instead, each *file* has an associated block size which is determined when the file is initially created. The `dfs.block.size` parameter determines the default block size for all

newly created files. It doesn't affect files that already exist in the filesystem and clients sometimes override it when they have special information about the files they'll create.

The `dfs.block.size` parameter value is expressed in bytes and is 67108864 (64MB) by default. The proper block size for a file depends on the data and how its processed, but for most use cases, 134217728 (128MB) is a more appropriate default. Hadoop MapReduce (specifically jobs that use input formats that subclass `FileIn putFormat`) wind up with a map task for each block of the file(s) processed as part of the job.[1] This means the file block size can significantly impact the efficiency of a MapReduce job for better or worse.

Example value: 134217728. Used by: Clients.

dfs.datanode.du.reserved

When the datanode reports the available disk capacity to the namenode, it will report the sum of the unused capacity of all `dfs.data.dir` disks. Since `mapred.local.dir` usually shares the same available disk space, there needs to be a way to reserve disk space for MapReduce applications. The value of `dfs.data node.du.reserved` specifies the amount of space, in bytes, to be reserved on *each disk* in `dfs.data.dir`. No disk space is reserved, by default, meaning HDFS is allowed to consume all available disk space on each data disk, at which point the node becomes read only. Instead, it is adviseable to reserve at least 10GB per disk for map task output by setting `dfs.datanode.du.reserved` to 10737418240. If the average MapReduce job produces a significant amount of intermediate output (again, this is map task output) or you have large disks (where each disk is greater than 2TB), feel free to increase the amount of reserved capacity accordingly.

Example value: 10737418240. Used by: DN.

dfs.namenode.handler.count

The namenode has a pool of worker threads that are responsible for processing RPC requests from clients as well as other cluster daemons. A larger number of handlers (i.e. worker threads) means a greater capacity to handle concurrent heartbeats from datanodes as well as metadata operations from clients. For larger clusters, or clusters with a large number of clients, it's usually necessary to increase `dfs.namename.handler.count` from its default of 10. A general guideline for setting `dfs.namenode.handler.count` is to make it the natural logarithm of the number of cluster nodes, times 20 (as a whole number). If the previous sentence makes you glaze over, use the following python snippet (where 200 is the number of nodes in the cluster in question):

```
esammer:~ hadoop01$ python -c 'import math ; print int(math.log(200) * 20)'
105
```

---

1. This isn't entirely true because MapReduce jobs operate on input splits—a logical window into a file—not an HDFS block, directly. For details on how Hadoop MapReduce divides jobs into tasks, see the section "FileInputFormat input splits" on page 238 of in Hadoop: The Definitive Guide (3rd ed).

Symptoms of this being set too low include datanodes timing out or receiving connection refused while trying to connect to the namenode, large namenode RPC queue sizes, and possibly high RPC latency. Each of these symptoms can be the effect of other problems, so it's difficult to say a change to `dfs.namename.handler.count` will correct the problem, but it's certainly something to check while troubleshooting.

Example value: 105 based on a 200 node cluster. Used by: NN.

dfs.datanode.failed.volumes.tolerated

The default behavior of the datanode is to fail outright when any of its local disks fail. With disk failures being relatively common in mid to large clusters, this isn't ideal. Loss of a datanode results in a drop in the observed replication factor and, in turn, causes the namenode to instruct a datanode with another copy of the data to replicate the data to recover. The dfs.datanode.failed.volumes.tolerated parameter specifies the number of disks that are permitted to die before failing the entire datanode.

Many wonder why not tolerate the failure of all disks, deferring the failure of the datanode until there are no functional disks left. This seems to make sense over an infinite time frame, but in reality, administrators respond to failed disks much sooner than the time it would take for all disks to fail from normal wear and tear. This leaves only the case where all disks fail in relatively rapid succession; an anomalous situation that should be invested immediately. In practice, a rapid failure of disks usually indicates a failure of the drive controller or a component thereof. While rare, if disks begin failing in series in a short amount of time, the best option is to isolate and fail the entire machine as soon as the pattern is detected.

The default value for `dfs.datanode.failed.volumes.tolerated` is 0 (zero) meaning any disk failure results in a failure of the datanode. Administrators may set this to a greater number to continue running in the face of a specified number of failures although exercise caution; failures in excess of one or two disks in a short span of time is probably indicative of a larger problem.

Example value: 1. Used by: DN.

dfs.hosts

Out of the box, all datanodes are permitted to connect to the namenode and join the cluster. A datanode, upon its first connection to a namenode, captures the namespace ID (a unique identifier generated for the filesystem at the time it's formatted), and is immediately eligible to receive blocks. It is possible for administrators to specify a file that contains a list of hostnames of datanodes that are explicitly allowed to connect and join the cluster, in which case, all others are denied. Those with stronger security requirements or who wish to explicitly control access will want to use this feature.

The format of the file specified by `dfs.hosts` is a newline separated list of hostnames or IP addresses, depending on how machines identify themselves to the cluster. See

"Hostnames, DNS, and Identification" on page 57 for more information on host identification.

Example value: */etc/hadoop/conf/dfs.hosts* Used by: NN.

dfs.host.exclude

Similar to dfs.hosts, HDFS supports the notion of explicitly excluding machines from the cluster by specifying a file that contains a newline separate list of hostnames or IP addresses. Host excludes are applied *after* includes, meaning that a machine name that appears in both files is excluded. The dfs.host.exclude parameter does double duty in that it is also the method by which datanodes are gracefully decommissioned. For information on the datanode decommissioning process, see "Decommissioning a Datanode" on page 197.

Example value: */etc/hadoop/conf/dfs.hosts.exclude* Used by: NN.

fs.trash.interval *(core-site.xml)*

Users invariably delete files accidentally (or worse, retroactively declare deletion an accident). HDFS supports a trash feature, similar to that of most desktop operating systems, that allows users to recover files that have been deleted. When enabled, a file is moved to a special directory called *.Trash* in the user's HDFS home directory upon deletion rather than being removed immediately. The fs.trash.interval specifies the amount of time (in minutes) the file is retained in the *.Trash* directory prior to being permanently deleted from HDFS. Users are free to move the file back out of the *.Trash* directory, as they would any other file, which effectively restores the file. The default value of zero indicates that the trash feature is disabled.

To be clear, there's no magic in the trash function; deferring the delete operation means that the space consumed by the file is still unavailable to new data until it is permanently deleted. Users can explicitly empty the trash by running the hadoop fs -expunge command or simply waiting the configured number of minutes. Files may be immediately deleted, skipping the trash altogether, by specifying the -skipTrash argument to the hadoop fs -rm command.

Trash only supported by the command line tools

The current releases of Hadoop, the trash functionality is only supported by the command line tools. Applications built against the HDFS APIs do not automatically get this functionality. Be sure and warn application developers of this as it has claimed a number of victims. There is discussion within the community about making trash a server-side feature that applies to all clients equally, although it hasn't yet been done.

Example value: 1440 (24 hours). Used by: NN, clients.

Formatting the Namenode

Before HDFS can be started, the namenode must be formatted. Formatting is a relatively simple operation, performed once, that creates the initial filesystem metadata on the namenode. The format command *must* be run as the OS user that you intend to be the HDFS super user (see "HDFS" on page 153 for more information on users and security in HDFS), on the namenode host, and after all dfs.name.dir directories have been created with the proper permissions. When run, the format operation creates an empty *fsimage* file, edit log, and a randomly generated storage ID. The first time datanodes connect to a namenode, they adopt the storage ID and will refuse to connect to any other namenode. Should you need to reformat the namenode, you must delete all data on the datanodes as well, which includes this storage ID information.

Formatting is a destructive operation

When you format the namenode, a new filesystem is initialized. If you reformat an existing namenode, not only is all existing metadata destroyed, but any existing block data on datanodes will be permanently orphaned and inaccessible. Exercise caution when performing a format operation and make sure that you truly intend to do so.

To format a namenode, execute the hadoop namenode -format command, as shown in Example 5-3.

Example 5-3. Formatting the namenode

```
[root@hadoop01 conf]# sudo -u hdfs hadoop namenode -format
12/07/30 11:43:49 INFO namenode.NameNode: STARTUP_MSG:
/************************************************************
STARTUP_MSG: Starting NameNode
STARTUP_MSG:   host = hadoop01/10.20.186.239
STARTUP_MSG:   args = [-format]
STARTUP_MSG:   version = 2.0.0-cdh4.0.1
STARTUP_MSG:   classpath = ...
STARTUP_MSG:   build = ...
************************************************************/
Formatting using clusterid: CID-e9486a4a-0f72-4556-a846-138db5c1e81e
12/07/30 11:43:49 INFO util.HostsFileReader: Refreshing hosts (include/exclude) list
12/07/30 11:43:49 INFO blockmanagement.DatanodeManager: dfs.block.invalidate.limit=1000
12/07/30 11:43:49 INFO util.GSet: VM type       = 64-bit
12/07/30 11:43:49 INFO util.GSet: 2% max memory = 17.77875 MB
12/07/30 11:43:49 INFO util.GSet: capacity      = 2^21 = 2097152 entries
12/07/30 11:43:49 INFO util.GSet: recommended=2097152, actual=2097152
12/07/30 11:43:49 INFO blockmanagement.BlockManager: dfs.block.access.token.enable=false
12/07/30 11:43:49 INFO blockmanagement.BlockManager: defaultReplication         = 3
12/07/30 11:43:49 INFO blockmanagement.BlockManager: maxReplication             = 512
12/07/30 11:43:49 INFO blockmanagement.BlockManager: minReplication             = 1
12/07/30 11:43:49 INFO blockmanagement.BlockManager: maxReplicationStreams      = 2
12/07/30 11:43:49 INFO blockmanagement.BlockManager: shouldCheckForEnoughRacks  = false
12/07/30 11:43:49 INFO blockmanagement.BlockManager: replicationRecheckInterval = 3000
12/07/30 11:43:50 INFO namenode.FSNamesystem: fsOwner                = hdfs (auth:SIMPLE)
```

```
12/07/30 11:43:50 INFO namenode.FSNamesystem: supergroup          = supergroup
12/07/30 11:43:50 INFO namenode.FSNamesystem: isPermissionEnabled = true
12/07/30 11:43:50 INFO namenode.FSNamesystem: HA Enabled: false
12/07/30 11:43:50 INFO namenode.FSNamesystem: Append Enabled: true
12/07/30 11:43:50 INFO namenode.NameNode: Caching file names occuring more than 10 times
12/07/30 11:43:50 INFO namenode.NNStorage: Storage directory /data/1/hadoop/dfs/nn has ↵
  been successfully formatted.
12/07/30 11:43:50 INFO namenode.FSImage: Saving image file ↵
  /data/1/hadoop/dfs/nn/current/fsimage.ckpt_0000000000000000000 using no compression
12/07/30 11:43:50 INFO namenode.FSImage: Image file of size 119 saved in 0 seconds.
12/07/30 11:43:50 INFO namenode.NNStorageRetentionManager: Going to retain 1 images ↵
  with txid >= 0
12/07/30 11:43:50 INFO namenode.FileJournalManager: Purging logs older than 0
12/07/30 11:43:50 INFO namenode.NameNode: SHUTDOWN_MSG:
/************************************************************
SHUTDOWN_MSG: Shutting down NameNode at hadoop01/10.20.186.239
************************************************************/
```

Once the namenode has been formatted, you can start the HDFS daemons (see "Starting and Stopping Processes with Init Scripts" on page 195).

Creating a /tmp Directory

Many applications in the Hadoop ecosystem expect to find a */tmp* directory in HDFS. Much like */tmp* in Linux, application commonly write temporary files and directories to this path while performing work. In order to be useful, this directory must be world writable so any user can create files, although users should not be able to modify or replace files they do not own. Set the permissions to 1777 (user read/write/execute, group read/write/execute, other read/write/execute, and sticky bit set) on */tmp* to make this so. See Example 5-4.

Example 5-4. Creating /tmp in HDFS

```
[root@hadoop01 conf]# hadoop fs -ls /
[root@hadoop01 conf]# sudo -u hdfs hadoop fs -mkdir /tmp
[root@hadoop01 conf]# sudo -u hdfs hadoop fs -chmod 1777 /tmp
[root@hadoop01 conf]# hadoop fs -ls /
Found 1 items
drwxrwxrwt   - hdfs supergroup          0 2012-07-30 11:52 /tmp
```

Namenode High Availability

As we've seen, any interruption in namenode service equates to an interruption in HDFS service. For mission critical Hadoop clusters, this has been a major concern for cluster administrators. Easily one of the most highly anticipated features of Hadoop 2.0.0 and CDH4, namenode high availability (HA or NN HA) enables either manual or automatic failover in the face of system failures. There are a number of steps necessary to enable HA, as well as a few dependencies that must first be satisfied.

Property names and command line tools

Since namenode high availability is a feature of Apache Hadoop 2.0 and CDH4, this section uses both the new configuration property names and the new command line tools present in those versions.

First, an enterprise class, highly available, NFS filer should be configured to export a volume capable of supporting the total size of the namenode metadata. This isn't necessarily different from the pre-HA days where it was recommended to keep a copy of metadata on an NFS mount. If you have an existing cluster where you've already configured this, you can reuse it for an HA configuration. Configuring and exporting NFS volumes is generally vendor specific, so we'll assume this has been done and the new volume is available at */mnt/filer/namenode-shared* on both namenodes. We'll refer to this as the *shared edits directory*. Typically, this volume should be mounted with the options `tcp`, `hard`, `intr`, at least `nfsvers=3`, and whatever `timeo` and `retrans` values make sense for your network. See `man 5 nfs` for more information on NFS mount options. The shared edits directory should have the same permissions as any other namenode metadata directory. See "Users, Groups, and Privileges" on page 60 for details.

If the shared edits path is not writable or becomes unavailable for any reason, the namenode process will abort. This is notably different than `dfs.name.dir` where a failed path is simply ignored. As this implies, if this path is inaccessible from both namenodes, both will abort and HDFS will become unavailable, hence the recommendation for a filer that is, itself, highly available. Remember that both namenode processes must be able to both read and write to this path. The easiest way to accomplish this is to ensure that the uid of the user the namenode process run as is the same on all namenodes. While it's a good policy to explicitly control the uid of system users so they're the same on servers in a data center, it's a requirement when using shared filesystems such as this.

NFS Is a (Temporary) Pain

Having a dependency on NFS and a shared edits directory is painful for many. An effort is underway to remove this dependency by adding a highly available journal service for the transaction log. When complete, this journal service will optionally replace the shared edits directory as a method of coordination between the namenodes in an HA deployment. For more information on this work, see the JIRA HDFS-3077 (*https://issues.apache.org/jira/browse/HDFS-3077*).

Using shared state on an NFS filer simplifies design, but creates a different problem; coordinated access. It is possible that, in specific failure scenarios, a namenode could become unavailable in a way where we can not know for sure if it is truly dead. When this happens, it's possible that the otherwise unreachable namenode continues to try and write to the shared edits directory. It's critical that this be prevented, as two processes writing to the same set of files can easily lead to data corruption. In an automatic failover configuration, this is further complicated by the fact that a human isn't around to mediate such a situation. To enforce exclusive access to the shared state, HA systems typically employ one or more fencing methods. How you fence a service depends greatly on the service in question, so this is a common place custom scripts are used. Hadoop support various fencing methods that must be configured (see "Fencing Options" on page 102) before HA will function.

The next step is to make the necessary configuration changes to the *core-site.xml* and *hdfs-site.xml* files. This involves the creation of a logical name for the highly available namenode service called the *nameservice-id*, the grouping of namenodes into that service using logical *namenode-ids*, defining namenode properties like the RPC and HTTP service ports, and configuring a set of fencing methods. All of this is required for both manual and automatic failover scenarios.

No more secondary namenode

Remember that in an HA deployment, the standby (inactive) namenode performs the work of the secondary namenode. See "Namenode High Availability" on page 17 for more information.

Fencing Options

In order to prevent data corruption during a forced state transition (in other words, when our partner dies and we must become active) a method of fencing is required. This is because, in cases where the misbehaving namenode stops responding, it's still possible that it's up and running and will attempt to write to the shared edits directory. To prevent this, Hadoop allows administrators to decide the best way to fence off the unhealthy namenode. Fencing methods are configurable, and normally, multiple different methods are specified in configuration. Each method listed is executed, in order, until one of them succeeds. Generally, methods should be ordered with more polite methods earlier and the severe options later. Typical fencing strategies in HA systems include asking the partner to give up control gracefully (e.g. RPC calls or `kill -15`), telling it stop forcefully (e.g. `kill -9`), killing power to the host (e.g. an RPC call to a managed power distribution unit or IPMI management card to cut power to the host, commonly called Shoot The Other Node In The Head or STONITH), or telling the service containing the shared state to deny communication with the host (e.g. RPC calls to an NFS filer asking it to block traffic to the host).

Confused? Do not pass go!

If an effective fencing strategy is not configured correctly it is possible to corrupt shared state information in most HA data storage systems. Hadoop is one of these systems. If the concepts behind HA and fencing aren't clear, take the time to do a little extra research. It will save you countless hours, and possible data loss, down the road.

Hadoop ships with one standard and two user-configurable fencing methods: sshfence and shell. Before any user-defined fencing method is attempted, Hadoop will attempt to use its own RPC mechanism to ask the active namenode to relinquish its role. If that's not possible, the user-defined fencing methods listed in dfs.ha.fencing.methods (see dfs.ha.fencing.methods (required) on page 105) are used. The sshfence method attempts to ssh into the active namenode host and kill the process listening on the service port, as identified by the fuser command. For this to work, ssh keys must be pre-configured for a user with sufficient privileges to kill the namenode process. The private key must not require a passphrase, although it should be protected by filesystem permissions such that only the HDFS super user can access it (usually this is user hdfs). The sshfence method optionally takes a colon separated username and port, surrounded by parenthesis, shown in Example 5-5.

Example 5-5. Specifying a custom username and port to the sshfence method

```
sshfence(someuser:port)
```

Failures due to down hosts

The sshfence method suffers from a conundrum. When the machine to fence is down, it's impossible to determine whether it's truly down (and, effectively, already fenced) or simply not responding. This is the classic inability to differentiate a host down from a network partition, described in "Network Partitions" on page 214. If the host to fence is down, this method will declare that it failed to fence the node. As a result, you must have a non-ssh based fencing method to fall back to.

The second fencing method is the shell method which, as you might expect, executes an arbitrary shell command. This allows you to perform arbitrarily complex fencing using IPMI, NFS filer level fencing, or other vendor specific functions. All Hadoop configuration properties are available as environment variables to the shell script with dots (".") replaced with underscores ("_"). Additionally, the special environment variables in Table 5-2 are also available for use.

Table 5-2. Fencing shell script environment variables

Variable	
$target_host	The host to be fenced.
$target_port	The RPC port of the host to be fenced.
$target_address	$target_host:$target_port
$target_nameserviceid	The nameservice-id to which the namenode to fence belongs.
$target_namenodeid	The namenode-id of the namenode to fence.

The script, along with any arguments, should be surrounded by parenthesis after the method name. A closing parenthesis may not appear in the arguments, themselves. See

Example 5-6 for an example of a fencing script invocation that makes use of some of the environment variables from Table 5-2.

Example 5-6. Specifying a shell script and arguments to the shell fence method

```
shell(/some/path/to/a/script.py --namenode=$target_host --nameservice=$target_nameserviceid)
```

An exit code of zero from the shell script is used to indicate fencing was successful. Any other status indicates failure, in which case further fencing methods are used. If all fencing methods fail, no failover is performed and the take over is aborted. At this point, human intervention is required because it's unclear that taking over wouldn't corrupt the metadata.

> **The song that never ends...**
>
> The shell fencing method has no builtin provision for a timeout. If your script never exits, for whatever reason, a take over will never happen and you'll have some clean up work to do by hand.

Basic Configuration

The following HA-related configuration properties exist, and should be set in *hdfs-site.xml* except where otherwise indicated.

`dfs.nameservices` *(required)*

The `dfs.nameservices` parameter is used by both the namenode HA and federation features. In the context of HA, this defines the logical name of the service being provided by a pair of namenode IDs. The logical name can be anything you want, and is analogous to a virtual IP (VIP). The value of this parameter will be used as the authoritative name of the HDFS service in other parameters like `fs.defaultFS`. Many of the other HA options refer to this as the *nameservice-id*.

Example: prod-analytics. Used by: NN, clients.

`dfs.ha.namenodes.`*nameservice-id* *(required)*

With the nameservice-id defined by `dfs.nameservices`, it's now necessary to specify which *namenode-ids* make up that service. The value of this parameter should be a comma separated list of logical namenode names (note these are different than the logical service name or nameservice-id). Currently, only two namenode-ids can be specified. Like the nameservice-id, the namenode-ids can be any name you choose, and will be used to define namenode specific configuration properties in an HA pair of namenodes.

Example property name: `dfs.ha.namenodes.prod-analytics`, property value: nn1,nn2. Used by: NN, clients.

`dfs.namenode.rpc-address.`*nameservice-id*`.`*namenode-id* *(required)*

This parameter specifies the colon separated hostname and port on which *name node-id* should provide namenode RPC service for *nameservice-id*.

Example property name: `dfs.namenode.rpc-address.prod-analytics.nn1`, property value: hadoop01.mycompany.com:8020. Used by: NN, clients.

`dfs.namenode.http-address.`*`namesevice-id`*`.`*`namenode-id`*

Optionally, it is possible to specify the hostname and port for HTTP service for a given *namenode-id* within *nameservice-id*.

Example property name: `dfs.namenode.http-address.prod-analytics.nn1`, property value: hadoop01.mycompany.com:50070. Used by: NN.

`dfs.namenode.shared.edits.dir` *(required)*

Each namenode in an HA pair must have access to a shared filesystem defined by this property. The active namenode will write transactions to this location while the standby will constantly read and apply changes to its in-memory version of the metadata. The value should be expressed in the form of a *file://* URL.

Example: *file:///mnt/namenode/prod-analytics-edits*. Used by: NN.

`dfs.client.failover.proxy.provider.`*`nameservice-id`* *(required)*

When namenode HA is enabled, clients need a way to decide which namenode is active and should be used. This property specifies the class name of the plugin to use when locating the active namenode. Today, Hadoop only ships with a single plugin, but it still must be specified explicitly. Like many of the HA properties, this too supports specification by *nameservice-id*.

Example property name: `dfs.client.failover.proxy.provider.prod-analytics`, property value: `org.apache.hadoop.hdfs.server.namenode.ha.ConfiguredFailover` `ProxyProvider`. Used by: Clients.

`dfs.ha.fencing.methods` *(required)*

This property specifies a new line–separated list of fencing methods. See "Fencing Options" on page 102 for an explanation of the available options.

Example: sshfence(hdfs:22)

shell(/some/path/fence-nfs-filer.sh --host=$target_host)

shell(/some/path/pdu-controller.sh --disable-power --host=$target_host). Used by: NN, ZKFC (see "Automatic Failover Configuration" on page 105).

Automatic Failover Configuration

By default, namenode HA requires manual failover to be performed by a human or another outside system. If you'd rather not try and force an intern to stare at monitoring software all day and flip a switch when something goes wrong, you can instead enable support for automatic failover. Enabling automatic failover adds two new components to the system:

- Apache ZooKeeper (*http://zookeeper.apache.org*)

  ZooKeeper is a separate Apache software project that provides a highly available service for distributed locking, coordination, and configuration, and is required[2] for an automatic failover HA deployment. It is included in CDH, although it's a separate package install.

- The ZooKeeper Failover Controller (ZKFC)

  The ZKFC (or sometimes, simply the *failover controller*) is a separate daemon that runs along side each namenode in an HA configuration that watches its health, maintains ZooKeeper session information, and initiates state transitions and fencing when necessary. Already included with Hadoop, no additional software installation is necessary, although some configuration is required.

The following additional parameters must be configured in *hdfs-site.xml* for automatic failover to function correctly.

`dfs.ha.automatic-failover.enabled` (*required for automatic failover*)
: Setting this property to true instructs the startup scripts to additionally start the failover controller process and manage namenode state transitions using Zoo-Keeper for coordination. When this is enabled, you must also properly configure the `ha.zookeeper.quorum` property to point at the ZooKeeper quorum that should be used by the failover controller.

  Optionally, you can use the property `dfs.ha.automatic-failover.enabled.`*name service-id* to configure this on a per-nameservice-id basis, rather than globally.

  Default value: false Example: true. Used by: NN, ZKFC, clients.

`ha.zookeeper.quorum` (*core-site.xml, required for automatic failover*)
: When using the HDFS automatic failover feature, ZooKeeper must be properly configured. This property specifies the nodes that make up the ZooKeeper quorum. Each quorum member is a colon separated host port pair, and quorum members are separated by commas. Since the availability of the namenode is dependent on the availability of ZooKeeper in this configuration, a quorum of at least three nodes should be used so that ZooKeeper itself is highly available.

  Example: zk-node1:2181,zk-node2:2181,zk-node3:2181. Used by: ZKFC.

Initialzing ZooKeeper State

Before the failover controller will work, the necessary state in ZooKeeper must first be initialized. Hadoop includes the `hdfs zkfc -formatZK` command (see Example 5-7) for exactly this purpose. This command should be run as the HDFS super user (the user

---

2. For more information about installing and configuring ZooKeeper, Apache Hadoop users can reference the Apache ZooKeeper (*http://zookeeper.apache.org*) website. CDH users should reference Cloudera's documentation portal (*https://ccp.cloudera.com/display/DOC/Documentation*).

with which you formatted HDFS) and assumes that ZooKeeper is up and running, and all HA configuration is complete.

Example 5-7. Initializing ZooKeeper for use with namenode high availability

```
[root@hadoop01 conf]# sudo -u hdfs hdfs zkfc -formatZK
12/07/19 17:22:37 INFO DFSZKFailoverController: Failover controller configured for ↵
  NameNode prod-analytics.hadoop01
12/07/19 17:22:38 INFO ZooKeeper: Client environment:↵
  zookeeper.version=3.4.3-cdh4.0.1--1, built on 06/29/2012 00:00 GMT
12/07/19 17:22:38 INFO ZooKeeper: Client environment:host.name=hadoop01
12/07/19 17:22:38 INFO ZooKeeper: Client environment:java.version=1.6.0_31
12/07/19 17:22:38 INFO ZooKeeper: Client environment:↵
  java.vendor=Sun Microsystems Inc.
12/07/19 17:22:38 INFO ZooKeeper: Client environment:↵
  java.home=/usr/java/jdk1.6.0_31/jre
12/07/19 17:22:38 INFO ZooKeeper: Client environment:java.class.path=...
12/07/19 17:22:38 INFO ZooKeeper: Client environment:↵
  java.library.path=//usr/lib/hadoop/lib/native
12/07/19 17:22:38 INFO ZooKeeper: Client environment:java.io.tmpdir=/tmp
12/07/19 17:22:38 INFO ZooKeeper: Client environment:↵
  java.compiler=<NA>
12/07/19 17:22:38 INFO ZooKeeper: Client environment:os.name=Linux
12/07/19 17:22:38 INFO ZooKeeper: Client environment:os.arch=amd64
12/07/19 17:22:38 INFO ZooKeeper: Client environment:↵
  os.version=2.6.32-220.el6.x86_64
12/07/19 17:22:38 INFO ZooKeeper: Client environment:user.name=hdfs
12/07/19 17:22:38 INFO ZooKeeper: Client environment:↵
  user.home=/var/lib/hadoop-hdfs
12/07/19 17:22:38 INFO ZooKeeper: Client environment:↵
  user.dir=/etc/hadoop/conf.empty
12/07/19 17:22:38 INFO ZooKeeper: Initiating client connection, ↵
  connectString=hadoop01:2181,hadoop02:2181 sessionTimeout=5000 watcher=null
12/07/19 17:22:38 INFO ClientCnxn: Opening socket connection to ↵
  server /10.1.1.131:2181
12/07/19 17:22:38 WARN ZooKeeperSaslClient: SecurityException: ↵
  java.lang.SecurityException: Unable to locate a login configuration occurred ↵
    when trying to find JAAS configuration.
12/07/19 17:22:38 INFO ZooKeeperSaslClient: Client will not SASL-authenticate ↵
  because the default JAAS configuration section 'Client' could not be found. ↵
  If you are not using SASL, you may ignore this. On the other hand, if you ↵
  expected SASL to work, please fix your JAAS configuration.
12/07/19 17:22:38 INFO ClientCnxn: Socket connection established to ↵
  hadoop01/10.1.1.131:2181, initiating session
12/07/19 17:22:38 INFO ClientCnxn: Session establishment complete on ↵
  server hadoop01/10.1.1.131:2181, sessionid = 0x138a1b2f1d20000, negotiated ↵
  timeout = 5000
12/07/19 17:22:38 INFO ActiveStandbyElector: Successfully created ↵
  /hadoop-ha/prod-analytics in ZK.
12/07/19 17:22:38 WARN ActiveStandbyElector: Ignoring stale result from old client ↵
  with sessionId 0x138a1b2f1d20000
12/07/19 17:22:38 INFO ZooKeeper: Session: 0x138a1b2f1d20000 closed
12/07/19 17:22:38 INFO ClientCnxn: EventThread shut down
```

Format and Bootstrap the Namenodes

Pick one of the two namenodes to use as the primary namenode for the format and bootstrap process. We'll refer to the other namenode as the standby. Don't worry about which one you pick; this only matters for the initial setup. Format the primary namenode using the standard `hdfs namenode -format` as you normally would in a non-HA configuration, as in Example 5-8. This will format both the primary namenode's local directories and the shared edits directory.

Example 5-8. Formating a namenode for high availability

```
[root@hadoop-ha01 ~]# sudo -u hdfs hdfs namenode -format
12/07/25 11:37:46 INFO namenode.NameNode: STARTUP_MSG:
/************************************************************
STARTUP_MSG: Starting NameNode
STARTUP_MSG:   host = hadoop-ha01/10.20.191.144
STARTUP_MSG:   args = [-format]
STARTUP_MSG:   version = 2.0.0-cdh4.0.1
STARTUP_MSG:   classpath = ...
STARTUP_MSG:   build = ...
************************************************************/
Formatting using clusterid: CID-4cd4303c-62bd-468b-8cc1-652e0b88a2ec
12/07/25 11:37:47 INFO util.HostsFileReader: Refreshing hosts (include/exclude) list
12/07/25 11:37:47 INFO blockmanagement.DatanodeManager: dfs.block.invalidate.limit=1000
12/07/25 11:37:47 INFO util.GSet: VM type       = 64-bit
12/07/25 11:37:47 INFO util.GSet: 2% max memory = 17.77875 MB
12/07/25 11:37:47 INFO util.GSet: capacity      = 2^21 = 2097152 entries
12/07/25 11:37:47 INFO util.GSet: recommended=2097152, actual=2097152
12/07/25 11:37:47 INFO blockmanagement.BlockManager: dfs.block.access.token.enable=false
12/07/25 11:37:47 INFO blockmanagement.BlockManager: defaultReplication        = 3
12/07/25 11:37:47 INFO blockmanagement.BlockManager: maxReplication            = 512
12/07/25 11:37:47 INFO blockmanagement.BlockManager: minReplication            = 1
12/07/25 11:37:47 INFO blockmanagement.BlockManager: maxReplicationStreams     = 2
12/07/25 11:37:47 INFO blockmanagement.BlockManager: shouldCheckForEnoughRacks = false
12/07/25 11:37:47 INFO blockmanagement.BlockManager: replicationRecheckInterval = 3000
12/07/25 11:37:47 INFO namenode.FSNamesystem: fsOwner          = hdfs (auth:SIMPLE)
12/07/25 11:37:47 INFO namenode.FSNamesystem: supergroup       = supergroup
12/07/25 11:37:47 INFO namenode.FSNamesystem: isPermissionEnabled = true
12/07/25 11:37:47 INFO namenode.FSNamesystem: Determined nameservice ID: prod-analytics❶
12/07/25 11:37:47 INFO namenode.FSNamesystem: HA Enabled: true❷
12/07/25 11:37:47 INFO namenode.FSNamesystem: Append Enabled: true
12/07/25 11:37:47 INFO namenode.NameNode: Caching file names occuring more than 10 times
12/07/25 11:37:48 INFO namenode.NNStorage: Storage directory /data/1/hadoop/dfs/nn has ↵
been successfully formatted.❸
12/07/25 11:37:48 INFO namenode.NNStorage: Storage directory /mnt/namenode-shared has ↵
been successfully formatted.❹
12/07/25 11:37:48 INFO namenode.FSImage: Saving image file ↵
/data/1/hadoop/dfs/nn/current/fsimage.ckpt_0000000000000000000 using no compression
12/07/25 11:37:48 INFO namenode.FSImage: Image file of size 119 saved in 0 seconds.
12/07/25 11:37:48 INFO namenode.NNStorageRetentionManager: Going to retain 1 images ↵
with txid >= 0
12/07/25 11:37:48 INFO namenode.FileJournalManager: Purging logs older than 0
12/07/25 11:37:48 INFO namenode.NameNode: SHUTDOWN_MSG:
```

```
/************************************************************
SHUTDOWN_MSG: Shutting down NameNode at hadoop-ha01/10.20.191.144
************************************************************/
```

❶ The nameservice of the HA pair.

❷ HA configuration has been detected and enabled.

❸ A local directory being formatted for the namenode.

❹ The shared edits directory being formatted.

The standby namenode needs to be bootstrapped with a copy of the metadata information from the primary namenode. Without fail, there's a command that automates this process as well. The hdfs namenode -bootstrapStandby command works by contacting the primary namenode and retrieving a copy of the metadata over the network. For this to work, we must first start the primary namenode and make it active. There's nothing special to starting a namenode in an HA configuration. In Example 5-9 we just use the init script.

Example 5-9. Starting the primary namenode

```
[root@hadoop-ha01 ~]# /etc/init.d/hadoop-hdfs-namenode start
Starting Hadoop namenode:                         [  OK  ]
starting namenode, logging to /var/log/hadoop-hdfs/hadoop-hdfs-namenode-hadoop-ha01.out
```

By default, the namenode will start in standby state until it's told to transition to an active state by either an administrative command or the failover controller. See Example 5-10 for an example of the typical namenode log output.

Example 5-10. Logs from a namenode starting in standby state

```
...
2012-07-25 11:53:50,128 INFO FSNamesystem: fsOwner            = hdfs (auth:SIMPLE)
2012-07-25 11:53:50,128 INFO FSNamesystem: supergroup         = supergroup
2012-07-25 11:53:50,128 INFO FSNamesystem: isPermissionEnabled = true
2012-07-25 11:53:50,129 INFO FSNamesystem: Determined nameservice ID: prod-analytics
2012-07-25 11:53:50,129 INFO FSNamesystem: HA Enabled: true
2012-07-25 11:53:50,131 INFO FSNamesystem: Append Enabled: true
2012-07-25 11:53:50,412 INFO NameNode: Caching file names occuring more than 10 times
2012-07-25 11:53:50,474 INFO Storage: Locking is disabled
2012-07-25 11:53:50,508 INFO FSImage: No edit log streams selected.
2012-07-25 11:53:50,515 INFO FSImage: Loading image file ↵
   /data/1/hadoop/dfs/nn/current/fsimage_0000000000000000000 using no compression
2012-07-25 11:53:50,516 INFO FSImage: Number of files = 1
2012-07-25 11:53:50,517 INFO FSImage: Number of files under construction = 0
2012-07-25 11:53:50,517 INFO FSImage: Image file of size 119 loaded in 0 seconds.
2012-07-25 11:53:50,517 INFO FSImage: Loaded image for txid 0 from ↵
   /data/1/hadoop/dfs/nn/current/fsimage_0000000000000000000
2012-07-25 11:53:50,522 INFO NameCache: initialized with 0 entries 0 lookups
2012-07-25 11:53:50,522 INFO FSNamesystem: Finished loading FSImage in 108 msecs
2012-07-25 11:53:50,756 INFO Server: Starting Socket Reader #1 for port 8020
2012-07-25 11:53:50,790 INFO FSNamesystem: Registered FSNamesystemState MBean
2012-07-25 11:53:50,813 INFO FSNamesystem: Number of blocks under construction: 0
```

```
2012-07-25 11:53:50,813 INFO StateChange: STATE* Leaving safe mode after 0 secs.
2012-07-25 11:53:50,813 INFO StateChange: STATE* Network topology has 0 racks ↵
  and 0 datanodes
2012-07-25 11:53:50,813 INFO StateChange: STATE* UnderReplicatedBlocks has 0 blocks
2012-07-25 11:53:50,890 INFO log: Logging to ↵
  org.slf4j.impl.Log4jLoggerAdapter(org.mortbay.log) via org.mortbay.log.Slf4jLog
2012-07-25 11:53:50,943 INFO HttpServer: Added global filter 'safety' ↵
  (class=org.apache.hadoop.http.HttpServer$QuotingInputFilter)
2012-07-25 11:53:50,945 WARN StaticUserWebFilter: dfs.web.ugi should not be used. ↵
  Instead, use hadoop.http.staticuser.user.
2012-07-25 11:53:50,945 INFO HttpServer: Added filter static_user_filter ↵
  (class=org.apache.hadoop.http.lib.StaticUserWebFilter$StaticUserFilter) to ↵
  context WepAppsContext
2012-07-25 11:53:50,945 INFO HttpServer: Added filter static_user_filter ↵
  (class=org.apache.hadoop.http.lib.StaticUserWebFilter$StaticUserFilter) to ↵
  context logs
2012-07-25 11:53:50,946 INFO HttpServer: Added filter static_user_filter ↵
  (class=org.apache.hadoop.http.lib.StaticUserWebFilter$StaticUserFilter) to ↵
  context static
2012-07-25 11:53:50,958 INFO HttpServer: dfs.webhdfs.enabled = false
2012-07-25 11:53:50,974 INFO HttpServer: Jetty bound to port 50070
2012-07-25 11:53:50,974 INFO log: jetty-6.1.26.cloudera.1
2012-07-25 11:53:51,176 INFO log: Started SelectChannelConnector@0.0.0.0:50070
2012-07-25 11:53:51,176 INFO NameNode: Web-server up at: 0.0.0.0:50070
2012-07-25 11:53:51,176 INFO Server: IPC Server Responder: starting
2012-07-25 11:53:51,178 INFO Server: IPC Server listener on 8020: starting
2012-07-25 11:53:51,182 INFO NameNode: NameNode up at: hadoop-ha01/10.20.191.144:8020❶
2012-07-25 11:53:51,182 INFO FSNamesystem: Starting services required for standby state❷
2012-07-25 11:53:51,184 INFO EditLogTailer: Will roll logs on active node at ↵
  hadoop-ha02/10.20.191.145:8020 every 120 seconds.
2012-07-25 11:53:51,196 INFO StandbyCheckpointer: Starting standby checkpoint thread...
```

❶ The namenode is up and running.

❷ Standby services are started by default.

If you *have* configured automatic failover, you should now start the failover over controller. It will connect to ZooKeeper, discover no other namenode is currently active,
see that the local process is healthy, and ask it to transition to active status. Example 5-11 illustrates the process of starting the failover controller and a sample of its log
output.

Example 5-11. Starting the failover controller and confirming the namenode becomes active

```
[root@hadoop-ha01 ~]# /etc/init.d/hadoop-hdfs-zkfc start
Starting Hadoop zkfc:                                    [  OK  ]
starting zkfc, logging to /var/log/hadoop-hdfs/hadoop-hdfs-zkfc-hadoop-ha01.out
[root@hadoop-ha01 ~]# less /var/log/hadoop-hdfs/hadoop-hdfs-namenode-hadoop-ha01.log
...
2012-07-25 12:03:31,164 INFO FSNamesystem: Stopping services started for standby state❶
2012-07-25 12:03:31,165 WARN EditLogTailer: Edit log tailer interrupted❷
java.lang.InterruptedException: sleep interrupted
  at java.lang.Thread.sleep(Native Method)
  at org.apache.hadoop.hdfs.server.namenode.ha.EditLogTailer$EditLogTailerThread↵
    .doWork(EditLogTailer.java:329)
```

```
          at org.apache.hadoop.hdfs.server.namenode.ha.EditLogTailer$EditLogTailerThread↵
          .access$200(EditLogTailer.java:274)
          at org.apache.hadoop.hdfs.server.namenode.ha.EditLogTailer$EditLogTailerThread$1↵
          .run(EditLogTailer.java:291)
          at org.apache.hadoop.security.SecurityUtil.doAsLoginUserOrFatal(SecurityUtil.java:438)
          at org.apache.hadoop.hdfs.server.namenode.ha.EditLogTailer$EditLogTailerThread↵
          .run(EditLogTailer.java:287)
2012-07-25 12:03:31,166 INFO FSNamesystem: Starting services required for active state❸
2012-07-25 12:03:31,168 INFO FileJournalManager: Recovering unfinalized segments in ↵
 /mnt/namenode-shared/current
2012-07-25 12:03:31,168 INFO FileJournalManager: Recovering unfinalized segments in ↵
 /data/1/hadoop/dfs/nn/current
2012-07-25 12:03:31,168 INFO FSNamesystem: Catching up to latest edits from old active ↵
 before taking over writer role in edits logs.
2012-07-25 12:03:31,168 INFO FSNamesystem: Reprocessing replication and invalidation ↵
 queues...
2012-07-25 12:03:31,169 INFO DatanodeManager: Marking all datandoes as stale
2012-07-25 12:03:31,179 INFO BlockManager: Total number of blocks          = 0
2012-07-25 12:03:31,179 INFO BlockManager: Number of invalid blocks        = 0
2012-07-25 12:03:31,180 INFO BlockManager: Number of under-replicated blocks = 0
2012-07-25 12:03:31,180 INFO BlockManager: Number of  over-replicated blocks = 0
2012-07-25 12:03:31,180 INFO BlockManager: Number of blocks being written   = 0
2012-07-25 12:03:31,180 INFO FSNamesystem: Will take over writing edit logs at txnid 1
2012-07-25 12:03:31,180 INFO FSEditLog: Starting log segment at 1
2012-07-25 12:03:31,622 INFO FSEditLog: Number of transactions: 1 Total time for ↵
 transactions(ms): 1Number of transactions batched in Syncs: 0 Number of syncs: 1 ↵
 SyncTimes(ms): 259 125
```

❶ Namenode receives a command to transition from standby to active and stops standby services.

❷ The thread that watches for changes in the edit log is interrupted. This is normal.

❸ The namenode transitions to active and starts the necessary services.

If you *have not* configured automatic failover, you can manually activate the primary namenode by running the command in Example 5-12. The arguments to the -fail over command are the namenode that should be standby followed by the namenode that should become active. It helps to remember the order by thinking "I want to transition from namenode *A* to *B*." Refer to the namenode web user interface or log files to confirm the transition completes successfully.

Example 5-12. Forcing failover using the haadmin command

```
[root@hadoop-ha01 ~]# sudo -u hdfs hdfs haadmin -failover hadoop-ha02 hadoop-ha01
Failover to NameNode at hadoop-ha01/10.20.191.144:8020 successful
```

From the standby namenode, run the hdfs namenode -bootstrapStandby command to copy the necessary metadata from the active namenode, shown in Example 5-13.

Example 5-13. Bootstrapping the standby namenode metadata

```
[root@hadoop-ha02 conf]# sudo -u hdfs hdfs namenode -bootstrapStandby
12/07/25 14:05:33 INFO namenode.NameNode: STARTUP_MSG:
/************************************************************
STARTUP_MSG: Starting NameNode
STARTUP_MSG:   host = hadoop-ha02/10.20.191.145
STARTUP_MSG:   args = [-bootstrapStandby]
STARTUP_MSG:   version = 2.0.0-cdh4.0.1
STARTUP_MSG:   classpath = ...
STARTUP_MSG:   build = ...
************************************************************/
=====================================================
About to bootstrap Standby ID hadoop-ha02 from:
           Nameservice ID: prod-analytics
         Other Namenode ID: hadoop-ha01
  Other NN's HTTP address: hadoop-ha01:50070
  Other NN's IPC  address: hadoop-ha01/10.20.191.144:8020
             Namespace ID: 299561556
             Block pool ID: BP-824539445-10.20.191.144-1343241467811
                Cluster ID: CID-4cd4303c-62bd-468b-8cc1-652e0b88a2ec
            Layout version: -40
=====================================================
Re-format filesystem in /data/1/hadoop/dfs/nn ? (Y or N) Y
12/07/25 14:05:47 INFO namenode.NNStorage: Storage directory /data/1/hadoop/dfs/nn ↵
  has been successfully formatted.
12/07/25 14:05:47 WARN namenode.EditLogInputStream: skipping 1048563 bytes at the end ↵
  of edit log '/mnt/namenode-shared/current/edits_0000000000000000001-0000000000000000001': ↵
  reached txid 1 out of 1
12/07/25 14:05:47 INFO namenode.TransferFsImage: Opening connection to ↵
  http://hadoop-ha01:50070/getimage?getimage=1&txid=0&storageInfo=-40:299561556:0:↵
  CID-4cd4303c-62bd-468b-8cc1-652e0b88a2ec
12/07/25 14:05:47 INFO namenode.TransferFsImage: Downloaded file ↵
  fsimage.ckpt_0000000000000000000 size 119 bytes.
12/07/25 14:05:47 INFO namenode.NameNode: SHUTDOWN_MSG:
/************************************************************
SHUTDOWN_MSG: Shutting down NameNode at hadoop-ha02/10.20.191.145
************************************************************/
```

Start the standby namenode and failover controller, if you have configured automatic failover, as you did on the primary namenode. Check the web user interface of each namenode; one should claim to be active and the other standby. To test that automatic failover is working correctly, simply stop the active namenode process using the init script or sending the process a kill signal. If you check the failover controller logs, you should see it detect the change in health status and yield active status by removing its lock in ZooKeeper. The standby namenode should detect this almost immediately and take over the active role. To test manual failover if you're not using automatic failover, simply run the same command in Example 5-12 with the order of the namenodes reversed.

Namenode Federation

Federation is a feature new to Apache Hadoop 2.0 and CDH4, created to overcome the limitation that all filesystem metadata must fit in memory. It differs from namenode high availability (described in "Namenode High Availability" on page 100) in that rather than a single namespace being served from one of two possible namenodes, multiple namenodes each serve a *different* slice of a larger namespace. It's possible to enable either federation or high availability, or even both simultaneously. Sometimes, federation is used to provide a different level of service to a slice of a global namespace. For example, it may be necessary to tune garbage collection parameters or enable HA for the path */hbase* but not the rest of the namespace. Clients of HDFS use a specialized plugin called *ViewFS* to view the logical, global namespace as a single entity. In other words, a client is unaware that it may be talking to different namenodes when it accesses different paths. In this way, federation is similar to Linux where there are physical devices that are mounted at a given path using */etc/fstab*.

As first glance, it doesn't seem that federation is different from simply having multiple discreet clusters, save for the client plugin to view them as a single logical namespace. One of the major differentiating factors, however, is that each datanode in a federated cluster stores blocks for each namenode. When each namenode is formated, it generates a *block pool* in which block data associated with that namenode is stored. Each datanode, in turn, stores data for multiple block pools, and communicates with each namenode. When a namenode receives a heartbeat from a datanode, it learns about the total space on the datanode consumed by other block pools, as well as non-HDFS data. The rationale behind having all datanodes participate in all block pools rather than simply having discreet clusters is that this achieves better total utilization of datanode capacity. Instead, if we were to have a separate set of datanodes entirely for the heavily used namenode *A*, datanodes for namenode *B* would be underutilized while namenode *A* datanodes struggled to keep up with load.

Configuring HDFS for a federated deployment for a new cluster is straight forward. First, a logical nameservice-id is configured for each namenode that will participate in the federated namespace, using the `dfs.nameservices` property in *hdfs-site.xml*. Each *nameservice-id* can be either a single *namenode-id*, as is commonly the case in federation, or a pair of namenode-ids, for a highly available deployment. For now, we'll focus solely on the federation configuration. Datanodes send heartbeats to *all* nameservice-ids listed in `dfs.nameservices`. Next, each nameservice-id is mapped to a host and RPC port by way of the `dfs.namenode.rpc-address.`*nameservice-id* property. This is how a logical nameservice is bound to a physical host. Other options exist that effect namenode behavior. Example 5-14 contains an *hdfs-site.xml* file with a federated cluster with two namenodes.

Example 5-14. HDFS configuration for a federated cluster

```xml
<?xml version="1.0"?>
<?xml-stylesheet type="text/xsl" href="configuration.xsl"?>

<configuration>

  <!-- Generic HDFS configuration properties... -->

  <!--
    Two namespaces defined: nn01 and nn02. Datanodes will store
    blocks for both.
  -->
  <property>
    <name>dfs.nameservices</name>
    <value>nn01,nn02</value>
  </property>

  <!-- Bind nn01 to hadoop-fed01.mycompany.com, port 8020. -->
  <property>
    <name>dfs.namenode.rpc-address.nn01</name>
    <value>hadoop-fed01.mycompany.com:8020</value>
  </property>

  <!-- Bind nn02 to hadoop-fed02.mycompany.com, port 8020. -->
  <property>
    <name>dfs.namenode.rpc-address.nn02</name>
    <value>hadoop-fed02.mycompany.com:8020</value>
  </property>

  <!--
    The list of directories in which each namenode will store
    its metadata.
  -->
  <property>
    <name>dfs.name.dir</name>
    <value>/data/1/hadoop/dfs/nn,/data/2/hadoop/dfs/nn</value>
  </property>

</configuration>
```

Once the configuration files have been updated and distributed to all hosts, each namenode must be formatted. Formatting a namenode in a federated cluster is the same as in a single namenode configuration, with the exception that each namenode must have the same cluster-id. A *cluster-id* is a unique identifier that distinguishes one logical cluster from another. If a cluster-id is not provided at the time a namenode is formatted, one is randomly generated for you. You can choose to come up with a unique cluster-id and format each namenode with it, or format the first namenode without a specified cluster-id and reuse it when formatting additional namenodes. In our examples, we'll specify a cluster-id of prod-analytics explicitly, but you can use whatever you want. Remember that the user that formats the namenode becomes the HDFS super user. In

Example 5-15, we run the format command using `sudo -u hdfs` so user `hdfs` becomes the super user.

Example 5-15. Formatting a namenode with a specific cluster-id

```
[root@hadoop-fed01 ~]# sudo -u hdfs hdfs namenode -format -clusterID prod-analytics
12/07/23 15:59:24 INFO namenode.NameNode: STARTUP_MSG:
/************************************************************
STARTUP_MSG: Starting NameNode
STARTUP_MSG:   host = hadoop-fed01/10.20.195.236
STARTUP_MSG:   args = [-format, -clusterID, prod-analytics]
STARTUP_MSG:   version = 2.0.0-cdh4.0.1
STARTUP_MSG:   classpath = ...
STARTUP_MSG:   build = ...
************************************************************/
Formatting using clusterid: prod-analytics
12/07/23 15:59:24 INFO util.HostsFileReader: Refreshing hosts (include/exclude) list
12/07/23 15:59:24 INFO blockmanagement.DatanodeManager: dfs.block.invalidate.limit=1000
12/07/23 15:59:24 INFO util.GSet: VM type       = 64-bit
12/07/23 15:59:24 INFO util.GSet: 2% max memory = 17.77875 MB
12/07/23 15:59:24 INFO util.GSet: capacity      = 2^21 = 2097152 entries
12/07/23 15:59:24 INFO util.GSet: recommended=2097152, actual=2097152
12/07/23 15:59:24 INFO blockmanagement.BlockManager: dfs.block.access.token.enable=false
12/07/23 15:59:24 INFO blockmanagement.BlockManager: defaultReplication         = 3
12/07/23 15:59:24 INFO blockmanagement.BlockManager: maxReplication             = 512
12/07/23 15:59:24 INFO blockmanagement.BlockManager: minReplication             = 1
12/07/23 15:59:24 INFO blockmanagement.BlockManager: maxReplicationStreams      = 2
12/07/23 15:59:24 INFO blockmanagement.BlockManager: shouldCheckForEnoughRacks  = false
12/07/23 15:59:24 INFO blockmanagement.BlockManager: replicationRecheckInterval = 3000
12/07/23 15:59:24 INFO namenode.FSNamesystem: fsOwner            = hdfs (auth:SIMPLE)
12/07/23 15:59:24 INFO namenode.FSNamesystem: supergroup         = supergroup
12/07/23 15:59:24 INFO namenode.FSNamesystem: isPermissionEnabled = true
12/07/23 15:59:24 INFO namenode.FSNamesystem: Determined nameservice ID: nn01
12/07/23 15:59:24 INFO namenode.FSNamesystem: HA Enabled: false
12/07/23 15:59:24 INFO namenode.FSNamesystem: Append Enabled: true
12/07/23 16:14:06 INFO namenode.NameNode: Caching file names occuring more than 10 times
12/07/23 16:14:06 INFO namenode.NNStorage: Storage directory /data/1/hadoop/dfs/nn ↵
  has been successfully formatted.
12/07/23 16:14:06 INFO namenode.NNStorage: Storage directory /data/2/hadoop/dfs/nn ↵
  has been successfully formatted.
12/07/23 16:14:06 INFO namenode.FSImage: Saving image file ↵
  /data/2/hadoop/dfs/nn/current/fsimage.ckpt_0000000000000000000 using no compression
12/07/23 16:14:06 INFO namenode.FSImage: Saving image file ↵
  /data/1/hadoop/dfs/nn/current/fsimage.ckpt_0000000000000000000 using no compression
12/07/23 16:14:06 INFO namenode.FSImage: Image file of size 119 saved in 0 seconds.
12/07/23 16:14:06 INFO namenode.FSImage: Image file of size 119 saved in 0 seconds.
12/07/23 16:14:07 INFO namenode.NNStorageRetentionManager: Going to retain 1 images ↵
  with txid >= 0
12/07/23 16:14:07 INFO namenode.FileJournalManager: Purging logs older than 0
12/07/23 16:14:07 INFO namenode.FileJournalManager: Purging logs older than 0
12/07/23 16:14:07 INFO namenode.NameNode: SHUTDOWN_MSG:

/************************************************************
SHUTDOWN_MSG: Shutting down NameNode at hadoop-fed01/10.20.195.236
************************************************************/
```

At this point, start the namenodes and datanodes, and verify that all datanodes are communicating with each namenode. Each namenode has two primary URLs: one that shows the view of the namespace managed by that namenode, and an aggregate cluster view that shows all namenodes that make up the cluster. The namenode view, available at the URL *http://mynamenode.mycompany.com:50070/dfshealth.jsp* (Figure 5-1), displays information about the slice of the namespace handled by that specific namenode. The page at *http://mynamenode.mycompany.com:50070/dfsclusterhealth.jsp* (Figure 5-2) shows only an aggregate view of each namenode, the number of datanodes connected to it, and total capacity. The cluster level view is useful for getting an overall picture of a federated cluster and is the same on all namenodes.

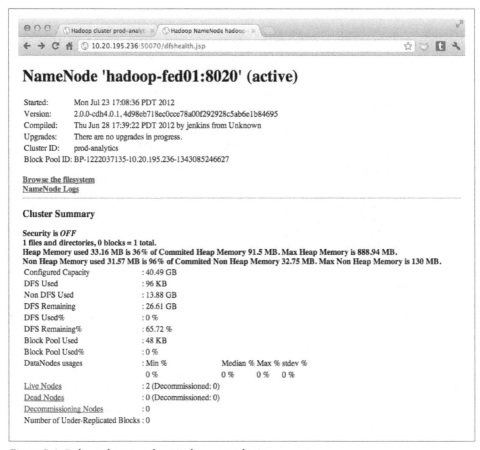

Figure 5-1. Federated namenode—single namenode view

From any one of the configured machines in the cluster, test operations against each namenode using the `hdfs dfs` commands. Since the cluster is federated (and we haven't yet configured ViewFS), you'll need to specify the namenode to talk to when executing each command using its hostname and port. In Example 5-16, we generate a one gig-abyte file and copy it into the two separate filesystem namespaces.

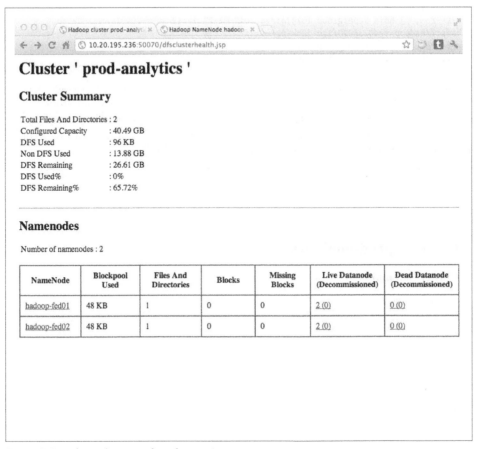

Figure 5-2. Federated namenode—cluster view

Example 5-16. Verifying HDFS federation functionality

```
# generate around 1GB of junk to play with
[root@hadoop-fed02 conf]# dd if=/dev/zero of=1gb-junk bs=1024 count=$((1024 * 1024))
# put a copy in the slice managed by hadoop-fed01
[root@hadoop-fed02 conf]# sudo -u hdfs hdfs dfs -put 1gb-junk \
  hdfs://hadoop-fed01:8020/1gb-junk-01
# put two copies in the slice managed by hadoop-fed02
[root@hadoop-fed02 conf]# sudo -u hdfs hdfs dfs -put 1gb-junk \
  hdfs://hadoop-fed02:8020/1gb-junk-02
[root@hadoop-fed02 conf]# sudo -u hdfs hdfs dfs -put 1gb-junk \
  hdfs://hadoop-fed02:8020/1gb-junk-02.2
# now prove to ourselves that each namenode only sees the files we expect
[root@hadoop-fed02 conf]# sudo -u hdfs hdfs dfs -ls hdfs://hadoop-fed01:8020/
Found 1 items
```

```
-rw-r--r--   3 hdfs supergroup 1073741824 2012-07-23 17:52 ↵
  hdfs://hadoop-fed01:8020/1gb-junk-01
[root@hadoop-fed02 conf]# sudo -u hdfs hdfs dfs -ls hdfs://hadoop-fed02:8020/
Found 2 items
-rw-r--r--   3 hdfs supergroup 1073741824 2012-07-23 17:52 ↵
  hdfs://hadoop-fed02:8020/1gb-junk-02
-rw-r--r--   3 hdfs supergroup 1073741824 2012-07-23 17:53 ↵
  hdfs://hadoop-fed02:8020/1gb-junk-02.2
```

If we now return to the cluster view, we'll see that one of our namenodes has twice as much data as the other (Figure 5-3). Note that, because we have two datanodes, each block can only be replicated twice. Namenode hadoop-fed01 should be managing one file and around 2GB of raw data, and hadoop-fed02 two files of 4GB of raw data. A total of 6GB of HDFS space is consumed on the entire cluster.

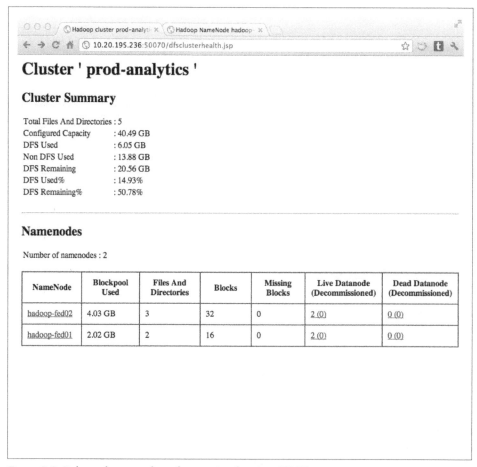

Figure 5-3. Federated namenode—after copying data into HDFS

If you look closely at Figures 5-2 and 5-3, you'll notice that the order in which the namenodes are listed is not necessarily the same between page loads. Make sure you're looking at the namenode you think you are when you load the page!

Client applications are free to access each namenode by name, as we did above, in a federated cluster. However, this means that each client needs to know which namenodes are responsible for which slices of the global namespace. In fact, nothing yet defines the global namespace. As far as clients are concerned, each namenode still looks like a separate HDFS cluster. The missing piece of the configuration puzzle is to configure ViewFS, and define which paths map to which namenodes.

Clients know to use ViewFS by the URL scheme used in the `fs.defaultFS` parameter. By setting this to *viewfs:///*, clients will load the ViewFS filesystem plugin which, in turn, will then look for *mount table* information within the configuration. The mount table is what defines the path to namenode mapping, much like the Linux */etc/fstab* file, and should be relatively self explanatory. It's possible to define multiple mount tables, each with different mapping information, and specify the mount table name using the `fs.defaultFS` URL of *viewfs://table-name/*. Omitting the `table-name` in the URL indicates the default mount table should be used.

Defining a mount table is done in the core-site.xml file. All mount table options are prefixed with the property name `fs.viewfs.mounttable.table-name`. The default mount table name is simply `default`, shown in Example 5-17.

Example 5-17. Client ViewFS mount table configuration

```
<?xml version="1.0"?>

<configuration>

  <!-- Typical core-site.xml configuration properties... -->

  <!-- Clients should use the default ViewFS mount table. -->
  <property>
    <name>fs.defaultFS</name>
    <value>viewfs:///</value>
  </property>

  <!-- Map /a to hadoop-fed01.mycompany.com:8020/ -->
  <property>
    <name>fs.viewfs.mounttable.default.link./a</name>
    <value>hdfs://hadoop-fed01.mycompany.com:8020/</value>
  </property>

  <!-- Map /b to hadoop-fed02.mycompany.com:8020/ -->
  <property>
    <name>fs.viewfs.mounttable.default.link./b</name>
    <value>hdfs://hadoop-fed02.mycompany.com:8020/</value>
  </property>
```

```
    <!-- Additional mounts... -->

</configuration>
```

Overlapping mounts

In Linux-like operating systems, it's possible to have overlapping mount points. For instance, one can have one mount point at */var* and a second mount at */var/log*. This is not currently supported in a federated cluster.

Using the same federated pair of namenodes we set up earlier and the configuration from Example 5-17, let's now run some simple tests to confirm everything is working as expected.

Example 5-18. Testing a ViewFS client

```
[root@hadoop-fed01 conf]# hdfs dfs -ls /a
Found 1 items
-rw-r--r--   3 hdfs supergroup 1073741824 2012-07-23 17:52 /a/1gb-junk-01
[root@hadoop-fed01 conf]# hdfs dfs -ls /b
Found 2 items
-rw-r--r--   3 hdfs supergroup 1073741824 2012-07-23 17:52 /b/1gb-junk-02
-rw-r--r--   3 hdfs supergroup 1073741824 2012-07-23 17:53 /b/1gb-junk-02.2
```

In Example 5-18, we see the test files we wrote to HDFS earlier. The files written to the host hadoop-fed01 in the root directory appear under */a* while the files from hadoop-fed02 appear under */b* because of the mapping table we've created. Clients no longer need to know which paths should be written to which namenodes, or even that multiple namenodes exist.

MapReduce

The following properties should be set in the *mapred-site.xml* file unless otherwise indicated. The format of *mapred-site.xml* is discussed in "The Hadoop XML Configuration Files" on page 87.

Identification and Location

mapred.job.tracker

Just as dfs.name.dir indicates the location of the namenode to datanodes and clients, mapred.job.tracker provides the same for tasktrackers and MapReduce clients. The mapred.job.tracker parameter is a hostname (or IP address) and port pair on which the jobtracker listens for RPC communication. For clients, it provides a method to quickly identify the proper machine to speak to in order to interact with the MapReduce framework.

The default value of mapred.job.tracker is the special string "local" which indicates the client is running in what is called *local mode*. In local mode, the client runs the entire MapReduce framework, albeit singly threaded, in the VM of the client itself. This is mostly useful in development and debugging scenarios and doesn't provide any of Hadoop's parallelism or fault tolerance. Additionally, when operating in local mode, clients do not use HDFS. Instead, all filesystem operations operate against the local host filesystem; the equivalent of having set `fs.default.name` to the value file:///. Due to the default value being the special string "local," there is no meaningful default port specified. The de facto standard port used in `mapred.job.tracker` is 8021, or one port higher than that of the namenode's port. Administrators, of course, are free to specify any value with the caveat of having deviated from what most reference material uses.

Example value: hadoop01.sf.cloudera.com:8021. Used by: JT, TT, clients.

`mapred.local.dir`

As described in Chapter 3, map tasks in a MapReduce job use the machine's local disk to store their intermediate output. The directories used are those specified by `mapred.local.dir`. As with `dfs.data.dir` for the HDFS datanode, `mapred.local.dir` supports the specification of a comma separated list of local filesystem directories with the assumption that each directory is a separate disk. Providing more than one directory allows map tasks to spread IO across multiple devices, thereby reducing a potential bottleneck in the processing pipeline.

There has been debate in the Hadoop community over whether `mapred.local.dir` and `dfs.data.dir` should share disks. The argument for sharing disks is that IO is spread over a greater number of spindles, some of which may not be currently doing IO on behalf of the datanode. Disk space utilization is higher as, if the cluster doesn't execute MapReduce jobs constantly, reserving complete disks for map output would mean they go largely unused. More spindles generally means greater throughput when operations are independent (which map tasks are). The downside to this is that, if the datanode is using the disks, reading or writing intermediate map output to the same device competes with the predictable sequential IO pattern of HDFS block reads or writes effectively creating random IO patterns. This interleaved IO effect can dramatically impact the performance of the map task outputting the data, any datanode operations during that time, and the reducers that are retrieving the map output during the shuffle phase. It's worth mentioning that the Linux kernel has some tricks for dealing with this kind of situation that involve how IO is scheduled, but it won't completely alleviate the pain.

If you choose to reserve dedicated disks for `mapred.local.dir`, there's no need to reserve disk space using `dfs.datanode.du.reserved` because the disks specified by `dfs.data.dir` would have exclusive use of the underlying disks. How many disks you reserve depends on how much map output each node needs to contend with. A more concrete example, given twelve 2TB disks in a worker node, ten disks may be used for the datanode while two are reserved for map output. If the machine is executing 12 map tasks, map output is being written to two disks, while reads are coming from ten.

Reserving disks for `mapred.local.dir` makes sense if you know a lot about the jobs that run and what they do, allowing for the proper allocation of intermediate data storage versus HDFS block data storage. Those new to Hadoop, have evolving needs, have ad-hoc analysis workloads, or who provide a large multitenant cluster as a service to a large organization, may find it makes more sense to share disks between intermediate and block data.

Example value: */data/1/mapred/local*, */data/2/mapred/local*. Used by: JT, TT.

Optimization and Tuning

`mapred.java.child.opts`

When the tasktracker launches child tasks, it does so in a separate JVM process. Administrators and developers can control the options passed to the `java` executable when it's launched. This is primarily useful to control the JVM heap size, garbage collection options, Java native library search paths, and JVM instrumentation agent settings. By far, the most common settings are related to the JVM memory footprint, though.

While not a definitive reference on the Oracle HotSpot VM, the options in Table 5-3 are the most commonly used.

Table 5-3. Common Oracle HotSpot JVM Options

Option	Description
-Xmx*Nu*	Set the maximum JVM heap size where *N* is a number and *u* is the unit it represents. Valid values for *u* are k for kilobytes, m for megabytes, and g for gigabytes. If *u* is not specified, the value is in bytes.
-Xms*Nu*	Set the initial JVM heap size. Some users choose to set the initial heap size when they know they will immediately allocate a large chunk of RAM and they'd rather do it up front. The values for *N* and *u* are the same as above.
-D*property*=*value*	Set application specific Java system properties such as garbage collection options.

 The default value of `mapred.child.java.opts` is set to -Xmx200m which is far too small for almost any type of data processing. Normal values range from 1GB to 4GB with the median value around 2GB.

Example value: -Xmx2g. Used by: Child tasks.

`mapred.child.ulimit`

In addition to setting the maximum heap size of the child task JVM in `mapred.child.java.opts`, it is possible to impose a limit on the amount of virtual memory a task is permitted to consume using standard process limits (on Linux, see `man 2 getrlimit`). This imposes a limit on how much *virtual* memory a process may consume before it is terminated. Virtual memory, in this context, is the address space of the process, meaning it includes physical memory, secondary storage such as swap, and resources like `mmap()`ed files. The value of `mapred.child.ulimit` is expressed in kilobytes and must be large enough to include the child JVM process. As a baseline, it should be roughly 1.5 times the size of the JVM max heap size so, for a 1GB heap size, a value of 1572864 (1.5GB or 1572864KB) would be appropriate.

Why Both mapred.child.java.opts and mapred.child.ulimit?

If the JVM memory consumption is limited by the maximum heap size, it may not be obvious why additional control is required over the process virtual memory limit. The problem is that the child JVM can, in turn, create additional processes which would not be limited by the heap size of the child itself. This is exactly how Hadoop Streaming - an API that permits non-Java mappers and reducers to be written and executed in Hadoop MapReduce - works; a user supplied script or program is created and executed under the control of the child JVM. The resource limitation imposed on the child JVM is inherited by any processes it creates which means administrators can exercise reasonable control over the total resources consumed on the cluster.

Example value: 1572864. Used by: Child tasks.

`mapred.tasktracker.map.tasks.maximum` *and* `mapred.tasktracker.reduce.tasks.maximum`

Each worker node in the cluster is configured with a maximum number of simultaneous map and reduce tasks it is capable of running in parallel. In an effort to control resource consumption, administrators can specify the number of each type of task independently. The reason for the two types of tasks having independent configuration is because they use the machine differently; map tasks have a data locality preference and use the network as little as possible, while reduce tasks have no locality preference and must always fetch their input over the network before processing it.

It is critical to understand that Hadoop MapReduce will run up to the sum of `mapred.tasktracker.map.tasks.maximum` and `mapred.tasktracker.reduce.tasks.maximum` tasks concurrently. Each task is run in a separate JVM with a max heap size commonly between 1GB and 4GB, depending on the type of jobs being executed (which is configured via `mapred.child.java.opts`). For example, setting `mapred.tasktracker.map.tasks.maximum` to 12 and `mapred.child.java.opts` to

-Xmx2g will result in at up to 24GB of RAM (plus some additional overhead for non-heap memory pools in the JVM) being used on the worker node *just for map tasks*. Each task also performs HDFS IO (most of which should be local) to read input and local disk IO for map task intermediate output so a sufficient number of drives and controller bandwidth is also required.

Oversubscribing the machine's CPU and disk IO will lead to degraded performance, but shouldn't cause outright failure of tasks while oversubscription of memory is far worse. If a worker node starts swapping performance will immediately and severely suffer. Imagine 12 tasks, each of which requires 4GB of RAM executing concurrently on a machine with 16GB of RAM and having to contend with one another for a single swap partition. It's possible that all tasks slow so much that they time out causing them to fail and be retried later. If the pattern of swapping and time out continues, tasks can exhaust their maximum number of retries causing the job to fail.

So where do you start when configuring the number of tasks for a machine? Start with a baseline configuration of one and a half tasks for each physical CPU core (rounded up the nearest whole number), assuming the balanced hardware configuration from "Worker Hardware Selection" on page 48, and adjust based on the observed behavior of the jobs that are commonly run. For example, with 12 physical cores, we would multiply 12 by 1.5 for 18 tasks total. Dividing these tasks by map and reduce slots can also be tricky. Again, as a baseline, start with roughly two thirds allocated to map task slots and the remaining one third as reduce task slots, or given our working example, 12 and 6, respectively (rounded up from 11.88 and 5.94).

Example value for `mapred.tasktracker.map.tasks.maximum`: 12, `mapred.task tracker.reduce.tasks.maximum`: 6. Used by: TT.

io.sort.mb

As map tasks produce output, it is stored in an in-memory circular buffer rather than being written directly to disk. The size of this buffer is controlled by the `io.sort.mb` parameter. When this buffer fills to a configured percentage (80% by default), a background thread begins spilling the contents of the buffer to disk in the directories specified by `mapred.local.dir`. If there are multiple `mapred.local.dir` directories, the map task will cycle through them in a round robin fashion. Prior to spilling to disk, this where the map output is partitioned and sorted by key. When the map task is complete, there may be many of these spill files. These files, which are already sorted by key, are merged into larger files and served to reducers by the tasktracker.

The value of `io.sort.mb` is specified in megabytes and, by default, is 100. Increasing the size of this buffer results in fewer spills to disk and, as a consequence, reduces the number of spill files that must be merged when the map task completes. The `io.sort.mb` parameter is one way administrators and job developers can trade more memory for reduced disk IO. The downside of this is that this buffer must be contained within the child task's JVM heap allocation, as defined by `mapred.child.java.opts`. For example, with a child heap size of 1GB and `io.sort.mb` set to 128, only 896MB is really available to the user's code.

For a 1GB child heap size, `io.sort.mb` can be set to 128MB as a baseline. Observe the average MapReduce job and note the amount of *map output records* versus the number of *spilled records*; if the latter is significantly higher than the former, it may be an indication that `io.sort.mb` should be increased. Bear in mind that developers can always override `io.sort.mb` at the job level (which is why it should not be marked as `final`), so if only a subset of jobs require special tuning, consider handling it that way. Remember that ultimately, all records output by map tasks must be spilled so, in the ideal scenario, these numbers are equal.

Example value: 128. Used by: Child tasks.

io.sort.factor

The sister parameter to `io.sort.mb` is `io.sort.factor` which defines the number of files to merge at once. There are two cases where files are merged in MapReduce: when a map task completes, spill files are merged, and after reducers have retrieved all map task output files and before the user reduce code is invoked. Both of these stages are part of the sort and shuffle phase of MapReduce.

To understand the merge operation, consider the example where we have a map task creating many spill files, each sorted by key. In order to reassemble the files into a single sorted file, we open some number of files (defined by `io.sort.factor`), and begin the iterative process of comparing the heads of the streams, picking the lowest key, and writing the result to a new file. This process is repeated until all streams are exhausted and a single new file contains the merged contents of the other files. At the end of each merge round, we check to see if there are more files and, if so, the entire process starts over.

Increasing the number of files merged in a single pass reduces the number of times data is read and written back to disk which, in turn, reduces disk IO. Of course, merging more files at once means using more memory so, like most things, there's a tradeoff to consider. With a child heap size greater than or equal to 1GB, start with `io.sort.factor` set to 64 when processing large datasets. If you observe a large amount of *local disk IO* during the sort and shuffle phase, it may be due to excessive merge rounds. The child task logs contain merge information at the INFO severity level.

Example value: 64. Used by: Child tasks.

mapred.compress.map.output

When the output of map tasks is spilled to disk, it is uncompressed by default. Enabling map output compression can significantly reduce the amount of disk IO as well as the amount of data that must be transferred across the network during the shuffle phase of a MapReduce job. Compression is a way of trading CPU time for disk IO because compression requires additional CPU cycles during both compression and decompression. If monitoring data shows that there is available CPU capacity during the sort and shuffle phase and the job is primarily bound by either network bandwidth or disk IO, enabling compression is almost certainly a win.

The compression algorithm or codec used to compress the map output is defined by the `mapred.map.output.compression.codec` parameter. Since map output need not be splittable, it is not important to select a compression codec that exhibits such a property. This leaves administrators and developers to select more or less aggressive compression codecs based on the resource consumption and state of the cluster. This parameter may be specified at the job level.

Example value: true. Used by: Child map tasks.

mapred.map.output.compression.codec

Hadoop MapReduce supports pluggable compression codecs or algorithms implemented as Java classes. The `mapred.map.output.compression.codec` is used to specify the codec that should be used to compress map output in MapReduce jobs. If no value is given, the codec `org.apache.hadoop.io.compress.DefaultCodec` is used. In most cases, it makes sense to use the `org.apache.io.compress.SnappyCodec` compression codec as it offers a balanced CPU usage to compression ratio. If excessive disk IO or network IO is observed and there is available CPU, administrators can test the more aggressive `org.apache.io.compress.GzipCodec`.

Example value: `org.apache.io.compress.SnappyCodec`. Used by: Child map tasks.

mapred.output.compression.type

If the output of a MapReduce job is to be written in SequenceFile format, `mapred.output.compression.type` specifies the type of compression to use. The available types are RECORD, which causes each value in the SequenceFile to be individually compressed, BLOCK, which causes all key value records to be compressed in groups of a given size, and NONE, which results in no compression. Note that compression *type* is different than the compression *codec*, which is the algorithm to use. The type indicates how the compression codec is applied; that is, to only record values, to a group or block of key value records, or not at all, as described above.

Deciding to use compression is usually straight forward. You may choose to compress data to reduce the required storage, to reduce the amount of disk or network IO required while reading or writing the data, or both. The real question is why exactly would one select RECORD over BLOCK compression, or vice versa. Consider, for a moment, that compression works by eliminating repeating data patterns and replacing this data with some form of marker. The more repetition there is within the data, the greater the achieved compression ratio. If the data being compressed is a single record value, it is unlikely (for most kinds of records) that there will be a significant amount of repeating data. In the case of BLOCK compression, however, a group of records, including both keys and values, are compressed together. In most cases, this is significantly more effective. The downside to BLOCK compression is that to access an individual record, the system must now decompress a block up to the location of the record of interest. In MapReduce, individual record level access is not what we are optimizing for, so this is a reasonable trade off. That said, if individual records in a SequenceFile are large and do contain enough data repetition to make compression desirable, you still have the option to use RECORD level compression. A SequenceFile containing images or other binary payloads would be a good example of when RECORD level compression is a good idea.

Remember that, in this context, the block being described is a group of key value records in a SequenceFile and not a block of a file in HDFS. To date, there is no automatic filesystem compression in HDFS. Instead, compression is always implemented by the writer and decompression by the reader.

Example value: BLOCK. Used by: Child tasks.

mapred.job.tracker.handler.count

The Hadoop jobtracker is the primary entry point to the system for clients submitting jobs, as well as the hub of cluster and job status. As a result, it fields a fair amount of RPC activity from clients and tasktrackers alike. Internally, the jobtracker maintains a worker thread pool to handle RPCs, much the same way that the namenode does. The mapred.job.tracker.handler.count controls the size of this thread pool.

By default, this thread pool is set to 10, but should be customized in almost all cases. Just like the namenode's dfs.namenode.handler.count parameter, mapred.job.tracker.handler.count should be set to the natural logarithm of the cluster size times 20. See dfs.namenode.handler.count on page 96 for more information.

Example value: 105. Used by: JT.

mapred.jobtracker.taskScheduler

Once a MapReduce job has been divided into tasks, it is the responsibility of the jobtracker's task scheduler plugin to decide which tasks execute in which order on which tasktrackers. The order tasks are scheduled within a job and between jobs can depend on a great many factors (all of which are described in Chapter 7), but the most important is the scheduler plug-in. The mapred.jobtracker.taskScheduler parameter specifies the Java class name of the scheduler plugin that should be used by the jobtracker. By default, Hadoop MapReduce uses a first in, first out (FIFO) scheduler implemented by the class org.apache.hadoop.mapred.JobQueueTaskScheduler. While this is fine during development and basic functional testing, production clusters should always use either the fair scheduler or the capacity scheduler, both of which support multiple queues with meaningful resource controls.

Example value: org.apache.hadoop.mapred.FairScheduler. Used by: JT.

mapred.reduce.parallel.copies

During the shuffle phase of a MapReduce job, each reducer task must fetch intermediate map output data from each of the tasktrackers where a map task from the same job ran. In other words, there are *R* x *M* total copies that must be performed where *R* is the number of reducers and *M* is the number of mappers. If each reducer were to perform each copy sequentially, this process would take an unnecessarily long time and may not take full advantage of the available network bandwidth. Instead, reducers can perform some number of these copies in parallel, as defined by the `mapred.reduce.parallel.copies` parameter. If, for instance, `mapred.reduce.parallel.copies` is set to 10 and 8 reducers are running on a machine, that machine alone will perform 80 copies in parallel from some number of tasktrackers. These copies are not throttled by Hadoop, so some care must be taken to not completely monopolize the network, potentially starving clients writing new data to HDFS.

The default value of `mapred.reduce.parallel.copies` is 5 which is usually far too low. Instead, a value of natural logarithm of the size of the cluster, time four, is more appropriate.

Example value: 10. Used by: Child tasks.

`mapred.reduce.tasks`

When MapReduce jobs are executed, the user does not specify the number of map tasks that should be created. This is because the framework (specifically, the input format specified by the job) makes this decision based on the data, itself. However, the user does specify the number of reducers that should be executed. It's impossible for the framework to know how many reducers to create because the data on which they would operate has not yet been created by the mappers. The `mapred.reduce.tasks` parameter specifies the number of reduce tasks to use for the job. It is commonly overridden at the job level based on the user's *a priori* knowledge of the data or the work being performed.

The default value of `mapred.reduce.tasks` is 1. This is rarely what the user wants and, when used accidentally, can create a significant bottleneck as all intermediate map output must be shuffled to a single reducer. It also means that all map output must fit on a single machine which may not be possible for larger jobs. For these reasons, this parameter should be set to 50% of the total reducer slots on the cluster as a starting point and adjusted based on the average number of jobs running on the cluster at any given time and the amount of data processed by each reducer. The ideal scenario is for most jobs to have enough reducers that they complete as fast as possible, without each reducer handling too many or too few records, but not going through multiple rounds of reducers, when possible.

For example, a cluster with 20 nodes, each configured to run 6 reducers in parallel yields 120 total reducers. If no further information about the jobs running on the cluster is available, setting `mapred.reduce.tasks` to 60 is a fine place to start. This leaves available reduce slots for other jobs that are submitted while the job in question is executing.

Example value: 64. Used by: JT.

`tasktracker.http.threads`

Earlier, we covered `mapred.reduce.parallel.copies` which controls the number of copies each reduce task initiates in parallel during the shuffle phase. This, however, only describes the *client* side of the communication. Each tasktracker runs an embedded HTTP server which it uses to vend intermediate map output to these reduce tasks. The `tasktracker.http.threads` controls the number of threads available to handle requests, concurrently.

The proper number of HTTP threads scales with the number of total reduce slots in the cluster *and* the permitted parallel copies they may perform. For example, if a cluster has 20 nodes, each with 6 reduce slots, each allowed to perform 5 parallel copies, every tasktracker could potentially have up to 600 clients attempting to fetch data in parallel! Of course, it may not make sense to allow so many copies in parallel. Monitoring the network profile of jobs, detecting outliers, and tuning appropriately is usually required.

Example value: 64. Used by: TT.

`mapred.reduce.slowstart.completed.maps`

Earlier, we stated that reducers couldn't start until all mappers completed. While it is true that the user's reduce method can not run until all mappers have produced their intermediate data, it is possible to start reducers early and begin shuffling intermediate output as it's produced by map tasks, allowing the job to get a jump on the potentially costly operation of copying the data across the network. This comes at the cost of occupying reduce slots before the reduce method can be executed. We don't necessarily want reducers to start so early that they have little or nothing to do, but early enough so that most of the data is copied when the final map tasks complete so the reduce operation can begin right away.

The `mapred.reduce.slowstart.completed.maps` parameter indicates when to begin allocating reducers as a percentage (as a floating point number) of completed map tasks. In other words, a value of 0.5 means reducers will be started when 50% of the map tasks are completed in the job. The default value of 0.05 - 5% of maps completed - starts reducers very early, and is designed for slow or highly saturated networks. As it becomes easier to build large, line rate, non-blocking networks, it makes sense to increase this value accordingly.

The slow start threshold is coupled to the number of nodes in the cluster, the reducers per node, and the parallel copies per reducer. Having more machines in the cluster allows for running more reduce tasks, each of which transfers data during the shuffle phase. We also now know that each reducer copies data from tasktrackers in parallel, as controlled by `mapred.reduce.parallel.copies`. All of these parameters provide a way to *increase* the amount of bandwidth consumed in order to decrease the run time of the job. The slow start parameter provides a way to control *when* to start the transfer so reduce slots remain free until they're truly needed.

For clusters connected by a line rate, non-blocking, 1Gbps network, start with slow start set to 0.8 (80%). Monitor the network during peak MapReduce times, tuning this up (closer to 1) to start reducers later if data copies quickly, and down (closer to 0) to start reducers earlier. The combination of slow start, reducer count, parallel copies, and map output compression allow administrators to control slot usage and network bandwidth, and optimize resource utilization during the shuffle phase rather extensively.

Example value: 0.8. Used by: JT.

Rack Topology

Rack topology, in the context of Hadoop, defines how machines are physically located in rack in the data center. Combined with traditional network design and top of rack switching, this allows us to infer how close machines are to one another, logically, in terms of network connectivity. The physical locality of machines also has a bearing on other concerns such as power infrastructure, which is critical to understanding the possible fault domains in the system.

By communicating topology information to Hadoop, we influence the placement of data within the cluster as well as the processing of that data. Both the Hadoop distributed filesystem and MapReduce are aware of, and benefit from rack topology information, when it's available. We already understand that HDFS keeps multiple copies of each block and stores them on different machines. Without topology information, a cluster than spans racks could place all replicas on a single rack, leaving us susceptible to data availability problems in the case that an entire rack failed. Instead, when a file is written to HDFS, the first replica of each block is written to a random node, while the second and third replicas are written to two machines in a separate rack. This logic is called the *block placement policy*. It may seem strange not to place one replica in each of three racks at first, but doing so would cause the data to pass over the core switching infrastructure an extra time, burning precious and expensive bandwidth. Placing replicas two and three in the same rack keeps the data transfer local to the top of rack switch which scales with the number of racks in the cluster.

Hadoop MapReduce also uses the rack topology information when deciding on which machines to place map tasks. Ideally, each map task is run on a machine with a local copy of the data. This is called a *data local task* and is one of the primary tricks in Hadoop's bag. This, however, is not always possible, as active clusters may have many jobs with many tasks running in parallel, each competing for slots on specific machines. If a map task that needs to process block *A* must run, but all machines with a copy of *A* are busy, the jobtracker will look for a machine in the same rack as one of these machines and schedule the task there. When the task runs, the block is streamed across the network to the map task. The logic behind this decision is similar to that of placing the second and third replica of a block on two machines in the same rack during an HDFS write; network bandwidth is greater between two machines connected to the same top of rack switch than crossing over the core switching infrastructure. A task that processes data that isn't local to the machine, but is within the same rack is said to be *rack local*. While rare, it is possible that even this isn't possible, in which case the task is *non-local*. Hadoop keeps track of how many tasks, of each type, are executed for reporting purposes.

Rack topology is configured in Hadoop by implementing a script that, when given a list of hostnames or IP addresses on the command line, prints the rack in which the machine is located, in order. The implementation of the topology script is entirely up to the administrator and may be as simple as a shell script that has a hardcoded list of machines and rack names, or as sophisticated as a C executable that reads data from a relational database. One of the most common types of scripts is one that uses a CSV file of machine to rack mappings. See Examples 5-19 and 5-20.

Example 5-19. Python Hadoop rack topology script (/etc/hadoop/conf/topology.py)

```python
#!/usr/bin/python

import sys

class RackTopology:

  # Make sure you include the absolute path to topology.csv.
  DEFAULT_TOPOLOGY_FILE = '/etc/hadoop/conf/topology.csv'
  DEFAULT_RACK = '/default-rack'

  def __init__(self, filename = DEFAULT_TOPOLOGY_FILE):
    self._filename = filename
    self._mapping = dict()

    self._load_topology(filename)

  def _load_topology(self, filename):
    '''
    Load a CSV-ish mapping file. Should be two columns with the first being the
    hostname or IP and the second the rack name. If a line isn't well formed,
    it's discarded. Each field is stripped of any leading or trailing space. If
    the file fails to load for any reason, all hosts will be in DEFAULT_RACK.
    '''
    try:
      f = file(filename, 'r')

      for line in f:
        fields = line.split(',')

        if len(fields) == 2:
          self._mapping[fields[0].strip()] = fields[1].strip()
    except:
      pass

  def rack_of(self, host):
    '''
    Look up and a hostname or IP address in the mapping and return its rack.
```

```
  '''
  if self._mapping.has_key(host):
    return self._mapping[host]
  else:
    return RackTopology.DEFAULT_RACK

if __name__ == '__main__':
  app = RackTopology()

  for node in sys.argv[1:]:
    print app.rack_of(node)
```

Example 5-20. Rack topology mapping file (/etc/hadoop/conf/topology.csv)

```
10.1.1.160,/rack1
10.1.1.161,/rack1
10.1.1.162,/rack2
10.1.1.163,/rack2
10.1.1.164,/rack2
```

With our script (Example 5-19) and mapping file (Example 5-20) defined, we only need to tell Hadoop the location of the script to enable rack awareness. To do this, set the parameter topology.script.file.name in *core-site.xml* to the absolute path of the script. The script should be executable and require no arguments other than the hostnames or IP addresses. Hadoop will invoke this script, as needed, to discover the node to rack mapping information.

You can verify that Hadoop is using your script by running the command hadoop dfsadmin -report as the HDFS superuser. If everything is working, you should see the proper rack name next to each machine. The name of the machine shown in this report (minus the port) is also the name that is passed to the topology script to look up rack information.

```
[esammer@hadoop01 ~]$ sudo -u hdfs hadoop dfsadmin -report
Configured Capacity: 19010409390080 (17.29 TB)
Present Capacity: 18228294160384 (16.58 TB)
DFS Remaining: 5514620928000 (5.02 TB)
DFS Used: 12713673232384 (11.56 TB)
DFS Used%: 69.75%
Under replicated blocks: 181
Blocks with corrupt replicas: 0
Missing blocks: 0

-------------------------------------------------
Datanodes available: 5 (5 total, 0 dead)

Name: 10.1.1.164:50010
Rack: /rack1
Decommission Status : Normal
Configured Capacity: 3802081878016 (3.46 TB)
DFS Used: 2559709347840 (2.33 TB)
Non DFS Used: 156356984832 (145.62 GB)
DFS Remaining: 1086015545344(1011.43 GB)
DFS Used%: 67.32%
```

```
DFS Remaining%: 28.56%
Last contact: Sun Mar 11 18:45:47 PDT 2012
```

...

The naming convention of the racks is a slash separated, pseudo-hierarchy, exactly the same as absolute Linux paths. Although today, rack topologies are single level (that is, machines are either in the same rack or not; there is no true hierarchy), it is possible that Hadoop will develop to understand multiple levels of locality. For instance, it is not currently possible to model multinode chassis systems with multiple racks. If a chassis holds two discreet servers and the cluster spans multiple racks, it is possible that two replicas of a block could land in a single chassis, which is less than ideal. This situation is significantly more likely in the case of highly dense blade systems, although they have other problems as well (see "Blades, SANs, and Virtualization" on page 52).

Some users see rack topology as a way to span a Hadoop cluster across data centers by creating two large racks, each of which encompasses all the nodes in each data center. Hadoop will not berate you with errors if you were to try this (at least not initially), but rest assured it will not work in practice. It seems as though, with multiple replicas and the ability to impact how replicas are placed, you'd have everything you need. The devil, as they say, is in the details. If you were to configure a cluster this way, you'd almost immediately hit the network bottleneck between data centers. Remember that while rack topology doesn't necessarily prohibit non-local reads, it only reduces the chances, and either way, all writes would always span data centers (because replicas are written synchronously). The other major issue is that, when running MapReduce jobs, the jobtracker will see replicas in the other data center—and the nodes on which they reside—as viable candidates for scheduling in order to achieve data locality during processing. This is benign enough, as no data is transferred across the network, but the ensuing shuffle phase will have to transfer a significant amount of data between the data centers. The final pathological case with this configuration is that, assuming everything else were not to be a problem (which is unlikely), within a data center, replicas will view all racks as a single rack. This results in an inability to distinguish between a rack-local task and a non-local task to Hadoop, which generates a significant amount of data transfer across the core switches within a single data center that wouldn't normally occur.

Security

Configuring authentication, authorization, and the various subsystems within Hadoop to operate in a secure manner is a large undertaking. Due to this complexity, Chapter 6 is devoted to the topic, including the necessary configuration steps to enable Hadoop security.

Identity, Authentication, and Authorization

Multitenancy is a fancy word for supporting many independent entities within a single larger system. The ability to support multiple discreet entities in a system is generally useful when it is costly or complex to operate an instance of that system for each entity. An example of this is the ability to run multiple databases within a single database server, a feature supported by almost all RDBMS vendors. By bringing multiple users of a service together, we can take advantage of the economies of scale and offer greater service as a whole. A simple example of this in the context of Hadoop is that, if a large cluster is built to run hourly production MapReduce jobs, there are generally free resources between executions of those jobs. If we were to silo users by group or use case, these lulls in resource usage would be lost across all groups. Instead, it often (but admittedly not always) makes sense to combine smaller silo clusters into a single large cluster. Not only does this simplify operations, but it increases the available capacity to service consumers, on average, which improves system resource utilization.

Unfortunately, running multitenant systems comes with some obvious challenges. Controlling access to data and resources immediately becomes a point of concern, especially when the data is sensitive in nature. It may be that two different groups of users should not see each other's data or even not know one another exist. Controlling access to resources also becomes critical. It shouldn't be possible for one group to monopolize the resources of a shared system. Administrators and especially security and compliance staff expect to be able to monitor and audit user activity in multitenant systems to ensure policies are enforced. The degree of isolation within a multitenant system can be seen as the gating factor between silo and shared deployments. This is even more true of data storage and processing systems, and is the impetus for a deep review of identity, access, and authorization controls in a system such as Hadoop.

When a user performs an action in Hadoop, there are three significant questions:

1. Who does this user claim to be?

   The *identity* of the entity interacting with the cluster (where entity means a human user or another system) is who they purport to be. As humans, we identify using our names. In Linux, we use usernames, whereas the relational database MySQL, for instance, has its own notion of a user. The identity is an arbitrary label that is unique to an entity, and something to which we can attach meaning.

2. Can this user prove they are who they say they are?

   Anyone can claim to be your Uncle Larry or Aunt Susan, but can they prove it? We *authenticate* one another by confirming an identity using some kind of system. To enter a country, an individual must present a valid and authentic passport bearing a photo of the person, for instance (although some may say this is a weak form of subjective authentication). Linux provides multiple forms of authentication via plug-ins, although passwords are probably the most common. Authentication mechanisms vary in *strength* (the rigor with which they confirm a user's identity).

3. Is this user allowed to do what they're asking to do?

   Once a user has identified themselves and we are reasonably sure they are who they claim to be, only then does it make sense to ensure they have been *authorized* to perform the requested action. It never makes sense for a system to support authorization without first authenticating users; a person could simply lie about who they are to gain privileges they wouldn't otherwise have.

Hadoop operates in either the default, so called *simple mode* or *secure mode*, which provides strong authentication support via Kerberos. For many, the simple security mode is sufficient and offers reasonable protection from mistakes in a trusted environment. As its name implies, it's simple to configure and manage, relying primarily on the host for authentication. If, however, you are running Hadoop in an untrusted, multitenant environment or where accidental data exposure would be catastrophic, secure mode is the appropriate option. In secure mode, Hadoop uses the well-known Kerberos protocol to authenticate users and daemons themselves during all operations. Additionally, MapReduce tasks in secure mode are executed as the same OS user as the job was submitted, whereas in simple mode, they are executed as the user running the tasktracker.

The most important aspect to understand is that, regardless of whether simple or secure mode is configured, it controls only how users are authenticated with the system. Authorization is inherently service specific. The evaluation of the authenticated user's privileges in the context of the action they are asking to perform is controlled entirely by the service. In the case of HDFS, this means deciding if a user is permitted to read from or write to a file, for example. Authentication must always be performed before authorization is considered, and because it is commonly the same for all services, it can be built as a separate, generic service.

Identity

In Hadoop, there is a strong relationship between who a user is in the host operating system and who they are in HDFS or MapReduce. Furthermore, since there are many machines involved in a cluster, it may not be immediately obvious what is actually required in order to execute a MapReduce job. Hadoop, like most systems, uses the concepts of users and groups to organize identities. However—and this is the root of quite a bit of confusion—it uses the identity of the user according to the operating system. That is, there is no such thing as a Hadoop user or group. When an OS user, in my case, user esammer, executes a command using the hadoop executable, or uses any of the Java APIs, Hadoop accepts this username as the identity with no further checks. Versions of Apache Hadoop prior to 0.20.200 or CDH3u0 also allowed users to specify their identity by setting a configuration parameter when performing an action in HDFS or even running a MapReduce job, although this is no longer possible.

In simple mode, the Hadoop library on the *client* sends the username of the running process with each command to either the namenode or jobtracker, depending on the command executed. When in secure mode, the primary component of the Kerberos principal name is used as the identity of the user. The user must already have a valid Kerberos ticket in their cache, otherwise the command will fail with an incredibly cryptic message like Example 6-1.

Example 6-1. A typical failed authentication attempt with security enabled

```
WARN ipc.Client: Exception encountered while connecting to the
server: javax.security.sasl.SaslException: GSS initiate failed [Caused by
GSSException: No valid credentials provided (Mechanism level: Failed to
find any Kerberos tgt)]
```

Kerberos and Hadoop

As mentioned earlier, Hadoop supports strong authentication using the *Kerberos* protocol. Kerberos was developed by a team at MIT to provide strong authentication of clients to a server and is well-known to many enterprises. When operating in secure mode, all clients must provide a valid Kerberos ticket that can be verified by the server. In addition to clients being authenticated, daemons are also verified. In the case of HDFS, for instance, a datanode is not permitted to connect to the namenode unless it provides a valid ticket within each RPC. All of this amounts to an environment where every daemon and client application can be cryptographically verified as a known entity prior to allowing any operations to be performed, a desirable feature of any data storage and processing system.

Kerberos: A Refresher

To say Kerberos is "well-known" could be an overstatement. For many, Kerberos is shrouded in dense, intimidating terminology and requires specific knowledge to configure properly. Many implementations of Kerberos exist, and though there are RFCs[1] that describe the Kerberos protocol itself, management tools and methods have traditionally been vendor-specific. In the Linux world, one of the most popular implementations is MIT Kerberos (*http://web.mit.edu/kerberos/*) version 5 (or MIT krb5 for short), an open source software package that includes the server, client, and admin tools. Before we dive into the details of configuring Hadoop to use Kerberos for authentication, let's first take a look at how Kerberos works, as well as the MIT implementation.

A user in Kerberos is called a *principal*, which is made up of three distinct components: the primary, instance, and realm. The first component of the principal is called the *primary*, or sometimes the user component. The primary component is an arbitrary string and may be the operating system username of the user or the name of a service. The primary component is followed by an optional section called the *instance*, which is used to create principals that are used by users in special roles or to define the host on which a service runs, for example. An instance, if it exists, is separated from the primary by a slash and then the content is used to disambiguate multiple principals for a single user or service. The final component of the principal is the *realm*. The realm is similar to a domain in DNS in that it logically defines a related group of objects, although rather than hostnames as in DNS, the Kerberos realm defines a group of principals (see Table 6-1). Each realm can have its own settings including the location of the KDC on the network and supported encryption algorithms. Large organizations commonly create distinct realms to delegate administration of a realm to a group within the enterprise. Realms, by convention, are written in uppercase characters.

Table 6-1. Example Kerberos principals

Principal	Description
esammer@MYREALM.CLOUDERA.COM	A standard user principal. User esammer in realm MYR-EALM.CLOUDERA.COM.
esammer/admin@MYREALM.CLOUDERA.COM	The admin instance of the user esammer in the realm MYR-EALM.CLOUDERA.COM.
hdfs/hadoop01.cloudera.com@MYREALM.CLOUDERA.COM	The hdfs service on the host hadoop01.cloudera.com in the realm MYREALM.CLOUDERA.COM.

At its core, Kerberos provides a central, trusted service called the Key Distribution Center or *KDC*. The KDC is made up of two distinct services: the authentication server (*AS*), which is responsible for authenticating a client and providing a ticket granting

---

1. IETF RFC 4120 - The Kerberos Network Authentication Service (version 5) - *http://tools.ietf.org/html/rfc4120*

ticket (*TGT*), and the ticket granting service (*TGS*), which, given a valid TGT, can grant a ticket that authenticates a user when communicating with a Kerberos-enabled (or *Kerberized*) service. The KDC contains a database of principals and their keys, very much like */etc/passwd* and some KDC implementations (including MIT Kerberos) support storing this data in centralized systems like LDAP. That's a lot of verbiage, but the process of authenticating a user is relatively simple.

Consider the case where user `esammer` wants to execute the command `hadoop fs -get / user/esammer/data.txt`. When operating in secure mode, the HDFS namenode and datanode will not permit any communication that does not contain a valid Kerberos ticket. We also know that at least two (and frequently many more) services must be contacted: one is the namenode to get the file metadata and check permissions, and the rest are the datanodes to retrieve the blocks of the file. To obtain any tickets from the KDC, we first retrieve a TGT from the AS by providing our principal name. The TGT, which is only valid for an administrator-defined period of time, is encrypted with our password and sent back to the client. The client prompts us for our password and attempts to decrypt the TGT. If it works, we're ready to request a ticket from the TGS, otherwise we've failed to decrypt the TGT and we're unable to request tickets. It's important to note that our password has never left the local machine; the system works because the KDC has a copy of the password, which has been shared in advance. This is a standard *shared secret* or *symmetric key* encryption model.

It is still not yet possible to speak to the namenode or datanode; we need to provide a valid ticket for those specific services. Now that we have a valid TGT, we can request service specific tickets from the TGS. To do so, using our TGT, we ask the TGS for a ticket for a specific service, identified by the service principal (such as the namenode of the cluster). The TGS, which is part of the KDC, can verify the TGT we provide is valid because it was encrypted with a special key called the TGT key. If the TGT can be validated and it hasn't yet expired, the TGS provides us a valid ticket for the service, which is also only valid for a finite amount of time. Within the returned ticket is a session key; a shared secret key that the service to which we speak can confirm with the KDC. Using this ticket, we can now contact the namenode and request metadata for */user/esammer/data.txt*. The namenode will validate the ticket with the KDC and assuming everything checks out, then performs the operation we originally requested. Additionally, for operations that involve access to block data, the namenode generates a *block token* for each block returned to the client. The block token is then provided to the datanode by client, which validates its authenticity before providing access to the block data.

The TGT received from the KDC's AS usually has a lifetime of 8 to 24 hours, meaning it is only necessary to provide a password once per time period. The TGT is cached locally on the client machine and reused during subsequent requests to the TGS. The MIT Kerberos implementation, for instance, caches ticket information in the temporary file */tmp/krb5cc_uid* where *uid* is the Linux user's uid. To perform the initial authentication and retrieve a TGT from the KDC with MIT Kerberos, use the `kinit` command; to list cached credentials, use the `klist` command as in Example 6-2.

Example 6-2. Obtaining a ticket granting ticket with kinit

```
[esammer@hadoop01 ~]$ klist
klist: No credentials cache found (ticket cache FILE:/tmp/krb5cc_500)
[esammer@hadoop01 ~]$ kinit
Password for esammer@MYREALM.CLOUDERA.COM:
[esammer@hadoop01 ~]$ klist
Ticket cache: FILE:/tmp/krb5cc_500
Default principal: esammer@MYREALM.CLOUDERA.COM

Valid starting     Expires            Service principal
03/22/12 15:35:50  03/23/12 15:35:50  krbtgt/MYREALM.CLOUDERA.COM@MYREALM.CLOUDERA.COM
        renew until 03/22/12 15:35:50
[esammer@hadoop01 ~]$ hadoop fs -get /user/esammer/data.txt
...
```

Kerberos is an enormous topic, complex in its own right. Prior to embarking on a Kerberos deployment, it's critical to understand how hosts and services are accessed by users as well as other services. Without a coherent understanding of a system, it's likely that you will find that services that used to be accessible no longer work. For a detailed explanation of Kerberos, see Kerberos: The Definitive Guide (*http://shop .oreilly.com/product/9780596004033.do*) by Jason Garman (O'Reilly Media).

Kerberos Support in Hadoop

Now that we have some understanding of how Kerberos works conceptually, it's worth looking at how this applies to Hadoop. There are two primary forms of authentication that occur in Hadoop with respect to Kerberos: nodes within the cluster authenticating with one another to ensure that only trusted machines are part of the cluster, and users, both human and system, that access the cluster to interact with services. Since many of the Hadoop daemons also have embedded web servers, they too must be secured and authenticated.

Within each service, both users and worker nodes are verified by their Kerberos credentials. HDFS and MapReduce follow the same general architecture; the worker daemons are each given a unique principal that identifies each daemon, they authenticate, and include a valid ticket in each RPC to their respective master daemon. The workers authenticate by using a keytab stored on the local disk. Though tedious, the act of creating a unique principal for each daemon, for each host, generating the keytab, and getting it to the proper machine, is absolutely necessary when configuring a secure Hadoop cluster. Workers must have their own unique principals because if they didn't, the KDC would issue a similar TGT (based on the principal's key and timestamp) to all nodes, and services would see potentially hundreds of clients all attempting to authenticate with the same ticket, falsely characterizing it as a replay attack.

Multiple principals are used by the system when Hadoop is operating in secure mode and take the form *service-name*/*hostname*@KRB.REALM.COM where the *service-name* is hdfs in the case of the HDFS daemons and mapred in the case of the MapReduce daemons. Since worker nodes run both a datanode as well as a tasktracker, each node requires two principals to be generated: one for the datanode and one for the tasktracker. The namenode and jobtracker also have principals, although in smaller clusters where the one or both of these daemons run on a node that is also a slave, it is not necessary to create a separate principal as namenode and datanode can share a principal and the tasktracker and jobtracker can share a principal.

Since it isn't feasible to log into each machine and execute kinit as both user hdfs and mapred and provide a password, the keys for the service principals are exported to files and placed in a well-known location. These files are referred to as key tables or just *keytabs*. Exporting the keys to files may seem dangerous, but if the contents of the files are properly protected by filesystem permissions (that is, owned by the user the daemon runs as, with permissions set to 0400), the integrity of the key is not compromised. When the daemons start up, they use this keytab to authenticate with the KDC and get a ticket so they can connect to the namenode or jobtracker, respectively. When operating in secure mode, it is not possible for a datanode or tasktracker to connect to its constituent master daemon without a valid ticket.

Exporting keys to keytabs

With MIT Kerberos, exporting a key to a keytab will invalidate any previously exported copies of that same key unless the -norandkey option is used. It's absolutely critical that you do not export a key that has already been exported unless that's what you mean to do. This should only be necessary if you believe a keytab has become compromised or is otherwise irrevocably lost or destroyed.

Users performing HDFS operations and running MapReduce jobs also must authenticate prior to those operations being allowed (or, technically, checked for authorization). When an application uses the Hadoop library to communicate with one of the services and is running in secure mode, the identity of the user to Hadoop is the primary component of the Kerberos principal. This is different from simple mode where the effective uid of the process is the identity of the user. Additionally, the tasks of a MapReduce jobs execute as the authenticated user that submitted the job. What this means is that, in secure mode, each user must have a principal in the KDC database *and* a user account on every machine in the cluster. See Table 6-2.

Table 6-2. Comparison of secure and simple mode identity

	Simple	Secure
Identity comes from:	Effective uid of client process	Kerberos principal
MapReduce tasks run as:	Tasktracker user (e.g., mapred)	Kerberos principal

The requirement that all users have a principal can complicate otherwise simple tasks. For instance, assuming the HDFS super user is hdfs, it would normally be possible to perform administrative activities using sudo like in Example 6-3.

Example 6-3. Performing HDFS administrative commands with sudo

```
# Creating a new user's home directory in HDFS. Since /user is owned
# by user hdfs, it is necessary to become that user or the super user (which
# also happens to be hdfs).
[esammer@hadoop01 ~]$ sudo -u hdfs hadoop fs -mkdir /user/jane
```

Unfortunately, this doesn't work in secure mode because the uid of the process doesn't make us hdfs. Instead, it is necessary to authenticate as user hdfs with Kerberos. This is normally done using kinit, as we saw earlier. This has the unpleasant side effect of requiring that we share the password for the HDFS principal. Rather than share the HDFS principal password with all the cluster administrators, we can export the HDFS principal key to a keytab protected by restrictive filesystem permissions, and then use sudo to allow selective users to access it when they authenticate with kinit. HDFS also supports the notion of a super group that users can be a member of to perform administrative commands as themselves.

Running tasks as the user that submitted the MapReduce job solves a few potential problems, the first of which is that, if we were to allow all tasks to run as user mapred, each map task would produce its intermediate output as the same user. A malicious user would be able to simply scan through the directories specified by mapred.local.dir and read or modify the output of another unrelated task. This kind of lack of isolation is a non-starter for security-sensitive deployments.

Since the tasktracker runs as an unprivileged user (user mapred, by default, in the case of CDH and whatever user the administrator configures in Apache Hadoop), it isn't possible for it to launch task JVMs as a different user. One way to solve this problem is to simply run the tasktracker process as root. While this would solve the immediate problem of permissions, any vulnerability in the tasktracker would open the entire system to compromise. Worse, since the tasktracker's job is to execute user supplied code as a user indicated by the jobtracker, an attacker would trivially have full control over all worker nodes. Instead of running the tasktracker as root, when operating in secure mode, the tasktracker relies on a small setuid executable called the *task-con troller*. The task-controller is a standalone binary implemented in C that sanity checks its environment and immediately drops privileges to the proper user before launching the task JVM. Configured by a small key value configuration file called *taskcontroller.cfg* in the Hadoop configuration directory, the task-controller is restricted to executing tasks for users with a uid above a certain value (as privileged accounts usually have low numbered uids). Specific users can also be explicitly prevented from running tasks, regardless of their uid, which is useful for denying Hadoop daemon users from executing tasks. For the task-controller to execute tasks as the user who submitted the job, each user must have accounts on all machines of the cluster. Administrators are expected to maintain these accounts, and because of the potentially large number of machines to keep in sync, admins are encouraged to either use centralized account management such as LDAP or an automated system to keep password files up-to-date.

Configuring Hadoop security

Configuring Hadoop to operate in secure mode can be a daunting task with a number of external dependencies. Detailed knowledge of Linux, Kerberos, SSL/TLS, and JVM security constructs are required. At the time of this book, there are also some known gotchas that exist in certain Linux distributions and versions of the JVM that can cause you grief. Some of those are exposed below.

The high-level process for enabling security is as follows.

1. Audit all services to ensure enabling security will not break anything.

   Hadoop security is all or nothing; enabling it will prevent all non-Kerberos authenticated communication. It is absolutely critical that you first take an inventory of all existing processes, both automated and otherwise, and decide how each will work once security is enabled. Don't forget about administrative scripts and tools!

2. Configure a working non-security enabled Hadoop cluster.

   Before embarking on enabling Hadoop's security features, get a simple mode cluster up and running. You'll want to iron out any kinks in DNS resolution, network connectivity, and simple misconfiguration early. Debugging network connectivity issues and supported encryption algorithms within the Kerberos KDC at the same time is not a position that you want to find yourself in.

3. Configure a working Kerberos environment.

   Basic Kerberos operations such as authenticating and receiving a ticket-granting ticket from the KDC should work before you continue. You are strongly encouraged to use MIT Kerberos with Hadoop; it is, by far, the most widely tested. If you have existing Kerberos infrastructure (such as provided by Microsoft Active Directory) that you wish to authenticate against, it is recommended that you configure a local MIT KDC with one way cross realm trust so Hadoop daemon principals exist in the MIT KDC and user authentication requests are forwarded to Active Directory. This is usually far safer as large Hadoop clusters can accidentally create distributed denial of service attacks against shared infrastructure when they become active.

4. Ensure host name resolution is sane.

   As discussed earlier, each Hadoop daemon has its own principal that it must know in order to authenticate. Since the hostname of the machine is part of the principal, all hostnames must be consistent and known at the time the principals are created. Once the principals are created, the hostnames may not be changed without recreating all of the principals! It is common that administrators run dedicated, caching-only, DNS name servers for large clusters.

5. Create Hadoop Kerberos principals.

Each daemon on each host of the cluster requires a distinct Kerberos principal when enabling security. Additionally, the Web user interfaces must also be given principals before they will function correctly. Just as the first point says, security is all or nothing.

6. Export principal keys to keytabs and distribute them to the proper cluster nodes.

With principals generated in the KDC, each key must be exported to a keytab, and copied to the proper host securely. Doing this by hand is incredibly laborious for even small clusters and, as a result, should be scripted.

7. Update Hadoop configuration files.

With all the principals generated and in their proper places, the Hadoop configuration files are then updated to enable security. The full list of configuration properties related to security are described later.

8. Restart all services.

To activate the configuration changes, all daemons must be restarted. The first time security is configured, it usually makes sense to start the first few daemons to make sure they authenticate correctly and are using the proper credentials before firing up the rest of the cluster.

9. Test!

It's probably clear by now that enabling security is complex and requires a fair bit of effort. The truly difficult part of configuring a security environment is testing that everything is working correctly. It can be particularly difficult on a large production cluster with existing jobs to verify that everything is functioning properly, but no assumptions should be made. Kerberos does not, by definition, afford leniency to misconfigured clients.

Creating principals for each of the Hadoop daemons and distributing their respective keytabs is the most tedious part of enabling Hadoop security. Doing this for each daemon by hand would be rather error prone, so instead, we'll create a file of host names and use a script to execute the proper commands. These examples assume MIT Kerberos 1.9 on CentOS 6.2.[2]

First, build a list of fully qualified host names, either by exporting them from an inventory system or generating them based on a well-known naming convention. For example, if all hosts follow the naming convention of hadoop*N*.mycompany.com, where *N* is a zero padded sequential number, a simple shell script will do:

```
[esammer@hadoop01 ~]$ for n in $(seq -f "%02g" 1 10) ; do
  echo "hadoop${n}.mycompany.com"
done > hostnames.txt
[esammer@hadoop01 ~]$ cat hostnames.txt
```

2. You can install the MIT Kerberos 1.9 client and server packages on CentOS 6.2 using the commands yum install krb5-workstation and yum install krb5-server, respectively.

```
hadoop01.mycompany.com
hadoop02.mycompany.com
hadoop03.mycompany.com
hadoop04.mycompany.com
hadoop05.mycompany.com
hadoop06.mycompany.com
hadoop07.mycompany.com
hadoop08.mycompany.com
hadoop09.mycompany.com
hadoop10.mycompany.com
```

Using our host list as input, we can write a script to create the necessary principals, export the keys to keytabs, and bucket them by machine name.

 This script *will* regenerate keys of any existing principals of the same name, which will invalidate any existing keytabs or passwords. Always measure twice and cut once when running scripts that affect the KDC!

```
#!/bin/sh

[ -r "hostnames.txt" ] || {
  echo "File hostnames.txt doesn't exist or isn't readable."
  exit 1
}

# Set this to the name of your Kerberos realm.
krb_realm=MYREALM.MYCOMPANY.COM

for name in $(cat hostnames.txt); do
  install -o root -g root -m 0700 -d ${name}

  kadmin.local <<EOF
addprinc -randkey host/${name}@${krb_realm}
addprinc -randkey hdfs/${name}@${krb_realm}
addprinc -randkey mapred/${name}@${krb_realm}
ktadd -k ${name}/hdfs.keytab -norandkey \
  hdfs/${name}@${krb_realm} host/${name}@${krb_realm}
ktadd -k ${name}/mapred.keytab -norandkey \
  mapred/${name}@${krb_realm} host/${name}@${krb_realm}
EOF

done
```

This script relies on a properly configured Kerberos KDC and assumes it is being run on the same machine as the KDC database. It also assumes *etc/krb5.conf* is correctly configured and that the current user, root, has privileges to write to the KDC database files. It's also important to use the -norandkey option to ktadd, otherwise each time you export the key, it changes, invalidating all previously created keytabs containing that key. Also tricky is that the -norandkey option to ktadd works only when using kad min.local (rather than kadmin). This is because kadmin.local never transports the key over the network since it works on the local KDC database. If you are not using MIT

Kerberos, consult your vendor's documentation to ensure keys are protected at all times.

You should now have a directory for each hostname, each of which contains two keytab files: one named *hdfs.keytab* and one named *mapred.keytab*. Each keytab contains its respective service principal (for example, hdfs/*hostname@realm*) and a copy of the host keytab. Next, using a secure copy utility like `scp` or `rsync` tunnelled over `ssh`, copy the keytabs to the proper machines and place them in the Hadoop configuration directory. The owner of the *hdfs.keytab* file must be the user the namenode, secondary namenode, and datanodes run as, whereas the *mapred.keytab* file must be owned by the user the jobtracker and tasktrackers run as. Keytab files must be protected at all times and as such, should have the permissions 0400 (owning user read only).

On Encryption Algorithms

Kerberos keys can be encrypted using various algorithms, some of which are stronger than others. These days, AES-128 or 256 is commonly used to encrypt keys. For Java to support AES-256, an additional JCE policy file must be installed on *all* machines in the cluster as well as any client machines that wish to connect to it. The so-called JCE Unlimited Strength Jurisdiction Policy Files enable additional algorithms to be used by the JVM. This is not included by default due to US export regulations and controls placed on certain encryption algorithms or strengths.

Some Linux distributions distribute MIT Kerberos with AES-256 as the preferred encryption algorithm for keys, which places a requirement on the JVM to support it. One option is to install the unlimited strength policy file, as previously described, or Kerberos can be instructed not to use AES-256. Obviously, the latter option is not appealing as it potentially opens the system to well-known (albeit difficult) attacks on weaker algorithms.

The Unlimited Strength Jurisdiction Policy Files may be downloaded from *http://www .oracle.com/technetwork/java/javase/downloads/jce-6-download-429243.html*.

With the keytabs distributed to the proper machines, the next step is to update the Hadoop configuration files to enable secure mode. First, Kerberos security is enabled in *core-site.xml*.

hadoop.security.authentication
> The `hadoop.security.authentication` parameter defines the authentication mechanism to use within Hadoop. By default, it is set to `simple`, which simply trusts the client is who they claim to be, whereas setting it to the string `kerberos` enables Kerberos support. In the future, other authentication schemes may be supported, but at the time of this writing, these are the only two valid options.
>
> Example value: `kerberos`

hadoop.security.authorization
> Enabling `hadoop.security.authorization` causes Hadoop to authorize the client when it makes remote procedure calls to a server. The access control lists that affect

these permissions are configured via the *hadoop-policy.xml* file and allow per-service level control. For instance, it is possible to permit only users placed in the `mapred-admin` Linux group to invoke APIs that are part of the administration service (the `security.admin.operations.protocol.acl` policy). When enabling security, this feature should be enabled as well and meaningful ACLs configured.

Example: true

Example 6-4 shows core-site.xml with the proper security properties set.

Example 6-4. Updating core-site.xml to enable Hadoop security

```
<?xml version="1.0"?>
<configuration>

  <!-- Add these properties to the existing core-site.xml configuration. -->

  <property>
    <name>hadoop.security.authentication</name>
    <value>kerberos</value>
  </property>

  <property>
    <name>hadoop.security.authorization</name>
    <value>true</value>
  </property>

</configuration>
```

Next, *hdfs-site.xml* must be configured so HDFS knows the principals to use and the location of the keytabs. Hadoop datanodes will also refuse to start in secure mode unless the data transceiver port is below 1024 (a privileged port) so that must also be changed.

dfs.block.access.token
:   Block access tokens are temporary keys that allow an HDFS block to be read, written, deleted, or a host of other internal actions, by an authenticated user. This mechanism allows Hadoop to ensure that only the intended users are able to access data in HDFS. While disabled (`false`) by default, this parameter should be enabled (set to `true`) in a secure deployment.

dfs.namenode.keytab.file
:   The `dfs.namenode.keytab.file` parameter specifies the location of the keytab that contains the Kerberos principal key for the namenode. This is the file uploaded to each host and by convention, is placed in the Hadoop configuration directory.

    Example: */etc/hadoop/conf/hdfs.keytab*

dfs.namenode.kerberos.principal
:   The Kerberos principal the namenode should use to authenticate. The key for this principal must exist in the keytab specified by `dfs.namenode.keytab.file`. The special token _HOST can be used for the instance portion of the principal, in which

case the fully qualified domain name will be interpolated. Note that the _HOST token cannot be used anywhere else in the principal.

Example: hdfs/_HOST@MYREALM.MYCOMPANY.COM

dfs.namenode.kerberos.https.principal
Similar to `dfs.namenode.kerberos.principal` (see previous entry), this parameter specifies the Kerberos principal that should be used by the embedded HTTPS server. The key for this principal must also be in the keytab specified by `dfs.name node.keytab.file`. Note that the local part of this principal *must* be host, as shown in the example.

Example: host/_HOST@MYREALM.MYCOMPANY.COM

dfs.https.address
The hostname or IP address on which the embedded HTTPS server should be bound. It is valid to specify the wild card IP 0.0.0.0 to indicate the HTTPS server should listen on all interfaces.

Example: 0.0.0.0

dfs.https.port
The port on which the embedded HTTPS server should listen for requests.

Example: 50470

dfs.datanode.keytab.file
Exactly the same as `dfs.namenode.keytab.file`, the `dfs.datanode.keytab.file` specifies the keytab file containing the principal keys used by the datanode process. This can, and usually is, the same file as `dfs.namenode.keytab.file`.

Example: */etc/hadoop/conf/hdfs.keytab*

dfs.datanode.kerberos.principal
The Kerberos principal the datanode should use to authenticate. The key for this principal must exist in the keytab specified by `dfs.datanode.keytab.file`. The special token _HOST can be used for the instance portion of the principal, in which case the fully qualified domain name will be interpolated. Note that the _HOST token cannot be used anywhere else in the principal. This is commonly the same principal as `dfs.namenode.kerberos.principal`.

Example: hdfs/_HOST@MYREALM.MYCOMPANY.COM

dfs.datanode.kerberos.https.principal
Similar to `dfs.datanode.kerberos.principal`, this parameter specifies the Kerberos principal that should be used by the embedded HTTPS server. The key for this principal must also be in the keytab specified by `dfs.datanode.keytab.file`.

Example: host/_HOST@MYREALM.MYCOMPANY.COM

dfs.datanode.address
The hostname or IP address and port, separated by a colon, on which the data transceiver RPC server should be bound. It is valid to specify the wild card IP 0.0.0.0

to indicate the server should listen on all interfaces. With security enabled, this port *must* be below 1024 or the datanode will not start.

Example: 0.0.0.0:1004

`dfs.datanode.http.address`

The hostname or IP address and port, separated by a colon, on which the embedded HTTP server should be bound. It is valid to specify the wild card IP 0.0.0.0 to indicate the HTTP server should listen on all interfaces.

Example: 0.0.0.0:1006

`dfs.datanode.data.dir.perm`

When security is enabled, Hadoop performs extra checks to ensure HDFS block data cannot be read by unauthorized users. One of these checks involves making sure the directories specified by `dfs.data.dir` are set to restrictive permissions. This prevents user code from simply opening and reading block data directly from the local disk rather than using the HDFS APIs, which require a valid Kerberos ticket and perform authorization checks on the file. If the permissions are incorrect, the datanode will change the permissions to the value specified by this parameter.

Local read short-circuiting

HDFS supports a feature called local read short-circuiting (as implemented by HDFS-2246 (*https://issues.apache.org/jira/browse/HDFS-2246*)) in which a client application running on the same machine as the datanode can completely bypass the datanode server and read block files directly from the local filesystem. This can dramatically increase the speed of read operations, but at the cost of opening access to the underlying block data of *all blocks* to the client. When this feature is enabled, clients must be running as the same user as the datanode *or* be in a group that has read access to block data. Both scenarios break some of the invariants assumed by the security model and can inadvertently expose data to malicious applications. Take great care when enabling this feature on a secure cluster or setting `dfs.datanode.data.dir.perm` to anything other than 0700.

Example: 0700

See Example 6-5 for a sample *hdfs-site.xml* file configured for security.

Example 6-5. Updating hdfs-site.xml to enable Hadoop security

```
<?xml version="1.0"?>
<configuration>

  <property>
    <name>dfs.block.access.token.enable</name>
    <value>true</value>
  </property>
```

```
<!-- NameNode security config -->

<property>
  <name>dfs.namenode.keytab.file</name>
  <value>hdfs.keytab</value>
</property>

<property>
  <name>dfs.namenode.kerberos.principal</name>
  <value>hdfs/_HOST@MYREALM.MYCOMPANY.COM</value>
</property>

<property>
  <name>dfs.namenode.kerberos.https.principal</name>
  <value>host/_HOST@MYREALM.MYCOMPANY.COM</value>
</property>

<!-- DataNode security config -->

<property>
  <name>dfs.datanode.keytab.file</name>
  <value>hdfs.keytab</value>
</property>

<property>
  <name>dfs.datanode.kerberos.principal</name>
  <value>hdfs/_HOST@MYREALM.MYCOMPANY.COM</value>
</property>

<property>
  <name>dfs.datanode.kerberos.https.principal</name>
  <value>host/_HOST@MYREALM.MYCOMPANY.COM</value>
</property>

</configuration>
```

Lastly, *mapred-site.xml* must be configured; in many ways, it has similar parameters to *hdfs-site.xml*.

mapreduce.jobtracker.kerberos.principal
> Just like `dfs.namenode.kerberos.principal`, this specifies the Kerberos principal the jobtracker uses during authentication. Again, the key for this principal must be in the keytab specified by `mapreduce.jobtracker.keytab.file`. The _HOST token may be used in the instance part of the principal, in which case, it will be interpolated with the fully qualified domain name of the machine on which the jobtracker is running.
>
> Example: mapred/_HOST@MYREALM.MYCOMPANY.COM

mapreduce.jobtracker.kerberos.https.principal
> This parameter is used to specify the Kerberos principal for the embedded HTTPS server, just as its HDFS siblings.
>
> Example: host/_HOST@MYREALM.MYCOMPANY.COM

`mapreduce.jobtracker.keytab.file`

> The keytab file containing the jobtracker principal key. See `dfs.namenode.ker`
> `beros.principal` on page 147 for more information.
>
> Example: */etc/hadoop/conf/mapred.keytab*

`mapreduce.tasktracker.kerberos.principal`

> The Kerberos principal used by the tasktracker. See `mapreduce.jobtracker.ker`
> `beros.principal` on page 150 for more information.
>
> Example: mapred/_HOST@MYREALM.MYCOMPANY.COM

`mapreduce.tasktracker.kerberos.https.principal`

> The Kerberos principal used by the embedded HTTPS server. See `mapreduce.job`
> `tracker.kerberos.https.principal` on page 150 for more information.
>
> Example: host/_HOST@MYREALM.MYCOMPANY.COM

`mapreduce.tasktracker.keytab.file`

> The keytab file containing the tasktracker principal key. See `mapreduce.job`
> `tracker.keytab.file` on page 151 for more information.
>
> Example: */etc/hadoop/conf/mapred.keytab*

`mapred.task.tracker.task-controller`

> As we've seen, the tasktracker has a few strategies for launching child task JVMs.
> In simple security mode, the tasks are launched as the same user as the tasktracker
> itself, while in secure mode, the setuid `task-controller` executable is used. The
> tasktracker uses a Java plug-in that controls which strategy is used, which is defined
> by this parameter. By default, `mapred.task.tracker.task-controller` specifies the
> class name `org.apache.hadoop.mapred.DefaultTaskController`, which simply exe-
> cutes the child task with the same permissions as the parent tasktracker. In the case
> of a secure cluster, this should instead be set to `org.apache.hadoop.mapred.Linux`
> `TaskController`, which is the implementation that knows about the setuid `task-`
> `controller` executable.
>
> Example: `org.apache.hadoop.mapred.LinuxTaskController`

`mapreduce.tasktracker.group`

> In secure mode, the setuid `task-controller`, after sanitizing its environment,
> changes its effective user id and group id to the user running the MapReduce job
> and a specified group, respectively. This parameter is what specifies the group that
> should be used when this occurs. It's important that the effective group be con-
> trolled so the user task has the proper permissions when it creates files (for example,
> in the Hadoop log directory). This value should always match the effective group
> of the tasktracker itself. If it doesn't, the `task-controller` will exit with a non-zero
> status. This isn't important with simple security mode because the `task-control`
> `ler` isn't used.
>
> Example: `mapred`

The task-controller's configuration is separate from the three primary XML files and is required for it to function properly. Located in the Hadoop configuration directory, *taskcontroller.cfg* is a plain text file that works very much like a Java property file: one key value pair per line, separated by an equals sign. Unlike a property file, however, whitespace is not permitted between the equals sign and its key or value. See Example 6-6 for a sample *taskcontroller.cfg*. The following parameters are supported.

mapred.local.dir *(required)*
    A comma separated list of directories used for temporary data during MapReduce jobs. This should be the same list as specified in mapred.local.dir in the *mapred-site.xml* file. See mapred.local.dir on page 121 for more information.

hadoop.log.dir *(required)*
    The directory in which log data should be written. This should be the same path as specified in HADOOP_LOG_DIR in the *hadoop-env.sh* file. See "Logging Configuration" on page 90 for more information.

mapred.tasktracker.group *(required)*
    The group that the tasktracker process runs as. In CDH, this is mapred and whatever user the administrator chooses in Apache Hadoop. This group should not contain any users other than the user the tasktracker runs as. If it does, those users will be able to impersonate any user with a user id greater than what is specified in min.user.id.

min.user.id *(required)*
    The minimum uid of the user to run a task as. If a user with uid below this value submits a MapReduce job, the task-controller will refuse to execute the tasks, exiting with a non-zero status code, which will cause all tasks to fail. The default value of this is 1000 in CDH while Apache Hadoop has no default.

> A number of Linux distributions, notably CentOS and RHEL, start the uid numbering of user accounts at 500. This means that the CDH default of 500 will cause all tasks to fail by default.

banned.users
    Specific users can be banned from executing tasks on the cluster. By default, CDH includes users mapred, hdfs, and bin in this list whereas Apache Hadoop leaves this empty. At a minimum, you should always include user hdfs. By doing so, you can avoid the potential attack vector where a task running as hdfs could read or modify HDFS blocks stored on the local disks, circumventing the permission checks performed by the namenode.

Example 6-6. Sample taskcontroller.cfg

```
mapred.local.dir=/data/1/hadoop/mapred/local,/data/2/hadoop/mapred/local
hadoop.log.dir=/var/log/hadoop
mapreduce.tasktracker.group=mapred
```

```
banned.users=mapred,hdfs,bin
min.user.id=1000
```

Finally, after distributing the changed configuration files to all hosts in the cluster, you are now ready to restart all daemons and begin testing. It is strongly recommended that you start with the namenode and a single datanode first to make sure everything is in working order. Watch the log files for errors, especially those related to authentication and resolve any issues you find. Given the complexity of setting up security, it is common to miss a step the first time and have a little debugging to do. Take it slow, one daemon at a time, and for production clusters, *always* have a rollback plan.

Authorization

So far, we've discussed only how clients identify themselves and how Hadoop authenticates them. Once a client is authenticated, though, that client is still subject to authorization when it attempts to perform an action. The actions that can be performed vary from service to service. An action in the context of HDFS, for example, may be reading a file, creating a directory, or renaming a filesystem object. MapReduce actions, on the other hand, could be submitting or killing a job. Evaluating whether or not a user is permitted to perform a specific action is the process of *authorization*.

HDFS

Every filesystem operation in HDFS is subject to authorization. In an effort to exploit existing knowledge, HDFS uses the same authorization model as most POSIX filesystems. Each filesystem object (such as a file or directory) has three classes of user: an owner, a group, and "other," which indicates anyone who isn't in one of the two previous classes. The available permissions that can be granted to each of the three classes on an object are *read*, *write*, and *execute*, just as with Linux or other Unix-like systems. For example, it is possible to grant the owner of a file both read and write privileges. These permissions are represented by a single octal (base-8) integer that is calculated by summing permission values (see Table 6-3).

Table 6-3. HDFS permission values

Permission	Value
Read	4
Write	2
Execute	1

Using our previous example, to indicate the file owner has both read and write privileges, we would sum the read permission value of 4 and the write permission value of 2, giving us 6, which represents the combination of the two privileges. This representation is always unambiguous. That is, it is impossible for two combinations to yield the same sum. The special value of 0 (zero) means that a user has no permissions. Noteworthy, it is not meaningful (nor is it illegal) for a file to be executable in HDFS, although directories use the execute permission to indicate that a user may access its contents (if they know the name of the contained file or directory already) and metadata information (then read permission is also required to retrieve the children's names).

To represent the three classes of user—owner, group, and other—we use three integers, one for each class, in that order. For instance, a file that allows the owner to read and write, the group to read, and other users to read, would have the permissions 644; the 6 indicates read and write for the owner (4 + 2), whereas the subsequent fields are both 4, indicating only the read permission is available. To indicate the owner of a directory has read, write, and execute permissions, but no one else has access, the permissions 700 would be used.

In addition to the above permissions, three other special permissions exist: setuid, setgid, and sticky mode (or "the sticky bit"). The setuid permission in Linux changes the process effective user id to that of the file owner when the file is executed. Since files in HDFS cannot be executed, granting this means nothing. The setgid permission, when set on a directory in Linux, forces the group of all immediate child files and directories to that of the parent directory. However, this is the default behavior in HDFS, so there's no need to explicitly set the setgid permission on a directory. Like setuid, there is no meaning to setting setgid on a file in HDFS because files cannot be executed. The final permission is called the sticky bit and when set on a directory, means that only the owner of a file in that directory may delete or rename the file, even if another user has access to do so (as granted by the write permission on the directory itself). The exception to this rule is that the HDFS super user and owner of the directory always have the ability to perform these actions. This is exactly the behavior one desires for temporary directories where all users need to be able to write data, but only the owner of that data should be able to remove or change it. These permissions are granted by using an optional fourth octal number placed to the *left* of the standard set of three. Just like the read, write, and execute permissions, setuid, setgid, and sticky bit each have a designed value that may be summed to grant multiple permissions. (See Table 6-4.)

Table 6-4. The setuid, setgid, and sticky bit permissions

Permission	Value
Setuid	4
Setgid	2
Sticky bit	1

A value of 0 (zero) removes these permissions, if they are set. Example 6-7 shows typical HDFS interaction with Kerberos authentication and permissions set.

Example 6-7. Using the sticky bit permission in HDFS

```
# Authenticate as user esammer
[esammer@hadoop01 ~]$ kinit esammer
Password for esammer@PE.HADOOP.CLOUDERA.COM:
# Create a directory called test
[esammer@hadoop01 ~]$ hadoop fs -mkdir /user/esammer/test
# Change the permissions to enable sticky bit and set:
# owner: read, write, execute
# group: read, write, execute
# other: read, write, execute
[esammer@hadoop01 ~]$ hadoop fs -chmod 1777 /user/esammer/test
# Create an empty file as esammer
[esammer@hadoop01 ~]$ hadoop fs -touch /user/esammer/test/foo
# Authenticate as user esammer2
[esammer@hadoop01 ~]$ kinit esammer2
Password for esammer2@PE.HADOOP.CLOUDERA.COM:
# Attempt to remove the file foo.
esammer@hadoop01 ~]$ hadoop fs -rmr /user/esammer/test/foo
rmr: org.apache.hadoop.security.AccessControlException: Permission denied by sticky ↵
  bit setting: user=esammer2, inode="/user/esammer/test/foo":esammer:hadoop:-rw-r--r--
# Oops. The sticky bit stopped us from removing the file. Let's create a file of
# our own called bar.
[esammer@hadoop01 ~]$ hadoop fs -touchz /user/esammer/test/bar
# Switch back to user esammer.
[esammer@hadoop01 ~]$ kinit esammer
Password for esammer@PE.HADOOP.CLOUDERA.COM:
# We can see both files...
[esammer@hadoop01 ~]$ hadoop fs -ls /user/esammer/test/
Found 2 items
-rw-r--r--   3 esammer2 hadoop          0 2012-04-25 13:53 /user/esammer/test/bar
-rw-r--r--   3 esammer  hadoop          0 2012-04-25 13:52 /user/esammer/test/foo
# But because user esammer owns the directory, we can delete esammer2's file!
[esammer@hadoop01 ~]$ hadoop fs -rmr /user/esammer/test/bar
Deleted hdfs://hadoop01.cloudera.com/user/esammer/test/bar
```

MapReduce

Hadoop MapReduce, like HDFS, has a few different classes of users (four, to be exact).

Cluster owner

The cluster owner is the OS user that started the cluster. In other words, this is the user the jobtracker daemon is running as. This is normally user hadoop for Apache Hadoop and mapred for CDH. Like the HDFS super user, the MapReduce cluster owner is granted all permissions implicitly and should be used rarely, if ever, by administrators.

Cluster administrator

One or more users may be specified as cluster administrators. These users have all of the same powers as the cluster owner, but do not need to be able to authenticate as the Linux user that started the cluster. Granting users this power allows them to perform administrative operations while still retaining the ability to audit their actions individually, rather than having them use a shared account. Use of a shared account is also discouraged as it creates the need to share authentication credentials.

Queue administrator

When a job is submitted to the jobtracker, the user specifies a *queue*. The queue has an access control list (ACL) associated with it that defines which users and groups may submit jobs, but also which users may administer the queue. Administrative actions may be changing the priority of a job, killing tasks, or even killing entire jobs.

Job owner

Finally, the job owner is the user who submitted a job. A job owner always has the ability to perform administrative actions on their own jobs.

Defining the cluster owner is a side effect of simply starting the jobtracker so there's no explicit configuration of this user, per se. Cluster and queue administrators, on the other hand, are defined by the *mapred-site.xml* and *mapred-queue-acls.xml* files, respectively. Since these files define access control, it's important to make sure the files and their parent directory are writable only by the cluster owner or root. If users will be submitting jobs on the same machine as the jobtracker, the files and their parent directory must be world readable to allow users to submit jobs because they contain information used by the client as well as the server.

An access control list in Hadoop is a space-separated pair of comma-separated lists. The first list is the users that allowed to perform a given action; the second is the list of groups that are allowed to perform an action. It is possible for either or both of the lists to be empty, in which case, no users or groups may perform an action. If the ACL is simply an asterisk, everyone is allowed to perform an action. The table in Example 6-8 shows a few examples of setting access control lists for services.

Example 6-8. Sample Hadoop access control lists and their meanings

ACL	Description
"*"	Everyone is permitted.
" " (a single space)	No one is permitted.
"user1,user2 group1,group2,group3"	Users 1 and 2, and groups 1, 2, and 3 are permitted.
"user1 " (a user followed by a single space)	User 1 is permitted, but no groups.
" group1" (a single space followed by a group)	Group 1 is permitted, but no users.

> The quotes are not part of the ACL and should not be typed. They are shown here to highlight the space character.

By default, Hadoop MapReduce is wide open; any user may submit a job to any queue, and all users may perform administrative actions. For single-purpose clusters in a trusted environment, this is fine, but for multitenant clusters, this doesn't work. There are a number of parameters and extra files that need to be configured to define and enable queue ACLs. The first step is to modify *mapred-site.xml* to enable ACLs, define cluster administrators, and specify the queues that should exist.

`mapred.acls.enabled`

> Access control lists must be globally enabled prior to use. Hadoop does not enforce ACLs, even if they're defined, if this parameter is not set to true.
>
> Example: true. Default: false

`mapred.cluster.administrators`

> An ACL that defines users and groups that are cluster administrators.
>
> Example: "esammer mradmins,ops" (without quotes). Default: undefined.

`mapred.queue.names`

> Before attaching ACLs to queues, all queues must be predefined. This is done by simply providing a comma-separated list of queue names to the `mapred.queue.names` parameter. There should be no spaces between names. Some scheduler plug-ins—notably the FIFO scheduler, which is the default—do not support multiple queues. Both the capacity scheduler and fair scheduler plug-ins support multiple queues.
>
> Example: research,production-etl,adhoc. Default: default.

 While the *mapred-queue-acls.xml* file is reloaded dynamically, changes to *mapred-site.xml* require daemons be restarted before changes take effect.

The next step is to define ACLs for the queues named in `mapred.queue.names`. This must be done in the *mapred-queue-acls.xml* file, also located in the Hadoop configuration directory. Like the primary three configuration files, *mapred-queue-acls.xml* follows the same format; an XML file with a top level configuration element, which contains zero or more property elements, each of which is a name value pair. Each MapReduce queue is configured with an ACL, as described above, in a separate configuration property where the name of the property is `mapred.queue.`*`queue-name.privilege`* and the value is the ACL. The *queue-name* should be one of the queue names from the `mapred.queue.names` property, and *privilege* is one of the available queue privileges (see Table 6-5).

Table 6-5. MapReduce queue privileges

Privilege	Description
acl-submit-job	An ACL that controls who may submit MapReduce jobs to a queue.
acl-administer-jobs	An ACL that controls who may perform administrative actions on jobs in a queue.

If, for example, you want to create a production-etl queue and grant user jane and anyone in the prod group access to submit jobs to it, production-etl must be listed in mapred.queue.names in *mapred-site.xml*, and mapred.queue.production-etl.acl-submit-job should be set to "jane prod" (without quotes) in *mapred-queue-acls.xml*, as in Example 6-9.

Example 6-9. Sample mapred-queue-acls.xml file

```
<?xml version="1.0"?>
<configuration>

  <!--
    Allow user jane and group prod to submit jobs to the
    production-etl queue.
  -->

  <property>
    <name>mapred.queue.production-etl.acl-submit-job</name>
    <value>jane prod</value>
  </property>

  <!--
    Allow no users, and groups prod and hadoop-admins, to
    administer jobs in the production-etl queue. Note the
    space after the opening value element. This means the
    user list is empty.

    The cluster owner, cluster admins, and job owner can
    always administer their jobs.
  -->

  <property>
    <name>mapred.queue.production-etl.acl-administer-jobs</name>
    <value> prod,hadoop-admins</value>
  </property>

  <!-- Many queues may be defined... -->

</configuration>
```

The queues described thus far are independent of the capacity and fair scheduler plug-ins, although they are related. None of the three scheduler plug-ins (including the default FIFO scheduler) provide access control over which jobs are submitted to which queues. If you need this kind of functionality, the expectation is that the queue names, as defined by `mapred.queue.names`, will match the queues configured in the scheduler plug-in. This allows job submission and queue ACLs to be implemented generically, while the order and machines on which tasks are executed is controlled by the plug-in. In Chapter 7, we'll cover how each of the schedulers may be configured to suit different environments and use cases.

Other Tools and Systems

Many of the projects commonly used with Hadoop (the so-called ecosystem projects) rely simply on the HDFS and MapReduce access controls. This makes a lot of sense because some of these tools are just clients of the two Hadoop services. Pig, for instance, is a good example of this. A user writes a Pig script, which is interpreted on the client machine, logical and physical execution plans are created, and a series of MapReduce jobs are submitted to the cluster. The data accessed by the job is commonly a directory of files in HDFS and is therefore subject to the filesystem permissions of the user who submitted the job. In other words, there's nothing else to which access must be controlled.

But that, of course, is not always the case. Other ecosystem projects do have additional information or higher level constructs that must be secured in multiuser environments. Hive is a good example of this. While also a client-side application, Hive stores additional metadata about the data in HDFS and presents a relational database style abstraction[3] to the end user. This presents an interesting case where, even if we were to restrict a user from accessing the data contained in HDFS, they would still be able to see the metadata—the table names, field names and types, and so forth—managed by Hive. In multitenant environments, this may not be acceptable. Disclosing information about users' datasets to one another may be sufficient to reveal what they are doing or how. Because of this risk, each of the ecosystem projects, including Hive, are responsible for protecting any metadata they maintain.

Each ecosystem project has different controls for protecting metadata and must be configured independently. It isn't feasible to cover all of the nuances of each of these projects in detail here. This is meant to provide references for further reading.

Apache Hive

Because HiveQL bakes down into MapReduce jobs, operations are subject to all of the access controls of MapReduce queue ACLs and HDFS file permissions. Additionally, Hive provides RDBMS style users, groups, and roles, as well as GRANT statements to control access to its so-called database objects. This enables finegrained access control

---

3. This does not mean Hive makes Hadoop a relational database. Instead, it presents a familiar SQL-like interface to users to query data, but its execution engine is still MapReduce and subject to all the inherent functional and performance characteristics therein.

to higher order constructs like tables, columns, or even views. Of course, this is enforced only at the time the HiveQL query is written and submitted; the files in HDFS have no knowledge of this metadata and as a result, it can't be enforced further down the stack. Remember that for MapReduce jobs to work, the user submitting the job must be able to access the files in HDFS. This creates an interesting problem where a user may not have permission to view the data in a column of a table from Hive's perspective, but the user must have access to the complete files in HDFS, thereby allowing them to circumvent the object-level policy. We'll see possible solutions to this problem in "Tying It Together" on page 164.

For more information about configuring Hive object level access control, see *http:// cwiki.apache.org/confluence/display/Hive/LanguageManual+Authorization*.

Apache HBase

HBase is a distributed, column-oriented, low latency system for storing enormous tables, both in terms of rows and columns. Already a huge topic, HBase, as of version 0.92.x (also included in CDH4), has support for performing access control checks on each operation issued to a table. These operations include get (reading a record), put (storing a record), scan (reading a range of records), and delete, as well as the administrative or data definition operations like creating tables. HBase security is implemented as a coprocessor—a plug-in that, in many ways, works like a database trigger, firing authorization checking code before each operation is performed.

Users and groups may be granted permission to perform any combination of the above operations at the table, column family, or column qualifier granularity. In other words, it is possible to restrict access to tables, groups of columns, or individual columns within a group.

For more information about configuring HBase security, see *http://hbase.apache.org/ book/security.html* or *https://ccp.cloudera.com/display/CDH4DOC/HBase+Security +Configuration* for CDH users.

Apache Oozie

Oozie is a workflow system specifically built to work with Hadoop and MapReduce. Users (usually developers) write workflows in an XML language that define one or more MapReduce jobs, their interdependencies, and what to do in the case of failures. These workflows are uploaded to the Oozie server where they are scheduled to run or executed immediately. When Oozie executes a MapReduce job as part of a workflow, it is run by the Oozie server, which keeps track of job-level failures and status.

In a secure environment, the Oozie server must authenticate via Kerberos to submit MapReduce jobs to the cluster. It's important, however, that these jobs execute as the user that created the workflow and not as the user running the Oozie server. In order to launch MapReduce jobs with the proper identity, each workflow defines the user and group with which the jobs should run. Additionally, in a secure environment, the value of the specified user and group are checked against the identity of the authenticated user submitting the workflow. In other words, if I—authenticated as user esammer—attempt to submit a workflow to Oozie that specifies user janedoe, Oozie will refuse to accept the workflow.

Oozie has a very simple security model based on the notion of users and groups. All users can see all workflows, but only modify those owned by themselves or a group to which they belong. Any number of users may be designated as administrators who, additionally, may modify any workflows, and perform administrative functions. With its security features disabled, all users are effectively administrators in Oozie.

For more information about how Oozie security, see *http://incubator.apache.org/oozie/docs/3.1.3/docs/AG_Install.html* or for CDH, *https://ccp.cloudera.com/display/CDH4DOC/Oozie+Security+Configuration*.

Hue

Hue is a web-based application that provides an end user–facing application that can be used to interact with a Hadoop cluster. Out of the box, Hue comes with a job browser, job designer, filesystem browser, and Beeswax, a Hive user interface from which users can execute HiveQL queries. Like most web applications, Hue provides username and password authentication, and (Hue) application level access control lists. Users are assigned to groups and groups are given permission to launch specific Hue applications. Additionally, users may be marked as super users, in which case they may launch all applications as well as administer users and privileges. As of version 2.x (included with CDH4), Hue supports synchronization with LDAP services (Open-LDAP and Active Directory, specifically) for both users and groups.

For more information about Hue configuration, see *https://ccp.cloudera.com/display/CDH4DOC/Hue+Security+Configuration*.

Apache Sqoop

Sqoop is a tool that facilitates bidirectional exchange of data between HDFS and relational databases. With Sqoop, it's possible to import the contents of a table, the result of a SQL query, or even an entire database, to files in HDFS so they may be used in MapReduce jobs. The inverse operation of exporting data residing in HDFS to tables in an RDBMS is also fully supported for files with a known schema. Sqoop does this by running a MapReduce job with a controlled number map tasks, each making a number of parallel connections to a database and performing parallel SELECT or INSERT/UPDATE statements (for import to Hadoop and export from Hadoop, respectively). One of Sqoop's more interesting features is its ability to accept vendor specific plug-ins for high performance import and export. These plug-ins take advantage of native features of the RDBMS for faster operations and drop in with no coding required by the Sqoop user. At this time, high performance plug-ins are available for MySQL, PostgreSQL, Oracle, Teradata, Netezza, Vertica, and SQL Server.

Since Sqoop jobs run as MapReduce jobs, they can be controlled in all the same ways as any other MapReduce job. This includes managing HDFS permissions on files and directories to control access to data. The database credentials must be supplied with each invocation of the `sqoop` command-line tool.

Frequently, users want to perform incremental imports or exports of data. Sqoop supports a number of strategies for determining which rows have changed since the last run, but all of them require maintaining some kind of state between runs. Users may decide to manually preserve this information somewhere, but for recurring jobs in production, this usually isn't realistic. Another option is to use Sqoop's saved job feature, which stores both connection credentials and incremental state information in a directory on the local filesystem of the client machine in what is called the *metastore*. Administrators and users can then execute Sqoop jobs by their saved job name rather than requiring all the command-line options upon each invocation. If saved jobs are used, the metastore directory must be protected using standard filesystem permissions as you would with other sensitive files on the system, especially if you decide to allow Sqoop to also store database passwords.

To learn more about Sqoop, saved jobs, and managing Sqoop's metastore, see the full documentation at *http://sqoop.apache.org/docs/1.4.1-incubating/index.html* or *http:// archive.cloudera.com/cdh/3/sqoop/SqoopUserGuide.html* for CDH users.

 The Sqoop community is currently working on a proposal for Sqoop 2, which maintains the functionality of Sqoop, but realizes it as a persistent service rather than a command-line tool. For more information on Sqoop 2, be sure to check out *https://cwiki.apache.org/confluence/dis play/SQOOP/Sqoop+2*.

Apache Flume

Apache Flume is a distributed, fault tolerant, scale out streaming data collection system commonly used for collecting log events. Unlike many of the other Hadoop ecosystem projects, Apache Flume does not strictly require Hadoop, although it complements HDFS very well. Flume uses the abstraction of sources, channels, and sinks to wire together data flows that transport data from one end point to another. Some of the more common sources are an Avro RPC source to which applications can speak directly, syslog, a raw netcat-style source, and a source that executes a command and reads from its standard output. Sources put data into channels that act as queues that support different strategies that effect durability. Sinks take events from channels and depending on the implementation, store them in HDFS, forward them to another Flume agent over the network, and insert them into HBase or any other data store. It is also simple to implement custom sources, channels, sinks, and other components within Flume for special use cases.

Flume's role in the ecosystem is one of data ingestion and for most users, this means writing to HDFS or HBase. Since data is written to these kinds of systems, it's important that administrators be able to control the permissions on the resultant files. The proper way of dictating the permissions with which data is written is controlled by the configured sink and will vary from implementation to implementation. The HDFS sink, for example, uses the Hadoop library and just as any other HDFS client, takes on the identity of the effective user ID of the process. Flume's HDFS sink also fully supports Kerberos authentication using a keytab, in which case, the principal becomes the owner of files in HDFS.

Flume supports a wide array of data ingest configuration options. For more information, see *http://flume.apache.org/FlumeUserGuide.html* or *http://archive.cloudera.com/cdh4/cdh/4/flume-ng/FlumeUserGuide.html* for CDH users.

Apache ZooKeeper

Like Flume, Apache ZooKeeper doesn't have a direct dependency on Hadoop, but a number of ecosystem projects do make use of it. ZooKeeper is a quorum-based, highly available, distributed coordination service used to build centralized configuration storage, naming, synchronization, leader election, and group membership services. Those building specialized distributed systems may find ZooKeeper appealing, but for many, it is seen as infrastructure for HBase and some features of HDFS.

ZooKeeper organizes data into ZNodes. Like files in a traditional filesystem, ZNodes can store arbitrary bytes, have access control lists associated with them, and can be organized hierarchically. In ZooKeeper, there is no distinction between a "file" and a "directory" ZNode; a single ZNode may have data (like a file) but also have child ZNodes (like a directory). Since ZNodes are very commonly used to store internal state of other applications and critical coordination information, they can be protected by ACLs, as mentioned earlier. In keeping with the filesystem metaphor, ZooKeeper offers a shell where administrators can execute commands to perform the equivalent of the chmod and chown commands.

For more information about ZooKeeper, see *http://zookeeper.apache.org/doc/r3.4.3/* or *http://archive.cloudera.com/cdh4/cdh/4/zookeeper/* for CDH users.

Apache Pig, Cascading, and Crunch

Many of the Hadoop ecosystem projects are client side tools or languages that bake down to MapReduce jobs. This class of projects, of which Pig, Cascading, and Crunch are all members, run entirely on a client machine and maintain no external metadata. These projects can be seen as a facade for Hadoop MapReduce, simplifying the programming model and providing a higher level language in which to perform operations. Each with a slightly different way of interpreting the problem of making MapReduce accessible, they are fundamentally similar in their implementation. For Hadoop administrators, these projects are trivial to support as they provide no additional operational overhead beyond MapReduce, and by extension, no additional security constructs.

Tying It Together

With an ever-growing ecosystem of projects forming around Hadoop, each with its own requirements, it's hard to understand how these pieces come together to form a single data processing platform. Beyond simply making these tools function, administrators are responsible for ensuring a singular identification, authentication, and authorization scheme is applied consistently and in accordance with data handling policies. This is a significant challenge, to use a well-worn, albeit applicable, cliche. However, there are a few things one can do to reduce the pain of building a secure, shared Hadoop platform.

To secure or not to secure
> Do your homework and make an informed decision about whether or not you need Hadoop security. It is not as simple as setting `hadoop.security.authentication` to `kerberos` and getting on with life. The repercussions of Kerberizing a cluster are significant in that every client of the cluster must be able to properly handle authentication. It's easy to say and difficult to make a reality. Can you trust clients to identify themselves truthfully? If not, you have your work cut out for you. Create a map of all access points to the cluster, understand which must support multiple users through a single process, and create a strategy to handle authentication. There's no universal answer, although there are some established patterns you can use.

All users and groups on all nodes
> Enabling secure mode means that every (OS) user that submits a MapReduce job must have an account on every machine in the cluster. The account may be locked so that it isn't possible to log in to the machine, but the account must exist and have a valid shell. One way to do this is by brute force; maintain user accounts by hand on each machine. This simply doesn't scale and will cause trouble for you down the road. Instead, use a configuration management system like Puppet or Chef, use LDAP for centralized account management, or use a commercial tool to maintain accounts. You can also save yourself some heartache by ensuring users have the same UIDs on all machines as well.

Run a local Kerberos KDC
> Set up a local installation of MIT Kerberos and configure the Hadoop cluster as its own realm. Configure each machine in the cluster to use the realm you've chosen as its default realm (this will save you endless pain later as it obviates the need to configure principal rewrite rules). If you have a global identity management system like Active Directory, configure a one way cross realm trust from the local KDC to the global system so users can successfully authenticate. While this seems odd at first, Hadoop has proven its ability to perform a distributed denial of service attack

on corporate identity infrastructure simply by running a MapReduce job. Remember that every RPC requires communication with the KDC in secure mode and with a large enough cluster, with many tasks it's possible to create a noticeable impact on shared infrastructure (one such incident rendered users incapable of authenticating for email for a short time during an unusual spike in Hadoop activity).

Establish an HDFS hierarchy that reflects access

Remember that the HDFS directory structure, like any other shared filesystem, is not just an organization construct, but the way you enforce access to data. Think about applications and access, and design accordingly. Like a relational database schema, the filesystem directory structure can be difficult to change for production systems. This is an area where administrators and developers must work in tandem.

Use gateway services to federate access

In scenarios where finegrained access control is required, it is useful to create gateway services. A *gateway* (or sometimes, *proxy*) service is a daemon that receives a (usually higher level) request and performs an action on behalf of a user when allowing the user to directly perform the action wouldn't provide enough control.

A gateway, for instance, can be used to simulate column level access to files. Because all columns are stored in a single file, and the file is the level granularity with which access control can be controlled, it is necessary to intercept operations, apply the necessary checks, execute a modified version of the user's request, and place the result in a location they can access. It's imperative that the user not be given direct access to the source file, as this would allow access control to be circumvented. If, for instance, the preferred method of access was Hive, the gateway service could take a Hive query, rewrite it, and submit it to Hive proper as a privileged user, on their behalf.[4] In many ways, this is the same idea as the sudo command, which is familiar to many administrators. This does require custom development and application specific knowledge, so it's hard to make a recommendation that's generally applicable, but the technique is what is important.

---

4. Some may note that Hive has basic constructs for controlling table level access as well as creating views, so it should be possible to create a view that doesn't select the restricted column and give access to that instead. The problem with this is that since the user's MapReduce job generated by Hive runs as them, they still must have access to the underlying file, which means if they were to go to the command line, they could simply read the original file, circumventing the higher level controls.

## CHAPTER 7

Resource Management

What Is Resource Management?

In a perfect world, multiple groups of users, each with jobs with different service level agreements (SLAs), would be able to coexist on a shared system, blissfully unaware of one another. Disk space and IO, memory, CPU time, and network bandwidth would be limitless, and MapReduce jobs would run unimpeded by the mundane details of competing disk access patterns, activity oscillation throughout the work day, and poorly implemented algorithms that spew data to disk faster than your average administrator can rap a developer across the knuckles. We don't live in that world and the infinite elastic utopia where the locality of terabytes (or more) of data is meaningless is not yet upon us. The question then, is how do we create an environment where competing interests can coexist peacefully, all the while ensuring the right jobs receive the right resources at the right time?

Resource management is about controlling how much of a finite resource should be allocated to a given user, group, or job. The resources—generally bisected into the categories of storage and compute—should be appropriately distributed across whatever designations make sense within the larger organization. This can mean allocation by the person for whom the work is performed, although more commonly, it is by line of business, where each group has jobs of varying criticality. Resource allocation is related to authentication in that we must know who someone is before we know how much of something to allocate to them. Without authentication and authorization, a malicious user could take more than they should have by posing as someone else. Proper management of resources is one component of planning for, and building, a multitenant environment.

In the context of Hadoop, the resources we are primarily concerned with are disk space consumption and number of files in HDFS, and map and reduce slot usage, in the case of MapReduce.

HDFS Quotas

HDFS, like many filesystems, supports the notion of quotas on disk space consumption. Administrators can specify a limit on the physical size (that is, the size *after* replication) a file[1] or directory in HDFS may be. This means that the organization of the directory tree affects how quotas may be enforced on users of the system. For instance, a common directory structure for a shared systems would include shared data sets produced by ETL processes, business unit specific derived data sets, and private user directories for temporary output and ad-hoc analysis, as in Example 7-1.

Example 7-1. Sample directory structure with space quotas

```
/
   data/                    # shared data sets, machine generated, no quotas
     user-activity/
     syslog/
     purchases/
   groups/                  # a directory per group / biz unit
     research/              # 20TB quota
     fraud-analysis/        # 100TB quota
     ops/                   # no quota
   users/                   # 50TB quota for all users
     esammer/               # 1TB quota per user...
     janedoe/
     joesmith/
```

Setting a space quota on a directory, shown in Example 7-2, is done by using the hadoop dfsadmin -setSpaceQuota *size path* command, where *size* is the permitted quota size (in bytes) and *path* is the directory to which the quota should be applied.

Example 7-2. Set a 10GB quota on the path /user/esammer

```
[esammer@hadoop01 ~]$ hadoop dfsadmin -setSpaceQuota 10737418240 /user/esammer
```

To view the quotas for a file or directory, use the hadoop fs -count -q *path* command as in Example 7-3.

Example 7-3. Viewing the quota on the path /user/esammer

```
[esammer@hadoop01 ~]$ hadoop fs -count -q /user/esammer
none inf 10737418240 -12702365277055 3999 9969 7902694269476 ↵
  hdfs://hadoop01.sf.cloudera.com/user/esammer
```

Example 7-3 requires some explanation; at the time of this writing, the command doesn't print the column headers. Column one is the file count quota and two is the file count remaining column. In this example, there is no file count quota set and so an infinite number of files may still be created. The third and fourth columns are the space

---

1. Due to the immutability of files in HDFS, it's uncommon to place a quota on them. Instead, quotas are normally placed on directories.

quota and remaining space in bytes. Here, the space quota is 10737418240 (10GB) and -12702365277055 bytes are remaining, meaning this directory has exceeded its quota by more than 11TB (which is only possible because the quota was applied after the data was already written). Any attempt to put new files into this directory are denied and an error message is returned. The remaining fields are the total file count, directory count, total content size (in bytes), and path, respectively.

You may notice that the math above doesn't necessarily add up. How can a quota of 10GB minus a content size of 7TB (shown as 7902694269476 bytes in Example 7-3) produce a quota overage of 11TB? This is because the HDFS quota is applied to the physical (post-replication) size rather than the logical (pre-replication) size. Confusion stems from the fact that the `hadoop fs -count -q` command output does not display the post-replication size of the content. It's also not always possible to simply multiply the content size by the replication factor to get the post-replication size on disk as files within the directory may not have the same replication factor. Should a user violate a quota, he will receive an error message like that in Example 7-4.

Example 7-4. Attempting to put a file in a directory over its space quota

```
[esammer@hadoop01 ~]$ hadoop fs -put /etc/passwd /user/esammer/
put: org.apache.hadoop.hdfs.protocol.DSQuotaExceededException: The DiskSpace ↵
  quota of /user/esammer is exceeded: quota=10737418240 diskspace consumed=11840.0g
```

A final source of pain with HDFS quotas has to do with how quota accounting is performed. Because HDFS is a distributed filesystem and many clients can be writing data to a directory at once, it would be difficult to evaluate each byte written against the remaining quota. Instead, HDFS assumes a worst-case scenario—that an entire block will be filled when it's allocated—which can create unintuitive error messages (see Example 7-5) about quota violations. As an example, consider an empty directory with a quota of 1MB. Writing a 4KB file to this directory with a block size of 128MB (which will only occupy 12KB after replication, assuming a replication factor of 3) will actually cause a quota violation! This is because the accounting system sees this write as potentially taking 384MB (3 × the 128MB block size) and refuses the write. As a result, it really only makes sense to specify quotas in multiples of the block size.

Example 7-5. Quota space accounting can be unintuitive

```
# Starting with an empty directory and a 1MB quota
[esammer@hadoop01 ~]$ hadoop fs -count -q /user/esammer/quota-test
none inf 1048576 1048576 1 0 0 hdfs://hadoop01.sf.cloudera.com/user/esammer/quota-test
# Attempt to put a 4KB file (replication 3, 128MB block size)
esammer@hadoop01 ~]$ du /etc/passwd
4       /etc/passwd
# An exception is thrown telling us the disk space consumed is 384MB
# even though we know it will only occupy 12KB!
[esammer@hadoop01 ~]$ hadoop fs -put /etc/passwd /user/esammer/quota-test/
12/06/09 16:23:08 WARN hdfs.DFSClient: DataStreamer Exception: org.apache.hadoop
  .hdfs.protocol.DSQuotaExceededException: org.apache.hadoop.hdfs
```

```
.protocol.DSQuotaExceededException: The DiskSpace quota of /user/esammer/quota-test
is exceeded: quota=1048576 diskspace consumed=384.0m
```

Removing the quota from a directory is done using the `hadoop dfsadmin -clrSpaceQuota` *path* command.

Finally, HDFS supports quotas on the number of files that may be created within a directory. This has more to do with the architecture of the namenode, notably its requirement to fit all filesystem metadata in memory. Using file count quotas, it's possible to prevent users or processes from monopolizing the namenode resources and potentially causing a service interruption. The commands to set and clear file count quotas are similar to space quotas: `hadoop dfsadmin -setQuota number` *path* and `hadoop dfsad min -clrQuota` *path*, respectively. As we've already seen, the `hadoop fs -count -q` *path* displays both count and space quotas.

MapReduce Schedulers

Cluster compute capacity—the aggregate of worker node CPU, memory, network bandwidth, and disk IO—is a finite resource. Today, Hadoop represents these resources primarily in the form of map and reduce task slots (though that is changing; see "The Future" on page 193 for more information), as defined by administrators, as we saw in `mapred.tasktracker.map.tasks.maximum` and `mapred.task tracker.reduce.tasks.maximum` on page 123. Task slots (or just *slots*) are a proxy for system resources. In other words, an administrator configures the number of slots on a given machine based on some predetermined notion of what actual resources map and reduce tasks will need. This is often difficult because jobs may have varied resource consumption profiles, or where Hadoop is a new platform within an organization, the profile of jobs may be entirely unknown.

Slots are shared across jobs that are executing concurrently just as the Linux kernel shares resources between running processes. In Hadoop MapReduce, the scheduler—a plug-in within the jobtracker—is the component that is responsible for assigning tasks to open slots on tasktrackers. This ends up being a non-trivial problem. Accidentally scheduling CPU, memory, or disk IO intensive tasks on the same host can cause contention. Additionally, map tasks have a locality preference (they want to be on one of the machines that has a replica of the data they are to process) that the scheduler must take into account. Tasks also may belong to jobs submitted from different users, some of which have service level agreements that must be met, whereas others simply want a fair allocation of resources so they aren't deferred indefinitely.

An easier way to understand the problem is by looking at an existing system such as a relational database. Consider two users, each of whom submits a SQL query at roughly the same time. What do we expect? Most would assume that both queries execute and make progress concurrently. In fact, users are commonly unaware of one another until such a time that there is contention for database resources. Now, consider that one of these users is, in fact, a billing system processing a batch of transactions while the other is a curious analyst confirming that 18 to 25 year olds account for most mobile phone purchases in the last 30 days. The "right" decision is probably to prioritize the billing system operation over the analyst query, but what if the analyst started her query first? The point is that resource scheduling in a multiuser environment is just as important as what resources are available in aggregate.

When a MapReduce job is executed by the client, a list of input splits is first computed. Each split is a range of the data set to process, as determined by the input format. The jobtracker creates a map task for each input split and based on the job configuration, adds these tasks to a designated queue. The scheduler plug-in is what decides what tasks, from what queues, should be processed on what tasktrackers, in what order. Because there are different scheduling algorithms, each with their own benefits and optimizations, there are multiple scheduler plug-ins an administrator can choose from when configuring a cluster. Only one scheduler at a time may be configured, however.

It's important to point out that tasks within a job can always be reordered. There's no guarantee that map task 1 will execute before map task 2 because given a large enough cluster, all map tasks could potentially execute in parallel. In fact, that's the entire point of MapReduce: to achieve parallelism at the framework layer so the developer need not concern himself with the intricacies of scheduling and failure handling. This can be strange at first because when we think about processing a file, we tend to think of it occurring linearly from byte zero through to the end of the file. Freedom to reorder map tasks allows the framework to make placement decisions based not just on order of task arrival, but the currently available resources (in this case, map slots).

Consider the scenario where a tasktracker has available slots to run map tasks. The scheduler could simply schedule the next map task in line on that machine, but there's a significant chance that the data that map task is assigned to process is not local to that machine. Instead, the jobtracker looks through the queued map tasks and attempts to find a task that has a preference for the given machine. It's possible for the jobtracker to do this because each map task includes the range of the file it is to process and combined with the HDFS block size of the file, the jobtracker can figure out which block contains that portion of the file. The jobtracker also communicates with the namenode to figure out which hosts contain a replica of the block in question. With this information, it's possible to make an informed decision about which tasks should be scheduled based on the current available resources. Each scheduler implements data locality logic like this in addition to other features they may support.

The FIFO Scheduler

The first in, first out (FIFO) scheduler is the default scheduler in Hadoop. As the name implies, it uses a simple "first come, first served" algorithm for scheduling tasks. For example, given two jobs—A and B—submitted in that order, all map tasks in job A will execute before any tasks from job B. As job A map tasks complete, job B map tasks are scheduled (Figure 7-1). This is simple enough, but suffers from a trivial monopolization problem.

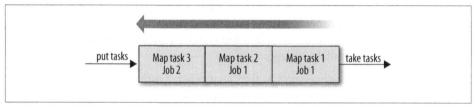

Figure 7-1. A single FIFO queue

Take the hypothetical case where Jane, our resident data scientist, submits a job to find frequently co-occuring product page views in activity data of a large commerce website over the last month. With traffic in excess of 1TB per day, this query scans over 30TB of data or approximately 245,760 map tasks, assuming a 128MB HDFS block size (30TB divided by the 128MB block size yields the number of map tasks, give or take). A 400 node cluster with 10 map slots per node would allow for 4000 map tasks to processed concurrently, only a fraction of the almost quarter million tasks that need to be performed to complete the query. Any job that is subsequently submitted needs to wait a considerable amount of time before any tasks will be scheduled. From the outside, the job will appear to simply make no progress, which can frustrate end users and violate SLAs for critical automated jobs.

The FIFO scheduler supports five levels of job prioritization, from lowest to highest: very low, low, normal, high, very high. Each priority is actually implemented as a separate FIFO queue. All tasks from higher priority queues are processed before lower priority queues and as described earlier, tasks are scheduled in the order of their jobs' submission. The easiest way to visualize prioritized FIFO scheduling is to think of it as five FIFO queues ordered top to bottom by priority. Tasks are then scheduled left to right, top to bottom. This means that all very high priority tasks are processed before any high priority tasks, which are processed before any normal priority tasks, and so on. An obvious problem with this form of scheduling is that if high priority tasks keep arriving, no normal priority tasks will ever be processed, for instance. Most users, when given the chance to prioritize their jobs, will always select the highest possible option. As a result, priorities no longer have meaning and magnanimous (and honest) users are trampled in the process. Figure 7-2 shows three of the five queues with map tasks in each queue. Tasks are taken and scheduled right to left, top to bottom, so even though job 1 may have been submitted first, job 3 will actually be the first job to receive resources.

Beyond prioritized task scheduling, the FIFO scheduler does not offer much in the way of additional features (compared to what we'll see later in the Capacity and Fair Schedulers). For small, experimental, or development clusters, the FIFO scheduler can be adequate. Production clusters, however, should use one of the other two schedulers covered next.

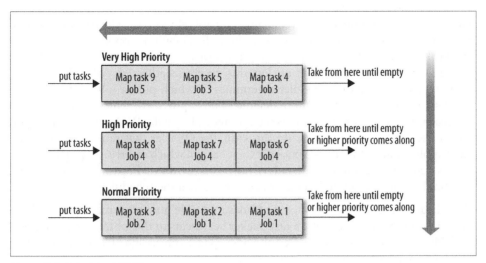

Figure 7-2. Prioritized FIFO queues

Configuration

The scheduler is configured by specifying the class name of the scheduler implementation to be used by the jobtracker in the `mapred.jobtracker.taskScheduler` parameter in *mapred-site.xml*. The name of the implementation class of the FIFO scheduler is `org.apache.hadoop.mapred.JobQueueTaskScheduler`. There is, however, no explicit configuration changes required to use the FIFO scheduler as it's the default.

The Fair Scheduler

The Fair Scheduler—sometimes called the Fair Share Scheduler or the FS scheduler—is an alternative scheduler to the default FIFO scheduler. It was developed to solve some of the problems that arise when using the FIFO scheduler in high traffic multitenant environments. Primarily, these problems center on the issues of resource starvation and (lack of) SLA guarantees, as described earlier. As part of his doctorate research, and while interning at Facebook and later Cloudera, Matei Zaharia (*http://www.cs.berkeley.edu/~matei/*), a Ph.D. student at the University of California, Berkeley, developed the Fair Scheduler. It is widely used in production environments and provides sane default behavior, out of the box.

A few base constructs provide the framework for resource scheduling and allocation in the Fair Scheduler. Jobs, which are submitted to queues, are placed into pools. Each pool is assigned a number of task slots based on a number of factors including the total slot capacity of the cluster, the current demand (where "demand" is the number of tasks in a pool) on other pools, minimum slot guarantees, and available slot capacity. Pools may optionally have minimum slot guarantees. These pools are said to have an SLA, with the minimum number of slots providing the vehicle for ensuring task scheduling within a given period of time. Beyond the minimum slot guarantees, each pool gets an equal number of the remaining available slots on the cluster; this is where the "fair share" portion of the name comes from. By default, no pools have minimums and so all pools simply receive an equal number of slots. Pools can be added dynamically, in which case, the number of slots they receive is adjusted. A MapReduce job property defines how the scheduler determines to which pool a job (and really, it's tasks) should be assigned. Again, a default value is provided, which is the property `user.name`. The `user.name` property is set automatically by the JVM to be the operating system user name of the process (in this case, the OS user that ran the MapReduce client application). This yields a pool per user, each of which receives an equal number of slots. Later we'll get into the details of how slots are divvied up amongst pools, but this should provide a primer on the critical concepts of the scheduler.

The scheduler uses a very specific set of rules to decide how resources (such as slots) are assigned to pools. Each time a tasktracker heartbeats to the jobtracker and reports available slots, the rules are evaluated and queued tasks are assigned for execution. The following are terms we'll use and some invariants.

Total capacity

In the context of scheduling, total capacity (or total cluster capacity) is the sum of all slots of each type (map slots and reduce slots) regardless of their state. A cluster with 10 tasktrackers, each with 8 map slots and 5 reduce slots, is said to have a total map slot capacity of 80 and a total reduce slot capacity of 50. If the slot configuration or number of tasktrackers is changed, the total cluster capacity changes. As Hadoop allows hot addition and removal of nodes even while jobs are running, total capacity is *not* a static number (and as a result, neither are its derivatives below).

Total available capacity

The total available capacity is the number of *open* slots in a cluster. An open slot is a slot that currently has no task assigned to it. Like total capacity, the total available capacity is divided into map and reduce capacity. The available capacity can never exceed the total capacity; you can never have more available slots than total slots.

Pool

A pool is a container for a group of jobs and the recipient of resource allocation. It is the Fair Scheduler's analog to a relational database resource group. Rather than configure what resources should be assigned to each job (a tedious and difficult process, as we may not know about all the jobs that could possibly exist in advance), we assign resources to a pool and then put jobs in pools.

Demand

A pool is said to have demand if and only if there are queued tasks that should be assigned to it. A pool with no queued tasks has no demand.

Fair share

The "fair" number of slots a pool should receive. How fair share is determined is described later.

Minimum share

An administrator-configured number of slots that a pool is guaranteed to receive. By default, pools have no minimum share. This is also simply called the *min-share* because of its configuration property name.

The first step in deciding how to allocate slots is to determine the total cluster capacity; it is impossible to give out more slots than we have. Of those slots, only a subset may be available, so the available capacity is also determined. The jobtracker knows both of these numbers because it receives regular status updates from tasktrackers by way of their heartbeat messages. When assigning tasks, the scheduler first looks at the demand for each pool. A pool with no demand is not given any slots, even if it has a minimum share. I can hear every reader screaming "but what if a job comes along and..."—hang in there, we'll get there. The scheduler gives each pool with demand its minimum share—if there is one configured—before going any further. If the sum of the minimum shares of pools with demand is greater than the total capacity, the minimum shares of each pool are adjusted *pro rata*. With the minimum shares satisfied, the scheduler switches to allocating the remaining slots. This is the fair share assignment stage of scheduling. The goal is to assign free slots as evenly as possible. If you were to imagine each pool as a glass of water, the goal of fair share assignment is to get the water level as even as possible across the glasses.

This is a lot to take in so it helps to consider some example scenarios with various configurations. For each scenario, we'll use the example cluster size from earlier—80 map slots and 50 reduce slots—unless specified otherwise.

First, let's look at the default behavior of the Fair Scheduler where pools simply receive their fair share of the available resources. In this case, user mary submits a MapReduce job. The scheduler creates a pool called mary if it doesn't already exist, because it's configured to use the value of the property user.name as the pool name. The pool has demand because the MapReduce job submitted (let's assume) has 20 map tasks that need to be assigned and executed. Because this pool has no minimum share, we skip that portion of the scheduling algorithm and move on to fair share assignment. With no other pools with demand, the pool mary is given all 20 slots (the demand). Even though another 60 map slots are available, they are not given to the pool because they wouldn't be used. Doing so would defeat one of the primary goals of the scheduler: to achieve the highest possible utilization of the cluster.

Building on the previous example, assume Bob were to now also submit a job with a map task demand of 40 tasks. A new pool named bob is created and the fair share of all pools are adjusted. Dividing the total map task capacity of 80 slots over the two pools yields 40 each. Mary is only using 20 slots and Bob is looking for 40. This fits fine within the available capacity and Bob receives the complete 40 slots he wants. Mary continues uninterrupted because she's below her 40 slot fair share (Table 7-1).

Table 7-1. Fair scheduler example allocation—demand less than fair share, total capacity of 80 slots

Pool	Demand	Minshare	Actual Share
Mary	20	0	20
Bob	40	0	40

If Jane now comes along with a 120 map task job, a new pool is created and fair shares are adjusted again. Each pool is technically entitled to 26 tasks, but because Mary's demand is only 20 and we never allocate more slots than the demand, she receives only the 20 slots requested. This means more slots are left for other pools. Bob and Jane, each with a demand greater than the total capacity, are not able to run all tasks at once anymore. When there isn't enough available capacity, tasks simply queue and are given to a pool as slots become available, and tasks can then execute, as you'd expect. In this particular case, shown in Table 7-2, Bob and Jane receive 30 tasks each. The case where these three users submit their jobs at the exact same time is easy to understand, although rarely the case. Far more often, Mary and Bob's jobs would already be running when Jane came along (or some other staggered submission use case). In this case, Bob is said to be over his fair share and Jane under (or starved). When this occurs, the scheduler allows Bob's tasks to complete gracefully, and then gives the newly available slots to the pool that has been starved the longest—in this case, Jane. The system self-corrects over time, and ultimately, all demand is satisfied.

Table 7-2. Fair scheduler example allocation—total demand exceeds total capacity of 80 slots

Pool	Demand	Minshare	Actual Share
Mary	20	0	20
Bob	40	0	30
Jane	120	0	30

So far we've described the ad-hoc job submission case where end users are submitting MapReduce jobs. This is fine, but these jobs are not incredibly time-sensitive. Let's now assume a pool named `production` exists where automated ETL jobs run regularly. It's important that each job is given a certain number of map slots in order to complete within a specified window of time (which, of course, assumes you know the average time of each map task and approximately how many tasks each iteration of the job requires, but that's another story). As an administrator, we configure this pool to have a minimum map share of 50 slots of the total 80.

Let's now consider what would happen with a production job with a demand of 30 map tasks—Mary with a demand of 40, and Bob with a demand of 30 (see Table 7-3). With only 80 tasks total, we're clearly over-subscribed. Not everyone will get what they want, or at least not Mary and Bob. Remember that minimum share allocation always occurs before fair share allocation and that we never give out more than a pool's demand. In this case, production receives the requested 30 slots (because it has a minimum share of 50) straight away. The remaining slots are divided according to the fair share assignment, which results in both Mary and Bob receiving 25 slots.

Table 7-3. Fair scheduler example allocation—demand less than minshare, total capacity of 80 slots

Pool	Demand	Minshare	Actual Share
Mary	40	0	25
Bob	30	0	25
Production	30	50	30

If the production job were to have a demand of 60 (in excess of its 50 slot minimum share), the numbers, shown in Table 7-4, change drastically with production receiving its full minimum share of 50 while Mary and Bob receive only 15 slots each.

Table 7-4. Fair scheduler example allocation—demand greater than minshare, total capacity of 80 slots

Pool	Demand	Minshare	Actual Share
Mary	40	0	15
Bob	30	0	15
Production	60	50	50

In addition to, or in place of a minimum share, pools may also have a *weight*. Pools with greater weight receive more slots during fair share allocation (weight does not impact minimum share allocation). The weight of a pool simply acts as a multiplier; a weight of 2 means the pool receives two slots to every one slot the other pools receive. By default, pools have a weight of 1. Let's look at an example (Table 7-5) where Bob has a demand of 60, Mary has a demand of 80, but Bob additionally has a weight of 2. The effects of a pool's weight aren't apparent until the total demand is greater than the total capacity. This is because when demand can be met for all jobs, there's no need to give one job special treatment over another. Neither pool in this example has a minimum share configured in the interest of simplicity, although that is a perfectly valid configuration.

Table 7-5. Fair scheduler example allocation—a pool with a weight, total capacity of 80 slots

Pool	Demand	Weight	Actual Share
Mary	80	1	26
Bob	60	2	53

Job priorities, like those supported in the FIFO scheduler, are also supported in the Fair Scheduler. When a priority is set, it simply affects the weight of the job; the higher the priority, the greater the weight, and the more tasks assigned during fair share allocation. Since the priority mechanism works by way of the weight, and weight is only accounted for during fair share allocation, the job priority does not affect minimum share allocation.

The important take-aways from this are:

- Minimum shares are always satisfied before fair shares.
- Pools never receive more slots than their demand, even if there's a minimum share in place.
- During fair share assignment, slots are allocated in an attempt to "fill the water glasses evenly."
- Pools can a have a weight that is only considered during fair share allocation.

So far, we've talked only about slot allocation to pools, but it's possible that two jobs could be submitted to the same pool. A trivial example of a situation where more than one job would exist in a single pool at the same time would be user Mary submitting two MapReduce jobs. The Fair Scheduler uses another instance of itself to schedule jobs *within* each pool. Remember that with its default behavior, resources are simply divided evenly. Normally, these resources are split across pools, but within a pool, they're split across jobs. The end result is almost always what you want; each MapReduce job within a pool makes progress without being unfair to other pools. In other words, if Mary receives 40 slots, she can run one job with 40 slots, two jobs with 20 each, and so on. For the remaining specialized cases, it's also possible to enforce FIFO scheduling *within* a pool. This tends to make sense for pools that hold jobs that access external resources and need to be accessed by one job at a time.

Earlier, we talked about how the Fair Scheduler does not reserve slots for pools configured with minimum shares unless there is demand for those pools. Instead, the scheduler attempts to use as much of the cluster as possible by allowing other pools to dynamically take over that capacity when it's not in use. When a job is submitted to a pool with a minimum share and those slots have been given away, there are two options: wait for the running tasks to complete and take the slots as they free up, or forcefully reclaim the necessary resources promised by the minimum share configuration. For jobs operating with an SLA, it's usually not acceptable to delay execution, especially when it's unclear how long we'd have to wait for those resources. The Fair Scheduler deals with this problem by preempting tasks and stealing the slots back to fulfill a starved pool's minimum share. To be clear, language like "forcefully reclaim" and "preempt" are euphemisms for "kill," in the context of Hadoop. This is because, as we've seen, the unit of work in a MapReduce job is the task. It's not possible to suspend a task like an operating system, context switch to a higher priority task, and then resume the lower priority task where we left off later. Instead, the scheduler simply kills a task, which then goes back into the queue for retry at a later time. Any work performed by a task that is killed is thrown away. While somewhat wasteful, this does accomplish the goal of keeping the resources where they're needed most. To look at it another way, it's *more* wasteful to leave capacity reserved by minimum shares unused even when there's no work in those pools.

There are two types of preemption: minimum share preemption and fair share preemption. Minimum share preemption occurs when a pool is operating below its configured minimum share, whereas fair share preemption kicks in only when a pool is operating below its fair share. Minimum share preemption is the more aggressive of the two and is applied when a pool has been operating below its minimum share for longer than a configurable minimum share preemption timeout. Fair share preemption, on the other hand, is applied conservatively; a pool must be below half of its fair share for the configured fair share preemption timeout before preemption occurs. A pool below its minimum share will reap only up to its minimum share, whereas a pool below 50% of its fair share will reap all the way up to its full fair share during preemption. Preemption is disabled by default and must be explicitly configured.

Normally, the scheduler assigns a single map or reduce task during each tasktracker heartbeat, even if multiple open slots are available. The rationale behind this is that, by doing so, tasks are spread over a wider set of physical machines. In other words, if multiple tasks were assigned during a single heartbeat, tasks would tend to clump on machines that reported in more recently than others. This increases the impact of a faulty machine getting a hold of a large portion of a job. On the other hand, the downside to this approach is that small jobs require greater ramp up time because they must wait for multiple tasktrackers to heartbeat in and take on tasks. Luckily, the Fair Scheduler exposes an option that enables multiple task assignment within a single heartbeat. Enabling this option greatly increases the perceived speed of small jobs at the cost of potentially landing many tasks on a single misbehaving host. Those that maintain clusters used by analysts or data scientists directly may wish to enable this feature.

Another trick in the Fair Scheduler bag is *delayed task assignment* (sometimes called delay scheduling) and is also the result of research conducted by Zaharia et al (*http:// www.cs.berkeley.edu/~matei/papers/2010/eurosys_delay_scheduling.pdf*). The goal of delayed assignment is to increase the data locality hit ratio and as a result, the performance of a job, as well as the utilization of the cluster as a whole. Delayed assignment works by letting a free slot on a tasktracker remain open for a short amount of time if there is no queued task that would prefer to run on the host in question. This is counterintuitive at first; how could delaying task assignment increase overall job runtime? The concept is simple: tasks execute faster when operating on local data. The amount of delay introduced by leaving the slot available (or temporarily violating fairness) is more than made up for by increasing the overall data locality hit rate. Leaving the slot open temporarily sacrifices fairness by potentially selecting a task to execute in a free slot that it is not necessarily entitled to for an increase in locality. Delayed assignment can improve data locality and performance and in certain cases, noticeably so.

Choose the Fair Scheduler over the Capacity Scheduler if:

- You have a slow network and data locality makes a significant difference to job runtime. Features like delay scheduling can make a dramatic difference in the effective locality rate of map tasks.

- You have a lot of variability in the utilization between pools. The Fair Scheduler's preemption model affects much greater overall cluster utilization by giving away otherwise reserved resources when they're not used.

- You require jobs *within* a pool to make equal progress rather than running in FIFO order.

Configuration

Configuring the Fair Scheduler is broken up into two parts: global settings that are made in *mapred-site.xml*, and configuring any special pool settings that is done in a separate file. As described earlier, the scheduler class name—which in the case of the Fair Scheduler, is `org.apache.hadoop.mapred.FairScheduler`—must be specified in the `mapred.jobtracker.taskScheduler` parameter in *mapred-site.xml*. The following Fair Scheduler settings are supported in *mapred-site.xml*:

`mapred.fairscheduler.allocation.file` *(required)*
> Defines the absolute path to the pool allocation file. This file must exist when the jobtracker starts and must be a valid XML file. The allocation file is polled for changes every 10 seconds and if it has changed, it is reloaded and the pool configurations are updated dynamically. See the following for more information on configuring pools in the allocation file.
>
> Default value: none. Example: */etc/hadoop/conf/allocations.xml*

`mapred.fairscheduler.poolnameproperty`
> The `mapred.fairscheduler.poolnameproperty` property specifies the name of the job configuration property from which to take the name of the pool for assignment. That's a mouthful. Take the default as an example: `mapred.fairscheduler.poolnameproperty` is set to `user.name`. This causes the scheduler to use the value of the `user.name` parameter as the pool to which a job is assigned. If the user `user.name` is set to `jane`, this now becomes the pool that is used. Instead, if we set `mapred.fairscheduler.poolnameproperty` to `group.name`, the user's primary OS group (on Linux, at least) would be used as the pool name. If you wish to use the jobtracker's access control lists to control who may submit jobs to which queues and by extension, which pools, you *must* set `mapred.fairscheduler.poolnameproperty` to `mapred.job.queue.name`. Users submitting jobs may then specify the proper value of `mapred.job.queue.name`, which is then checked against the ACLs and submitted to a pool of the same name.
>
> Default value: `user.name`

`mapred.fairscheduler.preemption`

Globally enables (true) or disables (false) preemption in the Fair Scheduler. Task preemption is disabled by default. If you have pools that must operate on an SLA, you should configure their minimum shares appropriately, enable this parameter, and set an appropriate minimum share or fair share timeout.

Default value: false

`mapred.fairscheduler.allow.undeclared.pools`

Normally, the Fair Scheduler automatically creates new pools if a job is submitted to them. To disable this behavior and force only pools defined in the allocations file to be considered valid, set this parameter to false.

Default value: true

`mapred.fairscheduler.sizebasedweight`

A lesser used but interesting feature of the Fair Scheduler is the ability to dynamically set the weight of a pool based on the size of its demand. Enabling this feature dynamically allocates more slots to pools that have a large number of queued tasks. In other words, as a pool becomes backlogged, the scheduler gives it more resources to help it catch up. Remember that weight affects only fair share allocation so this adjusts only allocation of resources after minimum shares have been satisfied (which also means it cannot impact SLAs).

Default value: false

`mapred.fairscheduler.assignmultiple`

Globally enables or disables multiple task assignment during a single tasktracker heartbeat, as described earlier. Clusters with short, interactive jobs will see a noticeable wall clock speed increase from job submission to completion time when enabling this.

Default value: true

`mapred.fairscheduler.assignmultiple.maps`

When multiple assignment is enabled, this parameter dictates how many map tasks should be assigned in a single heartbeat. Setting this value to -1 (negative one) indicates an unlimited number of map tasks may be assigned.

Default value: -1

`mapred.fairscheduler.assignmultiple.reduces`

This parameter serves exactly the same function as `mapred.fairscheduler.assign multiple.maps`, but for reduce tasks.

Default value: -1

`mapred.fairscheduler.weightadjuster`

It is possible to write a plug-in for the Fair Scheduler that determines how the weight of pools is adjusted, dynamically. While describing the development of such a plug-in is out of scope for this book, setting this parameter to the class name is how the plug-in is configured.

Default value: none.

Example value: `com.mycompany.hadoop.mapred.MyWeightAdjuster`

`mapred.fairscheduler.eventlog.enabled`

The Fair Scheduler supports a specialized event log that traces all actions from new job submission, to task assignment, to preemption. Rarely used, enabling this parameter can be helpful in understanding the behavior of the scheduler.

Default value: false

`mapred.fairscheduler.preemption.only.log`

Rather than actually preempting tasks according to the pool configuration, it's possible to just log what would have happened to the scheduler's event log (which must be separately enabled). Setting this value to true will do this.

Default value: false

With the global settings in place, the remainder of the configuration is done in the allocations file. This is the same file specified by the `mapred.fairscheduler.alloca tion.file` parameter in *mapred-site.xml*. It's generally named *allocations.xml* or *fair-scheduler.xml* and located in the Hadoop configuration directory, but that's not a hard requirement (although that's what we'll use here). Based on the file extension, it's probably obvious that this is an XML file, although the format is different than the normal Hadoop configuration files. (See Example 7-6.)

Example 7-6. A minimal Fair Scheduler allocation file

```
<?xml version="1.0"?>

<!-- The world's least exciting Fair Scheduler configuration file. -->
<allocations>
</allocations>
```

The absolute minimum the allocations file must contain is the standard XML stanza followed by the `allocations` document tag. Starting the jobtracker with this configuration (and the proper `mapred.fairscheduler.allocation.file` value) will enable the Fair Scheduler with its default behavior, which allows pools to be dynamically created with no special minimum shares or weights defined. Changes made to the allocations file are dynamically reloaded by the jobtracker, as described earlier.

The following tags are supported within the document-level `allocations` tag.

`pool`

The `pool` element defines and configures a pool. It supports a number of child elements that define the minimum map and reduce shares, the minimum share preemption timeout, and other properties. See Tables 7-6 and 7-7.

Table 7-6. Attributes

Name	Description	Required
name	Defines the pool name.	Yes

Table 7-7. Child elements

Name	Description	Required
minMaps	Minimum map share. (Default: 0)	No
minReduces	Minimum reduce share. (Default: 0)	No
maxMaps	Maximum allowed concurrent map tasks. (Default: unlimited)	No
maxReduces	Maximum allowed concurrent reduce tasks. (Default: unlimited)	No
maxRunningJobs	Total maximum running jobs permitted concurrently. (Default: unlimited)	No
weight	The pool weight used during fair share allocation. (Default: 1)	No
minSharePreemptionTimeout	Time, in seconds, before preempting tasks when operating under minimum share. (Default: unlimited)	No
schedulingMode	Scheduling mode used within a pool, either FAIR (default) or FIFO.	No

user

In addition to defining certain resource limits per pool, it's possible to define such limits on a per-user basis as well. This is helpful when there's a requirement to assign jobs to pools by something other than username, but certain users should still receive special treatment. While the sole child element of maxRunningJobs isn't necessarily required, omitting it obviates the need to specify the user element at all. (See Tables 7-8 and 7-9.)

Table 7-8. Attributes

Name	Description	Required
name	The user's name.	Yes

Table 7-9. Child Elements

Name	Description	Required
maxRunningJobs	Total maximum running jobs permitted concurrently. (Default: unlimited)	No

userMaxJobsDefault

This element defines the *default* maximum number of concurrent jobs for all users and may be overridden by `user` elements.

Default: 0 (unlimited)

poolMaxJobsDefault

This elements defines the *default* maximum number of concurrent jobs for all pools. Specifying a `maxRunningJobs` element within a `pool` element overrides this value for the pool.

fairSharePreemptionTimeout

The global fair share preemption timeout defines (in seconds) how long a pool operates under 50% of its fair share utilization before preemption occurs. This element has no meaning unless preemption is globally enabled in the *mapred-site.xml* file.

Default: Java's `Long.MAX_VALUE`.

defaultMinSharePreemptionTimeout

The default minimum share preemption timeout defines (in seconds) how long a pool operates under its minimum share before preemption occurs. This element has no meaning unless preemption is globally enabled in the *mapred-site.xml* file. Pools may override this value using the `minSharePreemptionTimeout` child element of the `pool` element.

Default: Java's `Long.MAX_VALUE`.

defaultPoolSchedulingMode

By default, jobs within a pool are scheduled using the same algorithm as fair share allocation between pools. It is possible to change the default for all pools to be strictly FIFO ordered, by setting this element to `FIFO`. The only other option is `FAIR` which is the default. Pools may override this value using the `schedulingMode` child element of the `pool` element.

All of this can be a lot to take in. The following are a few example allocation file examples to get you started. The first example (Example 7-7) is a configuration file that defines a pool named `production-etl` with minimum shares of 40 and 20 map and reduce slots, respectively, and a `research` pool with a weight of 2 but no minimum shares. Minimum share preemption is configured to occur after five minutes and fair share preemption never occurs.

Example 7-7. Fair Scheduler pool configuration—production-etl, research

```
<?xml version="1.0"?>

<allocations>

  <defaultMinSharePreemptionTimeout>300</defaultMinSharePreemptionTimeout>

  <pool name="production-etl">
    <minMaps>40</minMaps>
```

```
    <minReduces>20</minReduces>
  </pool>

  <pool name="research">
    <weight>2</weight>
  </pool>

</allocations>
```

Next, Example 7-8 shows the same configuration, but now user `james` is limited to only three concurrent jobs, no matter what pool he uses.

Example 7-8. Fair Scheduler pool configuration—production-etl, research, user limits

```
<?xml version="1.0"?>

<allocations>

  <defaultMinSharePreemptionTimeout>300</defaultMinSharePreemptionTimeout>

  <user name="james">
    <maxRunningJobs>3</maxRunningJobs>
  </user>

  <pool name="production-etl">
    <minMaps>40</minMaps>
    <minReduces>20</minReduces>
  </pool>

  <pool name="research">
    <weight>2</weight>
  </pool>

</allocations>
```

The Capacity Scheduler

Finally, the Capacity Scheduler (sometimes called the *cap scheduler* for short) is another popular alternative to the default FIFO scheduler. Like the Fair Scheduler, the Capacity Scheduler was created to enable multiple groups to share a single large cluster, while maintaining certain guarantees on resource allocation. Originally developed by the Hadoop team at Yahoo!, the Capacity Scheduler is battle tested in some of the largest Hadoop clusters known.

The primary differences between the Fair and Capacity schedulers have to do with the philosophy behind the task scheduling algorithm. Additionally, there are some feature differences that would cause someone to choose one over the other, which are highlighted. To start, the Capacity Scheduler is a simpler and in some ways, a more deterministic scheduler than the Fair Scheduler. An administrator configures one or more queues, each with a *capacity*—a predetermined fraction of the total cluster slot capacity. This is akin to the Fair Scheduler's minimum share definition, however it is reserved for the queue in question and is not given away in the absence of demand. During the tasktracker heartbeat, slots are given to queues (analogous to the Fair Scheduler pools, in this context), with the most starved queues receive slots first. Queue starvation is measured by dividing the number of running tasks in the queue by the queue's capacity or in other words, its percentage used. Any additional slots beyond the sum of the queue capacities defined may be freely assigned to any queue, as needed, by the scheduler.

Within a queue, jobs for the same user are FIFO ordered. Unfortunately, this means it's possible for two jobs submitted by the same user within a queue to block another, although capacity is still distributed appropriate across queues. Similar to the FIFO scheduler, however, jobs can be prioritized within a queue. This limitation may or may not be an issue for you, depending on your use case and environment. Administrators can optionally disable intra-queue prioritization of jobs as well.

One of the more significant features of the Capacity Scheduler is the ability to control allocation based on physical machine resources. The previously covered schedulers work exclusively in terms of slots, but the Capacity Scheduler additionally understands scheduling tasks based on (user defined) memory consumption of a job's tasks as well. When properly configured, the scheduler uses information collected by the tasktracker to aid in scheduling decisions. An administrator may specify a default virtual and physical memory limit on tasks that users may optionally override upon job submission. The scheduler then uses this information to decide on which tasktracker to place the tasks, taking into account any other tasks currently executing on the host. Checks exist to ensure these so-called high memory jobs are not starved for resources in the face of jobs without such a requirement.

JVM garbage collection pauses can become an issue in high activity clusters. This tends to be a side effect of how the jobtracker initializes jobs submitted to the cluster and how it handles memory. Tasks are represented within the jobtracker as Java objects and placed in a list-like data structure. When many large jobs are submitted in rapid succession, the amount of memory required to create and manage these objects and their associated state can add up considerably. Task objects are constantly being created during submission, modified during execution, and destroyed when they age out of the system. Ultimately, this leads to object churn and manifests as long pauses during garbage collection. Some of this can be mitigated by fancy garbage collector tuning, however, a better answer is to simply manage memory more effectively. The Capacity Scheduler supports a feature where job initialization is performed lazily, which can reduce the required memory footprint of the jobtracker. This feature allows an administrator to specify a maximum number of jobs to initialize, per user, per queue. Of course, a running job must have all of its task objects in memory, so these limits apply to those that aren't yet ready to run.

Choose the Capacity Scheduler over the Fair Scheduler if:

- You know a lot about your cluster workloads and utilization and simply want to enforce resource allocation.

- You have very little fluctuation within queue utilization. The Capacity Scheduler's more rigid resource allocation makes sense when all queues are at capacity almost all the time.
- You have high variance in the memory requirements of jobs and you need the Capacity Scheduler's memory-based scheduling support.
- You demand scheduler determinism.

Configuration

Like the other schedulers, the first step in configuring the Capacity Scheduler is to set the value of `mapred.jobtracker.taskScheduler` to its class name, `org.apache.hadoop.mapred.CapacityTaskScheduler`. Just as with the Fair Scheduler, the Capacity Scheduler uses a separate file (unsurprisingly) called *capacity-scheduler.xml*, which also lives in the Hadoop configuration directory. In this file, the various queue capacities and other settings are defined, however it is still necessary to specify the queue names in the *mapred-site.xml* file in the `mapred.queue.names` parameter. The *capacity-scheduler.xml* file follows the same key value format of the three standard Hadoop XML configuration files.

Queue settings are defined using the same pseudo-hierarchical naming convention as other Hadoop parameters. Here is a list of the supported Capacity Scheduler configuration parameters.

On deprecated memory related parameters

Some of parameters to control memory-aware scheduling in the Apache Hadoop and CDH documentation are actually deprecated in the code. Rather than cover the deprecated parameters (which were a little confusing), the newer, simpler parameters are shown in the following list. You may find that these parameters are not covered in the published documentation for certain releases, but they do work and should be used instead. To reduce confusion, explicit version numbers have been listed for these parameters.

`mapred.capacity-scheduler.queue.`*queue-name*`.capacity`

Sets the capacity for the queue named *queue-name*. The defined *queue-name* must match one of the queues named in the `mapred.queue.names` parameter in *mapred-site.xml*. The value of this parameter is an integer and specifies the percentage of the total available cluster slots to be reserved for tasks in this queue. This applies to both map and reduce slots. For example, a value of 82 would reserve 82% of map *and* reduce slots for the named queue. The sum of the capacities of all queues must be less than or equal to 100. If there are any queues without a configured capacity, each receives an even share of any unallocated capacity.

Default value: none. Example value: 30.

`mapred.capacity-scheduler.queue.`*`queue-name`*`.maximum-capacity`   *(AH   1.x+,*
CDH3u0+)

> Places an upper limit on how much of the cluster, beyond the queue's defined
> capacity, a queue is permitted to use (defined as a percentage of capacity). This
> parameter exists to prevent a queue with long running tasks from grabbing and
> holding excess capacity that, when needed by another queue that's starved for
> capacity, can not be returned quickly. It exists to mitigate the lack of preemption
> in the Capacity Scheduler. A simple example use of this feature would be a queue
> with a capacity of 30 and a maximum capacity of 80. This value must be greater
> than or equal to the queue's capacity. The default value of -1 (negative one) indi-
> cates that a queue has no limit on the maximum capacity it can use.
>
> Default value: -1 (no maximum capacity limit)

`mapred.capacity-scheduler.queue.`*`queue-name`*`.supports-priority`

> Enabling this option (a value of true) instructs the scheduler to respect the priority
> with which jobs are submitted to *queue-name*.
>
> Default value: false

`mapred.capacity-scheduler.queue.`*`queue-name`*`.minimum-user-limit-percent`

> The maximum percentage (specified as an integer from 0 to 100) of slots within a
> queue that a user will receive when there is contention for them. For example, a
> value of 25 means no user will receive more than 25% of the queue resources if
> there are multiple users running jobs within a queue. When there isn't contention,
> all queue resources are divided evenly amongst users. In other words, if the queue
> capacity was 50% of 200 total cluster slots (yielding 100 slots for this queue) and
> this parameter was 25, a single user would receive all 100 slots, two users would
> receive 50 slots, three users would receive 33 slots, and beyond that, users would
> never receive more than 25 slots. A value of 100 means there is no per-user limit.
>
> Default value: 100

`mapred.capacity-scheduler.queue.`*`queue-name`*`.user-limit-factor`   *(AH   1.x+,*
CDH3u0+)

> Related to the minimum user limit percentage, the user limit factor defines a mul-
> tiplier of the queue's capacity to which a user is limited regardless of excess cluster
> capacity. For instance, the value of 2 means no user will ever receive more than 2×
> the queue's capacity. Given a queue capacity of 20% of a 100 slot cluster, a single
> user would never occupy more than 40 slots (20% of 100 is 20 slots, times a mul-
> tiplier of 2 is 40 slots). The default value of 1 limits a single user to the capacity of
> the queue.
>
> Default value: 1

`mapred.capacity-scheduler.queue.`*`queue-name`*`.maximum-initialized-jobs-per-user`

> The number of jobs per user that should be eagerly initialized within a queue. If
> this property is not defined, the value of `mapred.capacity-scheduler.default-max`
> `imum-initialized-jobs-per-user` is used.

Default value: value of `mapred.capacity-scheduler.default-maximum-initialized-jobs-per-user`.

`mapred.capacity-scheduler.queue.`*queue-name*`.maximum-initialized-active-tasks` *(AH 1.x+, CDH3u0+)*

The maximum number of tasks that can be initialized within a given queue. When this value is exceeded, tasks are queued on disk rather than in memory.

Default value: value of `mapred.capacity-scheduler.default-maximum-active-tasks-per-queue`

`mapred.capacity-scheduler.queue.`*queue-name*`.maximum-initialized-active-tasks-per-user` *(AH 1.x+, CDH3u0+)*

The maximum number of tasks that can be initialized within a given queue for a given user. When this value is exceeded, tasks are queued on disk rather than in memory.

Default value: value of `mapred.capacity-scheduler.default-maximum-active-tasks-per-user`

`mapred.capacity-scheduler.queue.`*queue-name*`.init-accept-jobs-factor` *(AH 1.x+, CDH3u0+)*

Allows for queue level overrides of the related `mapred.capacity-scheduler.default-init-accept-jobs-factor`. See later entries for a full explanation of this parameter.

Default value: value of `mapred.capacity-scheduler.default-init-accept-jobs-factor`

`mapred.capacity-scheduler.default-maximum-active-tasks-per-queue` *(AH 1.x+, CDH3u0+)*

The scheduler wide default number of maximum initialized active tasks permitted in memory per queue. When there are more tasks than this value, they are queued to disk. This value can be overridden by individual queues by using `mapred.capacity-scheduler.queue.`*queue-name*`.maximum-initialized-active-tasks`.

Default value: 200000

`mapred.capacity-scheduler.default-maximum-active-tasks-per-user` *(AH 1.x+, CDH3u0+)*

The scheduler wide default number of maximum initialized active tasks permitted in memory, per user. When there are more tasks than this value, they are queued to disk. This value can be overridden by individual queues by using `mapred.capacity-scheduler.queue.`*queue-name*`.maximum-initialized-active-tasks-per-user`.

Default value: 100000

`mapred.capacity-scheduler.default-init-accept-jobs-factor` *(AH 1.x+, CDH3u0+)*

The Capacity Scheduler includes some support for protecting itself against inadvertent denial of service attacks. One measure is to stop accepting new job submissions to queues after the number of queued and running jobs exceeds a threshold.

To ensure new job acceptance is performed with some degree of fairness across queues, the scheduler makes some assumptions. One of these is that the queue capacity (which, remember, is expressed as a percentage of cluster slot capacity), while normally applied to task slots, can also be used as the percentage of resources to use for new job acceptance. In other words, if a queue is allocated 45% of all cluster slots, the scheduler will allow it 45% of the maximum system job count before it begins rejecting new jobs. This parameter acts as a multiplier to that job count. Continuing the example, a queue with 45% capacity, the default maximum system job count of 5,000, and this value set to 20, would accept up to 45,000 new jobs before rejecting additional submissions (45% of 5,000 is 2,250, times 20 equals 45,000). Keep in mind that this value is the default for queues that do not explicitly specify a value for `mapred.capacity-scheduler.queue.`*`queue-name`*`.init-accept-jobs-factor`. Unless a queue's capacity is unusually small or you reduce max system jobs, there probably isn't a compelling reason to modify this value. The notable exception is the case where cluster resources—both jobtracker and total cluster slots—are in almost absurd demand, in which case this can act like throttling connections on an HTTP server.

Default value: 10

`mapred.capacity-scheduler.default-supports-priority` *(AH 1.x+, CDH3u0+)*
Sets the default value for queues that do not explicitly set `mapred.capacity-scheduler.queue.`*`queue-name`*`.supports-priority`. Enabling this parameter causes the scheduler to take job priorities into account when scheduling, otherwise they're ignored.

Default value: false

`mapred.capacity-scheduler.init-poll-interval`
Internally, the Capacity Scheduler polls the queues for new jobs to initialize. It's possible to control the frequency (defined in milliseconds) at which this polling occurs. Polling too often results in wasted CPU resources, whereas polling too infrequently means that jobs that should be scheduled can't because they're not yet ready. This is an advanced parameter that most users shouldn't need to modify.

Default value: 5000 (5 seconds)

`mapred.capacity-scheduler.init-worker-threads`
Job initialization is handled by a group of worker threads within the capacity scheduler and is configured using this parameter. When the number of worker threads is fewer than the number of job queues, threads initialize jobs in a round-robin fashion. If this parameter's value is greater than or equal to the number of queues, each queue has a dedicated thread to perform job initialization. There are never more initialization worker threads spawned than job queues. This is an advanced parameter that most users shouldn't need to modify.

Default value: 5

`mapred.capacity-scheduler.maximum-system-jobs` *(AH 1.x+, CDH3u0+)*

Defines the maximum jobs that can be initialized at any one time within the scheduler.

Default value: 5000

`mapred.cluster.map.memory.mb` *(AH 0.20.x+, CDH3u0+) (set in mapred-site.xml)*

Specifies the size of a map slot in megabytes. This is used by the scheduler to know how much (virtual) memory the administrator expects a map slot to support. When a user submits a job that asks for more memory per map task than this, it is simply counted as occupying more than one slot. For example, if this parameter were set to 2048 (2GB) and a user submitting a job specifies that their map tasks need 4096 (4GB), the scheduler will count each map task as two slots and schedule it accordingly. This parameter *must* be set for memory-aware scheduling to function.

Default value: -1 (meaning memory-aware scheduling is disabled)

`mapred.cluster.reduce.memory.mb` *(AH 0.20.x+, CDH3u0+) (set in mapred-site.xml)*

This parameter serves exactly the same purpose as `mapred.cluster.map.mem ory.mb` above, but for reduce slots. This parameter *must* be set for memory-aware scheduling to function.

Default value: -1 (meaning memory-aware scheduling is disabled)

`mapred.cluster.max.map.memory.mb` *(AH 0.20.x+, CDH3u0+) (set in mapred-site.xml)*

Related to `mapred.cluster.map.memory.mb` (note the subtle difference in the names), this parameter places a limit on the amount of memory a user may request for map tasks when submitting a job. Setting this parameter to 8192 (8GB), for example, would prevent a user from requesting more than 8GB per map task and as a more tangible result, more than 4 map slots per map task (assuming `mapred.clus ter.map.memory.mb` was set to 2048). This parameter *must* be set for memory-aware scheduling to function.

Default value: -1 (meaning memory-aware scheduling is disabled)

`mapred.cluster.max.reduce.memory.mb` *(AH 0.20.x+, CDH3u0+) (set in mapred-site.xml)*

The reduce task counterpart to `mapred.cluster.max.map.memory.mb`, this parameter affects the limit on the maximum amount of memory a user may request for reduce tasks. This parameter *must* be set for memory-aware scheduling to function.

Default value: -1 (meaning memory-aware scheduling is disabled)

Let's look at a simple Capacity Scheduler configuration file in Example 7-9. We'll assume we're working with a cluster of 80 map slots and 30 reduce slots, and the same pool names from the Fair Scheduler example.

Example 7-9. Capacity Scheduler queue configuration—production-etl, research

```xml
<?xml version="1.0"?>

<configuration>

  <!--
    50% of the cluster capacity is given to the production-etl queue.
  -->
  <property>
    <name>mapred.capacity-scheduler.queue.production-etl.capacity</name>
    <value>50</value>
  </property>

  <!--
    Allow production jobs to be prioritized.
  -->
  <property>
    <name>mapred.capacity-scheduler.queue.production-etl.supports-priority</name>
    <value>true</value>
  </property>

  <!--
    Don't allow the research group to occupy more than 30% of the cluster.
  -->
  <property>
    <name>mapred.capacity-scheduler.queue.research.maximum-capacity</name>
    <value>30</value>
  </property>

  <!--
    No single user is permitted to take up more than 50% of the research
    queue capacity.
  -->
  <property>
    <name>mapred.capacity-scheduler.queue.research.minimum-user-limit-percent</name>
    <value>50</value>
  </property>

  <!-- Scheduler-wide defaults. -->

  <!--
    Permit up to 10K jobs.
  -->
  <property>
    <name>mapred.capacity-scheduler.maximum-system-jobs</name>
    <value>10000</value>
  </property>

</configuration>
```

The Future

Today, it's possible to build large shared Hadoop clusters and support multiple groups of users while maintaining service level agreements in both storage and processing capacity. It is, however, necessary to have detailed knowledge of how various workloads perform with respect to system resources and to encapsulate that behavior in how task slots are provisioned. Ideally, this wouldn't be the case. Research has been well under way for some time now to improve the state of the art with respect to both how resources are tracked and how they're allocated to cluster users. The problem is that, while it's trivial (at least theoretically) to track host level resource consumption, tracking this information at the process granularity is a little bit trickier. Systems like Hadoop have additional layers of complexity introduced as a result of being multiuser systems, but also because they accept arbitrary code. In the world of the relational database, where it's possible to build dataset statistics and where the environment where one interacts with the data is so highly structured, it is simpler (although still not necessarily as simple as one might expect) to measure resources consumed during a given operation. In fact, using information about the data, most relational databases have a reasonable ability to anticipate resource consumption before an operation begins (assuming it's up to date). Hadoop isn't there yet.

The power of Hadoop lies in its ability to take in, process, and store massive amounts of data in various formats. This comes with the baggage of not necessarily having the luxury of a centralized mechanism to compute, store, and reference this type of information. Of course, all the tools to do so exist and are available, but it's up to the user to decide when and to what extent the cost of building and maintaining this information is important. In other words, Hadoop is a framework for those building custom data processing systems more than a shrink-wrapped, turn key, data management system. This isn't easy and many aren't in the business of building data management systems, and so there has to be a middle ground.

If you believe the hype (and you probably do, either voluntarily or at the demand of those around you, if you're reading this), Hadoop is fast becoming a larger platform for different forms of data processing. YARN is an indication of this. Sure, the YARN impetus was to scale the function of the jobtracker and enable the coexistence of different versions of the MapReduce libraries on the same hardware, but it also created the infrastructure necessary to allow those who *are* in the business of implementing data processing systems (such as the larger Hadoop community) to build new frameworks as applications on a meta-platform, a resource management framework in which one can build data processing systems with resource management features. Not only can we allocate resources within MapReduce, but consider multiple instances of MapReduce running in containers within YARN, sharing a single instance of HDFS. That is the future of Hadoop and we're seeing the beginning of it today.

Researchers, both in academia and the industry, are working on new ways to manage host resources in a more granular way. Today it is possible to make scheduling decisions based on memory consumption, but with Linux Control Groups (*http://www.kernel .org/doc/Documentation/cgroups/cgroups.txt*) (or more commonly, just *cgroups*) and better reporting of host resources to the scheduler, it will be possible make better decisions about task placement. Using a system like cgroups also greatly increases system stability as processes can be isolated from one another and resource limit violators killed quickly.

## CHAPTER 8

Cluster Maintenance

Hadoop clusters require a moderate amount of day-to-day care and feeding in order to remain healthy and in optimal working condition. Maintenance tasks are usually performed in response to events: expanding the cluster, dealing with failures or errant jobs, managing logs, or upgrading software in a production environment. This chapter is written in "run book form," with common tasks called out and simple processes for dealing with those situations. It's not meant to supplant a complete understanding of the system, and as always, the normal caveats apply when dealing with systems that store data or serve critical functions.

Managing Hadoop Processes

It's not at all unusual to need to start, stop, or restart Hadoop daemons because of configuration changes or as part of a larger process. Depending on the selected deployment model and distribution, this can be as simple as using standard service init scripts or by way of specialized scripts for Hadoop. Some administrators may use configuration management systems such as Puppet and Chef to manage processes.

Starting and Stopping Processes with Init Scripts

The most common reason administrators restart Hadoop processes is to enact configuration changes. Other common reasons are to upgrade Hadoop, add or remove worker nodes, or react to incidents. The effect of starting or stopping a process is entirely dependent upon the process in question. Starting a namenode will bring it into service after it loads the *fsimage*, replays the transaction log, sees some percentage of blocks (minimally replicated) from the datanodes, and is stable for some additional amount of time, as defined by the `dfs.safemode.extension` parameter. The percentage of blocks required by the namenode to start is controlled by the `dfs.safemode.threshold.pct` parameter, but is roughly 100%.[1] The datanode daemon will connect to its configured

---

1. Technically, it's 0.999, or 99.9%, for internal implementation reasons.

namenode upon start and immediately join the cluster. Once the namenode has registered the datanode, subsequent read and write operations may begin using it right away.

Stopping or restarting a namenode will render HDFS unavailable unless operating in a highly available pair. Datanodes can be safely stopped without interrupting HDFS service, although replication of their block data will occur, which creates load on the network. Stopping a tasktracker results in any currently executing child tasks being killed. These tasks will be retried later on another tasktracker. Any affected jobs will appear to slow down but will not fail unless the tasks in question were the final attempt to be made prior to failing the job.

1. Become user `root` (or use `sudo`).
2. Execute `/etc/init.d/`*`script operation`* where *`script`* is one of the daemon init scripts and *`operation`* is one of `start`, `stop`, or `restart`.
3. Confirm that the process started or stopped by checking its log files or looking for the process in the output of `ps -ef | grep `*`process`*.

The CDH init scripts are distributed within their own packages and must be installed separately, whereas Apache Hadoop is a single package that contains everything. CDH users: see "CDH" on page 80 for more information on installing init scripts.

Starting and Stopping Processes Manually

It is occasionally handy to be able to manually start a Hadoop daemon in the foreground as often happens when an administrator needs to debug odd behavior on a machine or when rapidly experimenting with different configuration parameters. Starting a process manually and running it in the foreground doesn't change its behavior, so all consequences of starting or stopping a process using the init scripts apply:

1. Become the user the process needs to run as (or use `sudo -u `*`username`* when executing commands).
2. Execute `hadoop `*`process`* to start the process, where *`process`* is one of the Hadoop daemons (see the help output of `hadoop` for a list). To stop the process, press Control+C or `kill `*`process-id`* from another terminal.

HDFS Maintenance Tasks

Adding a Datanode

Adding a datanode is done in response to a need for additional cluster capacity, usually in the case of additional storage requirements, although sometimes it is to increase aggregate IO bandwidth or to reduce the impact of losing a single machine. The addition of new datanodes to an existing HDFS cluster is an online or *hot* operation. For those that make use of the HDFS host include functionality, the IP address of the new host must be added to the include file, but the list of hosts can be dynamically refreshed without restarting the namenode:

1. Add the IP address of the datanode to the file specified by the `dfs.hosts` parameter. Each entry should be separated by a newline character.

2. Execute the command `hadoop dfsadmin -refreshNodes` as the HDFS superuser or a user with equivalent privileges.

3. If using rack awareness, update any rack information necessary for the new host.

4. Start the datanode process.

5. Check the namenode web UI or the output of `hadoop dfsadmin -report` to confirm that the new host is connected.

Steps 1 and 2 are required only if you are using the HDFS host include functionality.

Decommissioning a Datanode

A datanode may be decommissioned to remove it from the cluster gracefully while maintaining the replication factor of all blocks stored on the machine. The process can be lengthy, depending on the amount of data on the host, the activity of the cluster, and the speed of the network. Due to the length of the decommissioning process, it is not common for this to be done prior to brief host outages such as those caused by OS reboots or rolling restarts due to configuration changes. If it is imperative that all copies of a block data remain completely available, use the decommissioning function.

 The decommissioning process relies on the HDFS host include and exclude files. If you are not using these files, it is not possible to gracefully decommission a datanode.

Decommissioning a datanode results in increased network activity while HDFS creates new replicas of the block data on other datanodes in the cluster. When the process begins, the namenode UI will indicate that the decommissioning of one or more nodes is currently in progress. Upon completion, the status changes to decommissioned. At that point, the datanode process can be safely stopped:

1. Add the IP address of the datanode to the file specified by the `dfs.hosts.exclude` parameter. Each entry should be separated by a newline character.

2. Execute the command `hadoop dfsadmin -refreshNodes` as the HDFS super user or a user with equivalent privileges.

3. Monitor the namenode web UI and confirm the decommission process is in progress. It can take a few seconds to update.

4. Go get coffee or, for datanodes with a lot of data, go home for the night. Decommissioning can take hours or even days! When the process has completed, the namenode UI will list the datanode as decommissioned.

5. Stop the datanode process.

6. If you do not plan to reintroduce the machine to the cluster, remove it from the HDFS include and exclude files as well as any rack topology database.

7. Execute the command `hadoop dfsadmin -refreshNodes` to have the namenode pick up the removal.

Checking Filesystem Integrity with fsck

There are a few pathological conditions that can occur in HDFS. A file in HDFS can become corrupt if all copies of one or more blocks are unavailable, which would leave a hole in the file of up to the block size of the file, and any attempt to read a file in this state would result in a failure in the form of an exception. For this problem to occur, all copies of a block must become unavailable fast enough for the system to not have enough time to detect the failure and create a new replica of the data. Despite being rare, catastrophic failures like this can happen and when they do, administrators need a tool to detect the problem and help them find the missing blocks.

By default, the `fsck` tool generates a summary report that lists the overall health of the filesystem. HDFS is considered healthy if—and only if—all files have a minimum number of replicas available. A dot is printed for each file examined; the summary includes information about the number of total blocks, the average replication factor, available capacity, the number of missing blocks, and other important metrics:

```
[esammer@hadoop01 ~]$ sudo -u hdfs hadoop fsck /
FSCK started by hdfs (auth:SIMPLE) from /10.1.1.132 for path / at ↵
 Fri May 25 10:48:52 PDT 2012
..........................................................................................
..........................................................................................
.............................................Status: HEALTHY
 Total size:    9113209169518 B
 Total dirs:    9206
 Total files:   14649 (Files currently being written: 10)
 Total blocks (validated):     87640 (avg. block size 103984586 B) ↵
   (Total open file blocks (not validated): 10)
 Minimally replicated blocks:  87640 (100.0 %)
 Over-replicated blocks:       0 (0.0 %)
 Under-replicated blocks:      0 (0.0 %)
 Mis-replicated blocks:        0 (0.0 %)
 Default replication factor:   3
 Average block replication:    2.2504907
 Corrupt blocks:               0
 Missing replicas:             0 (0.0 %)
 Number of data-nodes:         10
 Number of racks:              1
FSCK ended at Fri May 25 10:47:32 PDT 2012 in 960 milliseconds
```

```
The filesystem under path '/' is HEALTHY
```

Hadoop's `fsck` is unlike Linux `fsck` in that it isn't destructive by default. Rather than running on a device, it also differs by checking a path (note the slash at the end of the previous command line). As you might expect, it is also possible to check only subtrees of the filesystem by providing a path other than the root.

A number of additional command-line options are supported by `fsck`:

```
[esammer@hadoop01 ~]$ sudo -u hdfs hadoop fsck
Usage: DFSck <path> [-move | -delete | -openforwrite] [-files [-blocks ↵
[-locations | -racks]]]
        <path>  start checking from this path
        -move   move corrupted files to /lost+found
        -delete delete corrupted files
        -files  print out files being checked
        -openforwrite   print out files opened for write
        -blocks print out block report
        -locations      print out locations for every block
        -racks  print out network topology for data-node locations
                By default fsck ignores files opened for write, use -openforwrite to ↵
                report such files. They are usually tagged CORRUPT or HEALTHY ↵
                depending on their block allocation status
...
```

The `-files`, `-blocks`, and `-locations` options can be used to figure out exactly which files are affected by missing blocks, as well as which blocks fall on which datanodes. In the event of a failure, it's important to be able to read the detailed fsck output:

```
[esammer@hadoop01 ~]$ sudo -u hdfs hadoop fsck / -files -blocks -locations
FSCK started by hdfs (auth:SIMPLE) from /10.1.1.132 for path / at ↵
  Fri May 25 17:20:33 PDT 2012
/ <dir>
...
/hbase/usertable/a8a0829c1661099e80f4d619a4a8b77d <dir>❶
/hbase/usertable/a8a0829c1661099e80f4d619a4a8b77d/.regioninfo ↵
  866 bytes, 1 block(s): OK❷
0. blk_3620806743122792301_938094 len=866 repl=3 ↵
  [10.1.1.140:1004, 10.1.1.135:1004, 10.1.1.137:1004]❸

/hbase/usertable/a8a0829c1661099e80f4d619a4a8b77d/.tmp <dir>
/hbase/usertable/a8a0829c1661099e80f4d619a4a8b77d/value <dir>
/hbase/usertable/a8a0829c1661099e80f4d619a4a8b77d/value/7404071833681777848 ↵
  544152382 bytes, 9 block(s): OK❹
0. blk_-4483752819038443375_961039 len=67108864 repl=3 ↵
  [10.1.1.136:1004, 10.1.1.132:1004, 10.1.1.135:1004]
1. blk_-9090271957364756334_961045 len=67108864 repl=3 ↵
  [10.1.1.134:1004, 10.1.1.139:1004, 10.1.1.135:1004]
2. blk_-8663933707558762843_961045 len=67108864 repl=3 ↵
  [10.1.1.136:1004, 10.1.1.133:1004, 10.1.1.135:1004]
3. blk_-243708713912215859_961046 len=67108864 repl=3 ↵
  [10.1.1.131:1004, 10.1.1.136:1004, 10.1.1.135:1004]
4. blk_8889057014155026774_961047 len=67108864 repl=3 ↵
  [10.1.1.136:1004, 10.1.1.135:1004, 10.1.1.137:1004]
```

```
 5. blk_-8973735748029935709_961048 len=67108864 repl=3 ↵
    [10.1.1.131:1004, 10.1.1.136:1004, 10.1.1.135:1004]
 6. blk_2457643535020786460_961048 len=67108864 repl=3 ↵
    [10.1.1.131:1004, 10.1.1.133:1004, 10.1.1.135:1004]
 7. blk_-903758822242531603_961049 len=67108864 repl=3 ↵
    [10.1.1.131:1004, 10.1.1.133:1004, 10.1.1.135:1004]
 8. blk_4446759321669624116_961051 len=7281470 repl=3 ↵
    [10.1.1.137:1004, 10.1.1.132:1004, 10.1.1.135:1004]
...
/user/esammer/job17/part-00077 12500000000 bytes, 94 block(s):
 Under replicated blk_-3488281800025438592_84806. ↵
   Target Replicas is 3 but found 2 replica(s).❺
 Under replicated blk_-1241890260240671450_84813. ↵
   Target Replicas is 3 but found 2 replica(s).
 Under replicated blk_2951198656702268751_84813. ↵
   Target Replicas is 3 but found 2 replica(s).
 Under replicated blk_2030140999874428901_84815. ↵
   Target Replicas is 3 but found 2 replica(s).
...
 0. blk_2806218775441650422_84812 len=134217728 repl=3 ↵
    [10.1.1.136:1004, 10.1.1.135:1004, 10.1.1.139:1004]❻
 1. blk_-7693415728714491276_84812 len=134217728 repl=3 ↵
    [10.1.1.140:1004, 10.1.1.139:1004, 10.1.1.137:1004]
 2. blk_-4047400381436606420_84812 len=134217728 repl=3 ↵
    [10.1.1.136:1004, 10.1.1.134:1004, 10.1.1.139:1004]
 3. blk_6268554594414163694_84812 len=134217728 repl=3 ↵
    [10.1.1.132:1004, 10.1.1.136:1004, 10.1.1.139:1004]
 4. blk_437166175380747476_84813 len=134217728 repl=3 ↵
    [10.1.1.138:1004, 10.1.1.132:1004, 10.1.1.139:1004]
 5. blk_-3373529866329232880_84814 len=134217728 repl=2 ↵
    [10.1.1.137:1004, 10.1.1.139:1004]
 6. blk_-6567492536488398932_84815 len=134217728 repl=3 ↵
    [10.1.1.137:1004, 10.1.1.132:1004, 10.1.1.139:1004]
 7. blk_-5068856556266368904_84815 len=134217728 repl=3 ↵
    [10.1.1.138:1004, 10.1.1.137:1004, 10.1.1.139:1004]
...
/user/esammer/job18/part-00018: CORRUPT block blk_-7164267453697813302❼
 MISSING 125 blocks of total size 16648440800 B
 0. blk_2190128488155518392_86488 len=134217728 MISSING!
 1. blk_6387562258768894352_86505 len=134217728 MISSING!
 2. blk_-2266931705749612258_86516 len=134217728 MISSING!
...
Status: CORRUPT
 Total size:    9113209169518 B (Total open files size: 372 B)
 Total dirs:    9206
 Total files:   14649 (Files currently being written: 10)
 Total blocks (validated):    87640 (avg. block size 103984586 B) ↵
   (Total open file blocks (not validated): 10)
   ******************************
   CORRUPT FILES:     21
   MISSING BLOCKS:    3846
   MISSING SIZE:      514487882400 B
   CORRUPT BLOCKS:    3846
   ******************************
 Minimally replicated blocks:    83794 (95.611595 %)❽
```

```
Over-replicated blocks:        0 (0.0 %)
Under-replicated blocks:       4684 (5.3445916 %)❾
Mis-replicated blocks:         0 (0.0 %)
Default replication factor:    3
Average block replication:     2.1531606
Corrupt blocks:                3846❿
Missing replicas:              4684 (2.4822075 %)⓫
Number of data-nodes:          9
Number of racks:               1
FSCK ended at Fri May 25 17:20:34 PDT 2012 in 573 milliseconds

The filesystem under path '/' is CORRUPT
```

❶ Directories are marked with <dir> and have no blocks. They exist only within the metadata of the namenode.

❷ A regular file in HDFS, listed with its size, the number of blocks it contains, and its current status (either OK or CORRUPT).

❸ A block entry. This is the first block (blocks are zero-indexed) in the file. It has a length of 866 bytes and 3 replicas that can be found on the datanodes with the IP addresses 10.1.1.140, 10.1.1.135, and 10.1.1.137.

❹ A healthy file with nine blocks.

❺ A file with missing replicas. This is usually the result when a datanode fails and HDFS is in the process of creating new replicas. The file is said to be under-replicated but healthy because at least one replica exists for all blocks. A list of the under-replicated blocks appears immediately after the filename.

❻ The block list of a file with under-replicated blocks. Block number 5 (blk_-3373529866329232880_84814) displays a replication factor of 2; the other blocks have three replicas.

❼ A corrupt file, missing all replicas of at least one block. In this example, the file is missing 125 blocks, or more than 15GB of data.

❽ The number of blocks that are minimally replicated. These files are healthy and can still be read.

❾ Under-replicated blocks are those that do not currently have the desired number of copies. HDFS automatically repairs missing replicas over time by making new replicas from available replicas.

❿ A corrupt block (as opposed to a file) is one that has no available replicas.

⓫ The total number of missing blocks.

A truly healthy HDFS has no under-replicated, corrupt, or missing blocks. In the normal course of operation, occasional network failures or host reboots can affect temporary under-replicated blocks and aren't cause for a major concern. A complete datanode failure will result in a spike in the number of under-replicated blocks, followed by a slow decrease over time and should be monitored.

Running the `fsck` utility is a metadata-only operation. In other words, because all information `fsck` uses can be obtained from the namenode, there's no need for it to communicate with the datanodes in the cluster. The most interesting implication is that `fsck` always returns the current state of the filesystem, according to the namenode. The number of remote procedure calls made to the namenode can be high (ultimately, it depends on the number of files in HDFS), so take care to perform checks during off-peak times, when possible. At first glance, it may seem like `fsck` is a reasonable way to monitor HDFS health, but many of the metrics it provides can be accessed programmatically (and less computationally expensive) via the monitoring APIs. See Chapter 10 for more information on configuring metric collection and monitoring. To run the `fsck` utility:

1. Log in to the the machine running the namenode.
2. Become the HDFS superuser or a user with equivalent privileges.
3. Execute `hadoop fsck /` with the desired options.

> To filter the onslaught of dots that `fsck` generates during a check, try running `hadoop fsck / | grep -v -E '^\.'` instead. This command will filter all lines that begin with a dot, removing much of the noise and making the output more readable.

Balancing HDFS Block Data

Although the namenode attempts to distribute blocks evenly between datanodes when it's written, it is still possible for HDFS to become unbalanced. A poor distribution of block data can reduce data locality in MapReduce, increasing network utilization and reducing job performance, as well as wearing on the disks in some datanodes more than others. This issue normally occurs in one of three cases: the addition of a new datanode, mass deletion of data, or unevenly colocated clients.

> Although running the balancer regularly can help with disk utilization and MapReduce job performance, HBase is rather intolerant of it for reasons related to how region servers read and access data. HBase users should *not* run the balancer, even after adding new nodes. HBase regularly rewrites its data files (during a major compaction), which "fixes" block distribution and data locality anyway.

Adding a new datanode to an existing cluster creates an imbalance in block data because the new node's disks are empty, while the rest of the datanodes maintain their existing load. HDFS does not automatically move blocks to a node when it is added to the cluster. Although it's true that it will receive blocks from newly written files, HDFS will continue to distribute these blocks evenly across all datanodes within the cluster. If the namenode were to assign all new blocks to the new datanode instead, it would become a bottleneck, impeding data ingestion as well as MapReduce job output.

Rapid deletion of a large set of existing files may result in some datanodes having fewer blocks than others. This, of course, depends on how well the files in question were distributed with respect to one another—something not commonly measured. As a contrived example, consider a cluster of three nodes in which nine one-block files are written, each with a replication factor of 1 (in other words, each block corresponds to an entire file). Further, assume a pure round-robin distribution of blocks across the three nodes: datanode A would receive files 1, 4, and 7; datanode B 2, 5, and 8; and datanote C 3, 6, and 9. You can see how deleting a specific group of files such as 1, 4, and 7 could create disparity between nodes. Of course, the way the namenode chooses to place blocks is not that simple—files usually have more than one block and clusters have many more than three nodes—but this example should give you some idea of how the problem can occur.

One of the most common (and sneaky) ways HDFS can become unbalanced is when some nodes of the cluster nodes have colocated clients, while others do not. For lack of a better term, a *colocated client* is an HDFS client that is running on a node that is also a member of the HDFS cluster (or more precisely, a node that is a datanode). The reason this situation is important has to do with the intended use case of HDFS: Map-Reduce. In MapReduce, reducers write data to HDFS in almost all cases. Further, it's true that local disk IO is greater than writing to a disk across the network. It is for this reason that the namenode will assign the local machine as the destination for the first replica when an HDFS client is running on a datanode. If you consider that reducers are usually evenly distributed throughout the cluster, tasktrackers and datanodes are always colocated, and writing a local disk is faster than across the network, it makes sense that colocated clients should always pick their local disk for the first replica. In classic B-rated horror film tradition: what could possibly go wrong?

It turns out that in order to mitigate cost, it's not uncommon for some to select a subset of the cluster nodes to double as data ingest nodes on which they place services such as Flume or other processes that write data into HDFS. The problem with this is that the disks on these nodes fill faster than others because they're always selected for the first replica of every block written to HDFS. The tell-tale sign of unevenly colocated clients is to look at the disk usage of all of the datanodes relative to one another (a view available within the namenode web UI); machines that act as clients in addition to being datanodes will show significantly higher disk usage than others.

To be clear, there's nothing wrong with colocating clients with datanodes. In fact, this ability is a feature of HDFS and the block placement policy. The pathological case of uneven block distribution arises when clients are unevenly distributed within the cluster. In some cases, it can't be helped—there may be no other place where a client can be run. In these instances, running the balancer regularly might be sufficient, or might at least stave off the problem until other accommodations can be made.

The balancer works by first calculating the average block count per datanode and then examining each datanode's deviation from the average. If a node is below some percentage, it is said to be under-utilized; a node above some percentage is over-utilized.

This percentage is called the *threshold* and by default, it is 10%. Many administrators find that they run the balancer and it immediately exits, stating that the cluster is balanced. Usually, this is because the nodes are within the default threshold, which is a wide range (remember, it's plus/minus the threshold, so two nodes may have a difference of 20%). Specifying a threshold that is too small can lead to a balancer that never completes on an active cluster. If you're unsure, start with 5% and adjust accordingly.

The most notable effect of running the balancer is the amount of network bandwidth it can consume. Fortunately, it is possible to control the rate at which data is transferred over the network using the `dfs.balance.bandwidthPerSec` property. Bear in mind that this is actually a property of the datanode and not the utility itself, as the datanode is what actually performs the block transfers (it cannot be modified without restarting the datanodes). Additionally, `dfs.balance.bandwidthPerSec` is defined in bytes rather than bits, as you might expect.

Data transfer does not pass through the machine on which you run the balancer, although the balancer does need to be able to communicate with the namenode. Interrupting the balancer while it's running is perfectly fine; block transfers in progress are aborted and no new transfers will begin. Block replication is atomic from a client's perspective so there's no danger of a client seeing a partially replicated block. Balancing HDFS block data also requires administrator privileges, as with other administrative commands:

1. Become the HDFS superuser or a user with equivalent privileges (or use `sudo -u` *username* when executing commands).

2. Execute `hadoop balancer -threshold` *N* to run the balancer in the foreground, where *N* is the percentage of blocks within which datanodes should be with one another. To stop the process prematurely, press Control+C or `kill` *process-id* from another terminal. Alternatively, Apache Hadoop users can run the process in the background using the `start-balancer.sh` script; CDH users should use the `hadoop-0.20-balancer` init script.

3. Monitor the output (or log file, if you choose to run the balancer in the background) to track progress.

Dealing with a Failed Disk

With a large number of machines that each have many disks, it's not unusual for disks to fail. Both HDFS and MapReduce are built to tolerate disk failures, as you've seen, but at some point failed disks do need to be replaced. Disk failures in worker nodes are usually much simpler to handle than those that occur on master nodes. The process involves temporarily removing the node from the cluster, replacing the drives, and reintroducing the node. Worker processes such as the datanode and tasktracker can be stopped to remove the affected node from the cluster prior to performing maintenance, as described in "Starting and Stopping Processes with Init Scripts" on page 195. In extremely busy clusters, it may make sense (time permitting) to follow the decommissioning process (see "Decommissioning a Data-node" on page 197) for the datanode to maintain a full complement of replicas.

Technically Hadoop doesn't detect bad disks. Instead, it checks specific attributes of special directories such as the datanode block directories (`dfs.data.dir`) and MapReduce scratch space (`mapred.local.dir`). A path is said to be healthy and available if and only if the following are all true:

1. The specified path is a directory.
2. The directory exists.
3. The directory is readable.
4. The directory is writable.

A path that doesn't meet all of these criteria is reported as failed. Any blocks (in the case of the datanode) that were in this directory are assumed to be lost and are removed from the list of blocks that the datanode in question considers available. When the datanode detects one of these failures, it logs the condition and sends an updated block report to the namenode. The namenode then updates the replication count for the affected blocks and creates new replicas of the now under-replicated blocks.

The datanode will shut down if more disks than `dfs.datanode.failed.volumes.toler ated` fail. By default, this parameter is set to zero, which means that a single disk failure results in the entire datanode failing. Some believe that a machine should remove itself from the cluster in the face of any failures; others feel it's fine to tolerate some low number of failures. Either way, `dfs.datanode.failed.volumes.tolerated` should be a low number, as a large number of disk failures usually indicates a larger problem such as a failed controller. Follow these steps:

1. Stop any Hadoop-related processes (optionally following the decommissioning process for the datanode).
2. Replace any failed disks.
3. Follow the process for adding the node back into the cluster.
4. Run the Hadoop `fsck` utility to validate the health of HDFS. Over-replicated blocks are normal immediately after a node is reintroduced to the cluster, which is automatically corrected over time.

MapReduce Maintenance Tasks

Adding a Tasktracker

Tasktrackers, like datanodes, immediately connect to their master process (the job-tracker) upon startup. Each heartbeat sent to the jobtracker advertises the available number of map and reduce slots available on the node, with assignment taking place in the response to the heartbeat. Before starting the tasktracker, the datanode should be started and HDFS balanced. This isn't a technical requirement, so don't panic if the processes are started in the opposite order, but performing these tasks in this order ensures that when the tasktracker is assigned work, there is local block data. If the tasktracker is started before the datanode, there will be no data locally available and all block data will be streamed across the network. This situation can lead to a storm of network traffic that impacts data ingestion or other tasks running on the cluster. The steps are as follows:

1. Follow the procedure for adding a datanode to HDFS.
2. Run the balancer utility to distribute existing block data to the new datanode.
3. Start the tasktracker process.
4. Confirm that the jobtracker can communicate with the new tasktracker by checking the number of available tasktrackers in its web user interface.

Decommissioning a Tasktracker

Unlike the datanode, there is no graceful way to decommission a tasktracker. Administrators tend to rely on the task failure and retry semantics of MapReduce when removing a tasktracker from the cluster. That is, a tasktracker process is stopped with the assumption that any currently executing tasks will fail and be rescheduled elsewhere on the cluster. It is possible that a task on its final attempt is running on the tasktracker in question and that a final failure may result in the entire job failing. Unfortunately, in an active cluster, it's not always possible to detect and prevent this case from occurring. For this reason, developers should be strongly encouraged, if not required, to build production processes that are resilient to job failures (usually by monitoring their status and resubmitting them, should they fail). Ad hoc MapReduce jobs are usually less of a concern, although failures are still undesirable. To decommission a tasktracker:

1. Stop the tasktracker process.
2. Monitor currently executing MapReduce jobs to confirm that task failures are rescheduled and any job-level failures are properly addressed.

Killing a MapReduce Job

Sometimes it's necessary to kill a MapReduce job executing on the cluster. Normally, this is done in response to a user request (in the case of interactive, ad hoc jobs) or an errant production job. Killing a MapReduce job is akin to terminating a SQL query in a relational database; the job, including any outstanding tasks, is abandoned, and the client that initiated it is notified that it has failed to complete. Any temporary map output data as well as partially written reducer output is discarded. To kill the job, complete the following steps:

1. Become the HDFS superuser or a user with equivalent privileges (or use `sudo -u` *username* when executing commands).

2. Execute `hadoop job -list` or use the jobtracker web user interface to find the job ID of the job you wish to terminate.

3. Execute `hadoop job -kill` *jobID* to terminate the job.

4. Confirm that the job is terminated using `hadoop job -list` or by checking the jobtracker web user interface.

Killing a MapReduce Task

Although it is occasionally necessary to kill an entire MapReduce job, other times call for a lighter touch. The stateless paradigm of MapReduce task processing (save for the attempt counter) enables administrators to kill tasks of a job that may be misbehaving rather than the job itself. This approach can be useful if a specific task is causing a problem on a machine and the administrator would like the framework to relocate the work. By killing the task, we can force the jobtracker to reattempt the work elsewhere. Unfortunately, it's not guaranteed that the jobtracker will select another worker; sometimes the task will be immediately reassigned to the same machine. It does, however, force the task to reenter the scheduler queue, possibly delaying execution of the task and reducing temporary contention for system resources, for instance.

It is possible that a task is experiencing problems not because of the worker on which it executes but because of the data it is assigned to process. We'll discuss common reasons tasks fail in Chapter 9. To kill the task:

1. Become the HDFS superuser, a user with equivalent privileges, or the owner of the MapReduce job (or use `sudo -u` *username* when executing commands).

2. Locate the task attempt you wish to kill using `hadoop job -list-attempt-ids` *jobID* *taskType* *taskState*, where *jobID* is the job ID of the job that contains the task attempt, *taskType* is the type of task (such as map, reduce), and *taskState* is the current state of the task (such as running, completed). Alternatively, the jobtracker web user interface can be used to locate the task attempt ID.

3. Execute `hadoop job -kill-task` *taskAttemptId* to kill the task.

Dealing with a Blacklisted Tasktracker

With a large number of machines in a cluster, it's not uncommon for individual machines to fail for one reason or another. In some cases, these failures are *soft* failures, in which the machine continues to operate but throws spurious errors that cause MapReduce tasks to fail. To protect the cluster from misbehaving hosts, Hadoop MapReduce can temporarily blacklist machines, removing them from the available pool of workers, either for a single job or globally.

The heuristic for blacklisting a tasktracker is simple but effective. Any tasktracker with three or more failed tasks from a single job is ineligible to receive any further tasks for that job. This is Hadoop's penalty box. Tasks from others jobs may still be assigned to the (potentially) problematic tasktracker during this time. Tasktrackers may be black-listed at the job level from time to time, usually due to poorly written MapReduce code in which tasks rapidly fail due to an error in logic.

Sometimes, however, the failures are persistent over multiple MapReduce jobs. These failures are more severe, in that they impact the health of many unrelated jobs, each of which now has tasks that must be reattempted. If tasks continue to fail on the same tasktracker, the jobtracker adds the host to a global blacklist and it will not receive any work for 24 hours, by default. This issue is indicative of something wrong with the configuration of the host or the hardware itself and should be diagnosed at the first opportunity. Because the cluster can protect itself by quarantining tasktrackers this way, it's usually unnecessary to wake up a human in the middle of the night for such an incident. A rapid increase in the number of machines in the global blacklist, however, is cause for alarm and is almost always due to misconfiguration on an active cluster.

Currently, there is no graceful way to administratively remove a machine from the global blacklist. The jobtracker retains this information in memory. A less than polite way of forcing the jobtracker to forgive a host is to restart either the offending task-tracker (which will register as a new instance with the jobtracker upon restart) or the jobtracker, in which case the blacklist is cleared entirely. Restarting the jobtracker tends to be invasive, as it also discards all information about all currently executing MapReduce jobs.

There is a parameter called `mapred.jobtracker.restart.recover` that, when set to true, attempts to serialize the jobtracker's state to disk so that it may be preserved between restarts. Some users have reported that this feature, though desirable, is not always reliable. In some cases, the jobtracker is unable to recover its state when restarting and all job in-formation is lost. Additionally, enabling this parameter significantly in-creases the startup time of the jobtracker. For these reasons, many ad-ministrators choose to leave this feature disabled.

## CHAPTER 9

Troubleshooting

Throughout this book, the notion that Hadoop is a distributed system made up of layered services has been a repeating theme. The interaction between these layers is what makes a system like this so complex and so difficult to troubleshoot. With complex moving parts, interdependent systems, sensitivity to environmental conditions and external factors, and numerous potential causes for numerous potential conditions, Hadoop starts to look like the human body. We'll treat it as such (with my apologies to the medical field as a whole).

Differential Diagnosis Applied to Systems

A significant portion of problems encountered with systems, in general, remain so because of improper diagnosis.[1] You cannot fix something when you don't know what's truly wrong. The medical field commonly uses a differential diagnosis process as a way of investigating symptoms and their likelihood in order to properly diagnose a patient with a condition. Differential diagnoses, for those of us without an MD, is essentially a knowledge- and data-driven process of elimination whereby tests are performed to confirm or reject a potential condition. In fact, this isn't as exotic a concept as it initially sounds when you think about how our brains attack these kinds of problems. It does, however, help to formalize such an approach and follow it, especially when things go wrong and your boss is standing over your shoulder asking you every five minutes whether it's fixed yet. When things go wrong, take a long, deep, breath and put on your white coat.

1. Develop a patient history.

    Each patient (a host, cluster, network) has a story to tell. Gather a history of what has occurred most recently to the various components of the system that may help

---

1. I have no empirical data to back this argument up. Anecdotally, however, it has been true in teams I've been a part of, managed, or talked to, and I'd put money on it being universally so.

in diagnosis. Recent maintenance operations, configuration changes, new hardware, and changes in load are all points of interest.

2. Develop a list of potential diagnoses.

   Write them down on a whiteboard. Nothing is dumb, but each diagnosis should pass the sniff test. Nothing comes off the list without a test that disproves the diagnosis as a possibility.

3. Sort the list by likelihood.

   Given what you know about the probability that a condition occurs in the wild, but also in the context of the patient and the environment, sort the list of diagnoses. The most common ailments should float to the top of the list; they're common for a reason. Examine the patient history for anything that would change your mind about the probability something is the root cause of the problem. Hold tight to Occam's razor, and when you hear hooves, look for horses, not zebras (*http://en .wikipedia.org/wiki/Zebra_(medicine)*)—unless you're in an area where zebras are incredibly common.

4. Test!

   Systematically work down the list, performing tests that either confirm or reject a given condition. Tests that eliminate multiple potential conditions should be performed sooner rather than later. Update the list if you find new information that would indicate you missed a potential condition. If you do update the list, go back to step 3 and repeat the process.

5. Diagnosis.

   As you work through various tests, you'll either find the problem or come out with no diagnosis. If you eliminate all possibilities, you've either missed a possible diagnosis in step 2 or incorrectly eliminated one based on a bad test (or misinterpretation of the results).

The tests performed when diagnosing systems are actually faster (and certainly cheaper) than what doctors need to do. The complete battery usually includes OS utilities such as `top`, `vmstat`, `sar`, `iostat`, and `netstat`, but also Hadoop-specific tools such as `hadoop dfsadmin`, and `hadoop fsck`. Log files are how machines communicate with us, so make sure you're always listening to what they have to say.

All of this sounds silly—and we're not necessarily saving lives. That said, the process of critical evaluation of data to arrive at an informed decision is nothing to laugh at. This method of looking at problems and solutions works, but it's only as good as the information you have. We'll use this approach to diagnosing problems encountered with Hadoop and point out some specific examples where it was used to find rather unintuitive problems in production systems.

Common Failures and Problems

There's an abundance of things that can go wrong with Hadoop. Like other systems, it's subject to the host environment on which its daemons run, but additionally so on the union of all hosts within the cluster. It's this latter part that complicates any system to such a degree. All of the standard things that can happen on a single host are magnified when hosts and services become dependent upon one another. The management and configuration of any distributed system dramatically increases the universe of things that can go wrong, and Hadoop is no exception to that.

Just as doctors have the Diagnostic and Statistical Manual of Mental Disorders (*http:// www.psych.org/practice/dsm*), or DSM, to describe and codify the known universe of disorders, administrators too need a set of known conditions and criteria for classification. What follows is a short list of some of the more prevalent conditions found when diagnosing Hadoop.

Humans (You)

More than anything, humans tend to cause the most havoc when it comes to the health of systems and machines. Even the most innocuous, mundane tasks can easily result in downtime. This isn't specifically a Hadoop problem as much as it is a general system administration issue. I'll put my money where my mouth is on this one and share a story with you.

I was once dispatched to a data center to fix a redundant loop that failed on a large SAN backing a production relational database. The system was up and running but had simply lost a redundant link; it was degraded. After all due diligence and planning, I left the office and went to the data center, laptop in hand, to fix the problem. Once in the data center, I carefully opened the racks, checked the physical state of everything, and confirmed that there was sufficient capacity on one of power distribution units in the racks with the storage before I plugged in my laptop...or so I thought. I plugged in the laptop and powered it on and immediately tripped a circuit in the rack. I panicked for a second until I realized that all power was redundant, fed by different circuits. Unfortunately, everything switching over at once must have caused a spike in load, or maybe some fans spun up, but within a few seconds, the redundant circuit popped as well and in the cabinet containing the SAN controller. Everything went quiet in the aisle, as if in observance of a moment of silence for what I had just done. Turns out, I just wasn't careful enough when I read the PDU display on power consumption and someone else had run a couple power cables from the next rack over when installing some machines a few days earlier. We worked fast and fixed the problem, but we all learned a couple of lessons that day (especially me) about the *real* cause of failures.

In retrospect, it's easy to see all of the things that went wrong and how silly the whole situation was. It was entirely preventable (in fact, nothing like it ever happened again). You can never be careful enough. Every system administrator has a horror story. What's truly important is recognizing the *likelihood* of such a situation so that it takes a proper place in the diagnostic process.

Misconfiguration

Kathleen Ting, a manager on Cloudera's support team gave a talk (*http://bit.ly/cloudera _talk*) at HadoopWorld 2011 in New York City, supported by research done by Ari Rabkin, where she talked about common failures and their cause. She revealed that 35% of tickets handled by the Cloudera support team were due to some kind of misconfiguration, within either Hadoop or the operating system. Further, these tickets accounted for 40% of the time spent by the team resolving issues with customers. This is not to say that the users were necessarily twiddling configuration parameters randomly—in fact, many are advanced users of multiple projects in the Hadoop ecosystem—but that the interaction between the numerous parameters leads to all kinds of unintended behavior.

It's possible to dismiss that argument and say that Hadoop is still young technology, that this situation will improve in time. Take the Oracle relational database, one of the most widely deployed relational database systems today. Many agree that with its myriad parameters, it can be incredibly difficult to configure optimally. In fact, it's so specialized that it even has its own job title: Oracle Database Administrator. Now consider that Oracle, as a product, is about 32 years old. This kind of story is not unique (although maybe Oracle is an extreme example) in large, complex systems.

So what can be done to mitigate misconfiguration? Here are a few tips:

- Develop a solid understanding of the precedence of configuration value overrides.
- Start with the basic parameters required for operation, such as storage locations, hostnames, and resource controls. Make sure that the cluster works with the minimal necessary set before graduating to the performance- and security-related parameters.
- Before setting anything, make sure you have a good idea about what it does.
- Double-check the unit of each parameter you set. Many parameters are expressed in bytes; a few are in megabytes.
- With each release, look for any parameters that changed in meaning or scope. Audit your configuration files frequently.
- Use a configuration management and deployment system to ensure that all files are up-to-date on all hosts and that daemons are properly restarted to affect changes.
- Before and after making configuration changes, run a subset of MapReduce jobs to evaluate the performance and resource consumption impact of the changes.

Beyond Hadoop proper, operating system misconfiguration is an equal source of pain in maintaining health clusters. Common problems include incorrect permissions on log and data directories and resource limits such as the maximum allowed number of simultaneously opened files being set to their defaults. This problem tends to happen when the initial setup and configuration of machines is not automated and the cluster is expanded. Clusters configured by hand run a significant risk of a single configuration step being accidentally missed. Of course, those who read through the recommendations in Chapters 4 and 5 should be able to dodge most of the fun and excitement of misconfiguration, but it happens to the best of us. Always have it on your list of potential culprits when generating your list of potential conditions.

Hardware Failure

As sure as the sun will rise, hardware will fail. It's not unheard of to have problems with memory, motherboards, and disk controllers, but the shining gem of the problematic component kingdom is the hard drive. One of the few components with moving parts in the modern server, the hard drive suffers from physical wear and tear during normal operations. All drive manufacturers advertise one of a number of different measures of drive failure rates: mean time to failure (MTTR), mean time between failures (MTBF), or annualized failure rate (AFR). The way these numbers are calculated can be confusing, and it's worth noting that they all apply to averages over a given period of time for a specific population, not the specific devices living in your machines. In other words, expect failures at all times, regardless of advertised metrics. Have spare components at the ready whenever possible, especially for mission-critical clusters.

Unfortunately, hardware rarely fails outright. Instead, it tends to degrade over time, leading to subtle, temporary failures that are compensated for by software components. Hadoop is excellent at masking, by way of compensation, impending hardware failures. HDFS will detect corrupt data blocks and automatically create new, correct replicas from other healthy copies of the data without human intervention. MapReduce automatically retries failed tasks, temporarily blacklists misbehaving hosts, and uses speculative execution to compensate for under-performing hardware. All of these features double as masking agents, so although this functionality is critical, it is not a panacea. You shouldn't need to wake up in the middle of the night for a corrupt HDFS block, but you should always track the rate of anomalous conditions in an effort to root out bad hardware.

Resource Exhaustion

CPU cycles, memory, disk space and IO, and network bandwidth are all finite resources for which various processes contend in a cluster. Resource exhaustion can be seen as a specialized subclass of misconfiguration. After all, an administrator is responsible for controlling resource allocation by way of configuration. Either way, it does occur and it tends to be high on the list of things that go wrong in the wild.

Resource allocation can be seen as a hierarchy. A cluster contains many hosts, which contain various resources that are divided amongst any tasks that need to run. Orthogonally, both the Hadoop daemons and user tasks consume these resources. It's possible that a disk running out of space causes a Hadoop daemon to fail or a task hits its maximum JVM heap size and is killed as a result; these are both equal examples of resource exhaustion. Because Hadoop accepts arbitrary code from users, it's extremely difficult to know in advance what they might do. This is one of the reasons Hadoop has so many parameters to control and sandbox user tasks. The framework inherently does not trust user-supplied code and for good reason, as task failures due to bugs or job-level misconfiguration are extremely common.

You should measure and track task failures to help users identify and correct misbehaving processes. Repetitive task failures occupy task slots and take resources away from other jobs and should be seen as a drain on overall capacity. Conversely, starving the Hadoop daemons for resources is detrimental to all users and can negatively affect throughput and SLAs. Proper allocation of system resources to the framework and your users is just as critical in Hadoop as it is any other service in the data center.

Host Identification and Naming

Like resource exhaustion, host identification and naming must be explicitly called out as a special kind of misconfiguration. The way that a worker host identifies itself to the namenode and jobtracker is the same way clients will attempt to contact it, which leads to interesting types of failures where a datanode, because of a misconfigured */etc/ hosts* entry, reports its loopback device IP address to namenode and successfully heartbeats, only to create a situation in which clients can never communicate with it. These types of problems commonly occur at initial cluster setup time, but they can burn countless hours for administrators while they try and find the root cause of the problem. The Hadoop mailing lists, for instance, are full of problems that can ultimately be traced back to identification and name resolution problems.

Network Partitions

A network partition is (informally) described as any case in which hosts on one segment of a network cannot communicate with hosts on another segment of the network. Trivially, this can mean that host A on switch 1 cannot send messages to host B on switch 2. The reason why they cannot communicate is purposefully left undefined here because it usually doesn't matter;[2] a switch, cable, NIC, or even host failure of the recipient all look the same to the sender participating in the connection (or vice versa). More subtly, a delay in delivering messages from one host to another above a certain threshold is functionality identical to not delivering the message at all. In other words, if a host is unable to get a response within its acceptable timeout from another machine,

---

2. Cloudera engineer Henry Robinson wrote a fantastic blog (*http://www.cloudera.com/blog/2010/04/cap -confusion-problems-with-partition-tolerance/*) post covering this in the context of the CAP theorem.

this case is indistinguishable from its partner simply being completely unavailable. In many cases, that's exactly how Hadoop will treat such a condition.

Network partitions are dubious in that they can just as easily be the symptom or the condition. For example, if one were to disable the switch port to which a host were connected, it would certainly be the root cause of a number of failures in communication between clients and the host in question. On the other hand, if the process that should receive messages from a client were to garbage collect for an excessive period of time, it might appear to the client as if the host became unavailable through some fault of the network. Further, short of absolute hardware failure, many network partitions are transient, leaving you with *only* symptoms remaining by the time you investigate. An historical view of the system, with proper collection of various metrics, is the only chance one has to distinguish these cases from one another.

"Is the Computer Plugged In?"

Let's be honest: there's no simple script to follow when performing tests to confirm or reject a diagnosis. There are different frameworks you can use, though, to make sure you cover all bases. It isn't feasible to walk through a multihundred-line-long call-center-style script when you're in the middle of a crisis. Again, in contrast to the medical field, doctors are taught silly little mnemonics to help them remember the various systems to consider when troubleshooting human beings. Given that they (arguably) have a lot more on the line than most administrators dealing with a problematic cluster, we'll build on their wisdom and experience. Hang on—things are about to get a little cheesy.

E-SPORE

In the midst of all the action when a failure does occur, it's important to follow some kind of process to make sure you don't miss performing a critical test. Just as coming up with the complete list of potential causes of a failure is important, you must be able to correctly confirm or reject each using the appropriate tests. It's not unusual that administrators forget to check something, and it's not always clear where to start. When you're at a loss or when you want to make sure you've thought of everything, try E-SPORE. E-SPORE is a mnemonic device to help you remember to examine each part of a distributed system while troubleshooting:

Environment
> Look at what's currently happening in the environment. Are there any glaring, obvious issues? Usually something has drawn your attention to a failure, such as a user filing a ticket or a monitoring system complaining about something. Is this unusual, given the history of the system? What is different about the environment now from the last time everything worked?

Stack

Consider the dependencies in the stack. The MapReduce service depends on HDFS being up, running, and healthy. Within each service lives another level of dependencies. All of HDFS depends on the namenode, which depends on its host OS, for example. There's also the more specific dependencies within the services like the jobtracker's dependency on the namenode for discovering block locations for scheduling, or an HBase region server's dependency on the ZooKeeper quorum. The entire cluster also has shared dependency on data center infrastructure such as the network, DNS, and other services. If the jobtracker appears to be failing to schedule jobs, maybe it's failing to communicate with the namenode.

Patterns

Look for a pattern in the failure. When MapReduce tasks begin to fail in a seemingly random way, look closer. Are the tasks from the same job? Are they all assigned to the same tasktracker? Do they all use a shared library that was changed recently? Patterns exist at various levels within the system. If you don't see one within a failed job, zoom out to the larger ETL process, then the cluster.

Output

Hadoop communicates its ailments to us by way of its logs. Always check log output for exceptions. Sometimes the error is logically far from the original cause (or the symptom is not immediately indicative of the disease). For instance, you might see a Java `NullPointerException` that caused a task to fail, but that was only the side effect of something that happened earlier that was the real root cause of the error. In fact, in distributed systems like Hadoop, it's not uncommon for the cause of the error to be on the other side of the network. If a datanode can't connect to the namenode, have you tried looking in the namenode's logs as well as the datanode?

Resources

All daemons need resources to operate, and as you saw earlier, resource exhaustion is far too common. Make sure local disks have enough capacity (and don't forget about */var/log*), the machine isn't swapping, the network utilization looks normal, and the CPU utilization looks normal given what the machine is currently doing. This process extends to intra-process resources such as the occupied heap within a JVM and the time spent garbage collecting versus providing service.

Event correlation

When none of these steps reveal anything interesting, follow the series of events that led to the failure, which usually involves intermachine, interprocess event correlation. For example, did a switch fail that caused additional replication traffic due to lost datanodes, or did something happen to the datanodes that caused a switch to be overrun with replication traffic, causing its failure? Knowing the correct order of events and having this kind of visibility into the system can help you understand byzantine failures.

There's nothing cheesier than a retrofit mnemonic device, but some form of regimented approach is necessary to properly evaluate the state of a system when troubleshooting. At each stage, there are some obvious test cases to be performed. Resource consumption is simple and relatively easy to understand, for instance, with tools such as df, du, sar, vmstat, iostat, and so forth. At the other end of the spectrum are more advanced techniques such as event correlation that require far more Hadoop-specific knowledge about the noteworthy events that occur within a system and some infrastructure to be able to extract and visualize that data in various ways. At its simplest, this can be cluster topology changes (nodes joining and leaving the cluster), rapid changes in the observed metric values (when standard deviation of the last *N* samples is greater than some threshold), and user actions such as job submission or HDFS file changes. Exactly which tool you use is less important than having an understanding of the type of data to look at and how.

Treatment and Care

Once the root cause of a problem has been identified, only then should a specific course of action be taken. Far too often, so-called shotgun debugging[3] occurs in moments of crisis. This approach usually ends in a series of corrective actions being taken that aren't necessarily needed, which increases the risk of additional disruption or damage to the system. You should absolutely avoid the urge to make changes until you know there's a high likelihood you've found the root cause of a particular issue. It's also important that detailed notes are kept about what actions are eventually taken and why. Always ask yourself if you or another member of the team would be able to solve the same problem if it happened again in a month.

Often there are multiple options for treatment, each with associated risk and side effects. Clearly the best scenario is one in which a problem is detected, diagnosed, and "cured" permanently. That, of course, is not always possible. Resolution can be classified into a number of different buckets:

Permanent eradication
> The ideal case, in which a problem is simply solved. Usually, these are trivial, expected issues such as disk failures or an overly verbose log consuming disk space. An administrator fixes the issue, makes a note of what was done, and moves on with life. We should all be so lucky.

Mitigation by configuration
> Some problems have no immediate solution and must be mitigated until the root cause can be stamped out. These tend to be slightly more complicated cases in which the risk of making a permanent change is either too risky or would take too long. A common instance of this is a user's MapReduce job that repeatedly runs

---

3. Shotgun debugging describes an unfocused series of corrective actions being attempted in the hope that you hit the target. Like a shotgun, the lack of precision usually has significant unintended consequences.

out of memory while processing a given dataset. Even if it's decided that there is a better way of writing the job so as to not consume so much RAM, doing so at 3:00 in the morning without proper code review and testing probably isn't the time to do so. It may, however, be possible to mitigate the problem by temporarily increasing the amount of memory allotted to MapReduce jobs until such time the code can be fixed.

Mitigation by architecture

Similar to mitigating a problem by changing configuration, it's sometimes better to change the architecture of a particular system to solve a problem. One slightly more advanced instance of this being the case is in solving slot utilization and job runtime problems. Let's assume that a MapReduce job processing a large dataset runs hourly, and every time it runs, it produces tens of thousands of tasks that would otherwise monopolize the cluster. As you learned in Chapter 7, we can use either the Fair or Capacity Scheduler to prevent the job from taking over. The problem is that the job still may not complete within a desired window of time because it takes a lot of time to churn through all the tasks. Rather than try to figure out how to handle so many tasks, we can try to mitigate the problem by looking at ways of reducing the number of tasks. We can't very well magically reduce the size of the data, but we can look at how much data is processed by each task. Remember that in many cases, there's roughly one map task per HDFS block of data. It's possible that there are so many tasks because there are a large number of very small, one-block files. The solution to this problem is architectural and involves changing the way data is written to involve a smaller number of larger files. Look at the size of the input split processed by each map task in the job (contained in the task logs) and work with the development team to find a more efficient way of storing and processing the data.

Mitigation by process

Another way to look at the previous problem is to say that it's not a code or architecture problem but a process problem. Maybe the job and its input data is as optimized as things are going to get and there's no remaining room for improvement. Another possibility to consider is shifting the time at which the offending job executes. Maybe there's simply a better time it can run. If it's an ad hoc job, maybe there should be an upper bound on how much data a single job can process at once before it loses an SLA. Alternatively, it could be that a summarized or highly compressed version of the dataset should be built to facilitate the offending job, assuming that it's so critical that it must run. Some of these options are as much architectural changes as they are about changing the process by which the cluster is managed.

On "Reboot It" Syndrome

The propensity for rebooting hosts or restarting daemons without any form of investigation is the opposite of everything discussed thus far. This particular form of disease was born out of a different incarnation of the 80/20 rule, one in which 80% of the users have no desire or need to understand what the problem is or why it exists. As administrators, we exist within the 20% for whom this is not—nor can we allow it to become —the case. By defaulting to just restarting things, you're defaulting to the nuclear option, obliterating all information and opportunities to learn from an experience. Without meaningful experience, preventative care simply isn't possible.

Consider for a moment what would happen if doctors opted for the medical version of "reboot it." Maybe they'd just cut off anything that stopped working.

Detecting, reacting to, and correcting an issue is generally seen as the problem-solving process. Unfortunately, this is a problem in and of itself because it misses the real opportunity: to learn from the failure. Incorporating new experiences can, and should, influence future behavior and ability. This approach means detecting related problems faster and reducing the time to resolution, of course, but even that isn't the true win.

Imagine you're on a bike going down an enormous hill without brakes. You lose control of the bike, crash, and wind up in the hospital. Don't worry, though, because eventually you make a complete recovery. Months later, you find yourself at the top of a hill that looks remarkably similar to the one where you were injured. Worse, the bike has an odd familiarity to it as well. You begin to realize something. The uneasy feeling in your stomach is experience, and it's screaming at you to not go down the hill. That is the true value of experience: preventative maintenance. Being able to recognize and prevent a similar situation from occurring is what saves us from the repetition of unpleasant situations. It's true that you could buy a helmet or learn to roll when you hit the ground, but you could also not ride a bike with no brakes down a hill.

With administration of complex production systems, it's not as simple as deciding to not go down the hill. By the time you're on the bike at the hill, it's too late. Instead, you need to take action long before you find yourself in such a situation. Action, in this context, means updating processes, code, and monitoring to incorporate what you've learned as a result of the incident. Taken in aggregate, most agree that preventative maintenance is cheaper (expressed in terms of code, time, money, and availability) than emergency maintenance and is well worth the investment. Of course, this line of reasoning can be taken too far, to the point at which overreaction can mean that heavyweight processes are put in place that impede productivity and flexibility. Like most things, preventative care can be overdone, so care should be exercised. Each change should be evaluated in the context of the likelihood that the given problem would repeat in the future, or if it were truly annomolous. In other words, do not build systems and processes around the most uncommon case you have encountered. Every decision should be a function of probability of occurrence and the associated impact when it does occur.

One incredibly useful tool in the preventative maintenance toolbox is the postmortem. It doesn't need to be a formal process, beyond actually holding it, and it should be open to anyone who wishes to attend. Anyone involved in the incident should attend, and the person with the most knowledge of the situation should lead it. Start by summarizing the problem and the end result, and then walk through the timeline of events, calling out anything interesting along the way. If the incident involved multiple systems, have the person with the most knowledge of each system handle that part of the walkthrough. Allow attendees to ask questions along the way about the decisions that were made or comment on an approach that might have worked better. At the end, write a synopsis of what happened, why, what was done about it, and what you're doing to help prevent it in the future. Everyone should ask questions about the likelihood of a repeat occurrence, the resultant damage (in terms of time, money, data loss, and so on), and any other pertinent points that would be useful to know in the future.

Worth noting is that the postmortem is commonly avoided because it tends to make people feel like they're being singled out. This is a valid concern: no one likes to think they've done a bad job. But it's also extremely unfortunate, as the postmortem is one of the best ways to prevent similar situations going forward. Walking through the timeline can help everyone, including anyone who maybe made a less-than-stellar decision along the way, understand where they can change their thinking and improve in the future. The postmortem is absolutely not, nor should it ever be permitted to be, a blame session. It's critical that those participating be both respectful and cognizant of the fact that others are putting it out there for all the group to see, so to speak. Create an environment where making mistakes is forgivable, honesty is praised, and blame and derision are not tolerated, and you will have a stronger team and better systems as a result.

At the time of this writing, Amazon Web Services, a popular infrastructure as a service cloud provider, had a large power outage that impacted a large swath of EC2 users. One of these customers was Netflix, a rather public and large-scale customer of the service. Although the incident itself was short-lived (comparatively), Netflix had an extended outage due to the way some of their systems were built. In fact, one of the reasons they had such an outage was a fix they had made to their code as the result of a different failure they previously observed. The Netflix team rather bravely posted a fantastic example of a postmortem of the incident on their public tech blog (*http://bit .ly/Netflix_AWS_storm*).

War Stories

Talking about the theory and process of troubleshooting is useful, even necessary. However, it's equally important to see how these techniques apply to real-world scenarios. What follows is a number of cases of real production problems with some depth on what it took to detect and resolve each case. In certain cases, details have been changed or omitted to protect the innocent, but the crux of the issue remains.

A Mystery Bottleneck

A cluster of a few hundred nodes running HDFS and MapReduce, responsible for streaming data ingest of all user activity from various web applications, presented with "intermittent slow HDFS write rates." Most streams would write "fast" (later learned to be at a rate greater than 50MB per second), but occasionally, the write rate would drop for some but not all streams to less than 5MB per second. All nodes were connected via a near-line rate, nonblocking 1GbE network, with each 48-port top-of-rack switch connected to a core via four trunked 10GbE fibre links for a mild over-subscription rate of 1.2. Commonly used in large clusters, the core switch in use theoretically supported the necessary fabric bandwidth to not be a bottleneck. Each host in the cluster contained 8 JBOD-configured, 2TB SATA II drives, connected via a single SAS controller to a standard dual-socket motherboard sporting 48GB of memory.

What was interesting about the problem was the intermittent nature of the degraded write performance. This was a new cluster, which always brings a fair amount of suspicion, mostly because there's no existing data with which to compare. However, the hardware itself was a known quantity and the intermittent nature immediately suggested an outlier somewhere in the network. Discussing the problem with the cluster administrator, it was revealed that it wasn't actually that an entire HDFS write *stream* would be slow, but that within a write, the speed would appear to drop for a short period of time and then resolve itself. At a high level, it immediately sounded like a network problem, but where and why were the open questions.

Larger organizations, at which system and network administrators are in two separate groups, tend to suffer from an *us and them* problem, each claiming that various ephemeral issues are the fault of the other. Network administrators view the network as a service, happy to remain ignorant of the content of the packets that fly back and forth, and systems folks assuming that the network is a given. Things are further complicated by the opacity of the network. It's not always clear what the physical topology is, or what's shared versus dedicated bandwidth. Without a view of the network from the switch, it's impossible to see what the overall traffic pattern looks like, so black box –style testing is usually necessary.

Once the hardware, configuration, and cluster history information was available, a list of possible problems was made. Obviously some kind of network issue could be causing this kind of behavior. It could be a global network problem in which all traffic was affected, possibly due to dropped packets and retransmission. Of course, this seemed unlikely, given the aggregate traffic that the cluster was handling with the given equipment. This could really be the case only if the core switch were shared with some other, extremely spiky application, and even then, the drop in transfer rate seemed to affect only some streams. It could be that it was local to a single top-of-rack switch. That would account for why only some streams were affected. We'd need to know more about which datanodes were involved to say whether it was contained on a single rack or if it spanned the whole network. As much as the network was possible, it could be a problem with a specific group of datanodes on the host side. A group of datanodes could be misconfigured somehow, causing any write that included one or more of those nodes in the replication pipeline to be affected. The rule around network partitions—that a machine failure and a network failure are indistinguishable from one another when it comes to message loss—could easily be generalized to a situation such as this, in which a pattern of failure could be a switch or a group of machines, and that a slow machine is the same as a slow segment of the network (where the segment could be a small as a single port). Either way, it seemed like the pattern was key. If we could find when and where the degraded performance occurred, only then would it even be possible to find out why.

Unfortunately, there was no per-host network monitoring in place, so it wasn't a simple matter of looking at the distribution of traffic to machines. Even if it was available, it's still difficult to distinguish artificially limited traffic from an underutilized machine in the cluster. Luckily, the issue was easy to observe and replicate. The cluster administrator pointed out that he could perform an HDFS transfer with the command `hadoop -put some_file.log /user/joe` and with some luck, hit the issue. Using the output of the `hadoop fsck` command, it's possible to find all hosts involved in an HDFS write operation, which would be critical. Remember from Chapter 2 that when clients write to HDFS, a replication pipeline is formed for each block. This means that a different set of datanodes is selected for each block written to HDFS, which would easily explain the intermittent nature of the problem. Together, we constructed a test to help us find the pattern, shown in Example 9-1; we would run the command in a loop, writing to numbered files in HDFS, timing each iteration of the command, as there was a noticeable difference in speed when the issue occurred. Note that we were interested in the results for all commands rather than just slow commands, because if a node appeared in both a slow and a normal speed write, that would show us that it probably wasn't a problem on that machine, or that the problem wasn't a specific machine, but possibly a component *within* a machine, such as a single disk. If we looked at just the hosts involved in the slow iterations, we might incorrectly focus on a machine. It was also entirely possible that there would be no pattern here and the problem wasn't related to a specific machine (but I admit I was pretty convinced).

To simplify the test, we used a file that was just under the block size. This meant there was a single block per file and a single triplet of datanodes as a result.

Example 9-1. Test script used to generate HDFS traffic

```sh
#!/bin/sh

opt_source_file="$1"
opt_dest="$2"
opt_iterations="$3"

[ -f "$opt_source_file" ] || {
  echo "Error: source file not provided or doesn't exist: $opt_source_file"
  exit 1
}
```

```
[ -n "$opt_dest" ] || {
  echo "Error: destination path not provided"
  exit 2
}

[ -n "$opt_iterations" ] || {
  echo "Error: number of iterations not provided"
  exit 3
}

filename=$(basename $opt_source_file)
i=0

while [ "$i" -lt "$opt_iterations" ] ; do
  echo "Writing $opt_dest/$filename.$i"
  time hadoop fs -put "$opt_source_file" "$opt_dest/$filename.$i"
  i=$(($i + 1))
done
```

We ran our test, writing the output to a file for later reference. The next step was to build a list of which datanodes participated in each replication pipeline. The information we used was produced by the hadoop fsck utility. The output from this specific incident isn't available, but Example 9-2 gives you an idea of how the output can be used for this purpose. Note the options passed to the command and the full listing of each block and the three datanodes on which a replica resides.

Example 9-2. HDFS fsck output displaying block locations per file

```
[esammer@hadoop01 ~]$ hadoop fsck /user/esammer -files -blocks -locations
FSCK started by hdfs (auth:SIMPLE) from /10.0.0.191 for path ↵
  /user/esammer at Mon Jul 09 15:35:41 PDT 2012
/user/esammer <dir>
...
/user/esammer/1tb/part-00004 10995116200 bytes, 1 block(s):  OK
0. BP-875753299-10.1.1.132-1340735471649:blk_6272257110614848973_83827 ↵
  len=134217728 repl=3 [10.1.1.134:50010, 10.1.1.135:50010, 10.1.1.139:50010]
...
```

The fsck output was parsed, and the list of datanodes for each single-block file was sorted to make comparisons simpler, as in Example 9-3.

Example 9-3. Parsed fsck output with sorted datanodes

```
/user/esammer/1tb/part-00004   10.1.1.134:50010   10.1.1.135:50010   10.1.1.139:50010
/user/esammer/1tb/part-00005   10.1.1.135:50010   10.1.1.137:50010   10.1.1.140:50010
/user/esammer/1tb/part-00006   10.1.1.131:50010   10.1.1.133:50010   10.1.1.134:50010
...
```

Performing some basic counts of which datanodes were involved in slow files versus fast files, it became obvious that a single datanode was present in all slow writes and no normal speed writes. Direct scp file copies to the other two machines that appeared with the problematic host in each instance also ran at an expected rate, while the host in question was significantly slower. Using scp and bypassing Hadoop altogether eliminated it as a potential contributor to the problem. It was clearly the single host that was the issue.

All host-level checks looked normal. Resource consumption, hardware, and software health all looked normal on the host. Eventually, we convinced the network team to take one last look at the switch to which the host was connected. As it turned out, either a human being or a bad cable (we never got an answer) had caused the single switch port to negotiate at 100Mb, rather than 1Gb—a simple problem to fix.

This was a situation in which a lot of lessons were learned, and there was obviously room for improvement. Here are some of the take-aways this particular company had, as a result:

- Always assume that the problem is yours. If each group had made such an assumption and spent a few extra minutes when performing initial troubleshooting, this problem would have been caught much, much sooner. Specifically, when the networking group confirmed that there was no issue, they checked only a subset of the total number of ports that made up the cluster, missing the misconfigured port. The same may have also been true on the host side of the link (we never actually saw this).
- Hadoop is, as promised, really good at covering up odd degradations in hardware performance. The problem went unnoticed for some time before it was clear that it was even an issue.
- Implement comprehensive monitoring. Having all monitoring in place, and under a single pane of glass, would have saved quite a bit of time writing ad hoc scripts to locate the problem.

There's No Place Like 127.0.0.1

Mike (not his real name) was tasked with setting up a new Hadoop cluster. He used the standard golden CentOS image used for all other machines in the data center as a base from which to start, installed the software, and configured Hadoop as he had done before. Starting with HDFS, he formatted the namenode and proceeded to fire up the namenode daemon. As expected, the web user interface immediately responded, showing zero datanodes in the cluster. Next, he started a datanode process on the same machine that, within a few seconds, showed up in the user interface. Everything looked like it was on track.

The next step was to start each datanode, in turn, checking that the total available HDFS capacity grew with each new node that connected. At this point, some strange behavior was observed. No other datanodes seemed to be able to connect to the namenode. Mike started making a list of things that could cause this result:

- It's possible that the machine running the namenode was running a firewall that prevented other hosts from connecting to it. This firewall would explain why the local datanode could connect but no other process could.

- It's possible that the namenode was binding to the wrong IP address. We know that the namenode uses the value of `fs.default.name` is used to decide which IP to bind to. This case seemed unlikely because Mike used the correct hostname by which the machine should be addressed. (In our examples, we'll use es-op-n1 as the namenode and es-op-n2 as a separate worker machine.)

- The datanodes may have received incorrect configuration in `fs.default.name`, instructing them to communicate with the wrong machine. This case was even more unlikely because the same configuration files were deployed to all nodes.

- Some network problem could have partitioned the namenode from the rest of the new workers. This possibility was easily rejected out of the gate because Mike was able to make ssh connections from one machine to the other.

- The `dfs.hosts` and `dfs.hosts.exclude` lists could have been denying datanode registration. Again, this option was easily rejected because these files had not yet been configured and the default behavior of the namenode is to allow all datanodes to connect.

It was common for new CentOS images to have a default set of firewall rules configured, which seemed possible. Additionally, it was trivial to verify it, so Mike decided to knock it off the list right away:

```
[root@es-op-n1 ~]# iptables -nvL
Chain INPUT (policy ACCEPT 0 packets, 0 bytes)
 pkts bytes target prot opt in  out source      destination
   34  2504 ACCEPT all  --  *   *   0.0.0.0/0  0.0.0.0/0 state RELATED,ESTABLISHED
    0     0 ACCEPT icmp --  *   *   0.0.0.0/0  0.0.0.0/0
    1   382 ACCEPT all  --  lo  *   0.0.0.0/0  0.0.0.0/0
    0     0 ACCEPT tcp  --  *   *   0.0.0.0/0  0.0.0.0/0 state NEW tcp dpt:22
    4   240 REJECT all  --  *   *   0.0.0.0/0  0.0.0.0/0 reject-with
                                                         icmp-host-prohibited

Chain FORWARD (policy ACCEPT 0 packets, 0 bytes)
 pkts bytes target prot opt in  out source      destination
    0     0 REJECT all  --  *   *   0.0.0.0/0  0.0.0.0/0 reject-with
                                                         icmp-host-prohibited

Chain OUTPUT (policy ACCEPT 24 packets, 2618 bytes)
 pkts bytes target prot opt in  out source      destination
```

Sure enough, the standard set of rules allowing only established and related connections, ICMP, loopback device, and SSH traffic were permitted. All other traffic was being rejected. Also, the packet counter column for the REJECT rule clearly showed that it was increasing at a steady rate. Without even checking the logs, Mike knew this wouldn't work. He decided to temporarily disable iptables while working on the new configuration:

```
[root@es-op-n1 ~]# /etc/init.d/iptables stop
iptables: Flushing firewall rules:                      [  OK  ]
iptables: Setting chains to policy ACCEPT: filter       [  OK  ]
iptables: Unloading modules:                            [  OK  ]
[root@es-op-n1 conf]# iptables -nvL
Chain INPUT (policy ACCEPT 0 packets, 0 bytes)
 pkts bytes target prot opt in  out source     destination

Chain FORWARD (policy ACCEPT 0 packets, 0 bytes)
 pkts bytes target prot opt in  out source     destination

Chain OUTPUT (policy ACCEPT 0 packets, 0 bytes)
 pkts bytes target prot opt in  out source     destination
```

With that issue resolved, the user interface was checked again. After checking the datanode processes' logs and confirming that they were still alive and retrying, Mike checked the namenode user interface again. Still, though, no new datanodes connected. It was obvious that this *would have* been a problem, but it wasn't actually the sole issue. Something was still wrong, so Mike moved on to the next possibility in the list: binding to the wrong IP address. Again, this possibility was also easy to check using the net stat command:

```
root@es-op-n1 ~]# netstat -nlp
Active Internet connections (only servers)
Proto Recv-Q Send-Q Local Address    Foreign Address   State    PID/Program name
tcp    0      0 127.0.0.1:8020        0.0.0.0:*         LISTEN   5611/java
tcp    0      0 0.0.0.0:50070         0.0.0.0:*         LISTEN   5611/java
tcp    0      0 0.0.0.0:22            0.0.0.0:*         LISTEN   4848/sshd
...
```

Process id 5611 had the two ports open he expected—the namenode RPC port (8020) and the web user interface (50070)—however, the RPC port was listening only on the loopback IP address 127.0.0.1. That was definitely going to be a problem. If the hostname specified by fs.default.name was, in fact, the proper hostname to use—after all, Mike had used it when creating an SSH connection to the machine—why was this happening? As a first step, Mike checked on what the machine thought its hostname was:

```
[root@es-op-n1 ~]# hostname
es-op-n1
```

Not the fully qualified name, but that should work just fine. Next, he checked what the data center DNS had to say about the hostname:

```
[root@es-op-n1 ~]# host -t A -v es-op-n1
Trying "es-op-n1.xyz.com"
;; ->>HEADER<<- opcode: QUERY, status: NOERROR, id: 36912
;; flags: qr aa rd ra; QUERY: 1, ANSWER: 1, AUTHORITY: 0, ADDITIONAL: 0
```

```
;; QUESTION SECTION:
;es-op-n1.xyz.com.    IN    A

;; ANSWER SECTION:
es-op-n1.xyz.com. 0  IN    A      10.20.194.222

Received 60 bytes from 10.20.76.73#53 in 0 ms
```

According to DNS, es-op-n1 lived at 10.20.194.222, which was correct. It was possible that something in *etc/hosts* (which normally appears before DNS in the list of sources of name resolution) was to blame:

```
[root@es-op-n1 ~]# cat /etc/hosts
127.0.0.1   localhost localhost.localdomain localhost4 localhost4.localdomain4 es-op-n1
```

Aha! The name es-op-n1 was listed as an alias for localhost, which resolves to 127.0.0.1. That could easily cause the issue. Mike fixed this, after some grumbling about why anyone would configure a machine this way, restarted the namenode process, and checked `netstat` again:

```
[root@es-op-n1 ~]# netstat -nlp
Active Internet connections (only servers)
Proto Recv-Q Send-Q Local Address        Foreign Address   State   PID/Program name
tcp    0      0 10.20.194.222:8020   0.0.0.0:*         LISTEN  6282/java
tcp    0      0 0.0.0.0:50070        0.0.0.0:*         LISTEN  6282/java
tcp    0      0 0.0.0.0:22           0.0.0.0:*         LISTEN  4848/sshd
...
```

Everything was looking much better now. Checking the namenode web user interface revealed two datanodes connected, which made sense: one from the local machine and the first worker that had been retrying all along. Just to make sure, Mike started copying some files into HDFS to confirm that everything worked properly before moving on:

```
[root@es-op-n1 ~]# sudo -u hdfs hadoop fs -put /etc/hosts /hosts1
[root@es-op-n1 ~]# sudo -u hdfs hadoop fs -put /etc/hosts /hosts2
[root@es-op-n1 ~]# sudo -u hdfs hadoop fs -put /etc/hosts /hosts3
[root@es-op-n1 ~]# sudo -u hdfs hadoop fs -ls /
Found 3 items
-rw-r--r--   3 hdfs supergroup      158 2012-07-10 15:17 /hosts1
-rw-r--r--   3 hdfs supergroup      158 2012-07-10 15:18 /hosts2
-rw-r--r--   3 hdfs supergroup      158 2012-07-10 15:18 /hosts3
[root@es-op-n1 ~]# sudo -u hdfs hadoop fs -rm /hosts\*
Deleted /hosts1
Deleted /hosts2
Deleted /hosts3
```

Once again, everything appeared to be working, and Mike was happy.

## CHAPTER 10

Monitoring

An Overview

It's hard to talk about building large shared, mission-critical systems without having a way to know their operational state and performance metrics. Most organizations (I hope) have some form of monitoring system that keeps track of various systems that occupy the data center. No one runs a large Hadoop cluster by itself, and while a lot of time is spent on data integration, monitoring integration sometimes falls by the wayside.

Most monitoring systems can be divided into two major components: metric collection and consumption of the resultant data. Hadoop is another source from which metrics should be collected. Consumption of the data can mean presenting aggregate metrics as dashboards, raw metrics as time series data for diagnoses and analysis, and very commonly, rule evaluation for alerting. In fact, many monitoring systems provide more than one of these features. It helps to further divide monitoring into two distinct types: health monitoring, where the goal is to determine that a service is in an expected operational state, and performance monitoring, where the goal is to use regular samples of performance metrics, over time, to gain a better understanding of how the system functions. Performance monitoring tends to be harder to cover outside of the context of a specific environment and set of workloads, so instead we'll focus primarily on health monitoring.

Hadoop, like most distributed systems, constitutes a monitoring challenge because the monitoring system must know about how the multiple services interact as a larger system. When monitoring HDFS, for example, we may want to see each daemon running, within normal memory consumption limits, responding to RPC requests in a defined window, and other "simple" metrics, but this doesn't tell us whether the entirety of the service is functional (although one may infer such things). Instead, it can be necessary to know that a certain percentage of datanodes are alive and communicating with the namenode, or what the block distribution is across the cluster to truly know the state of the system. Zooming in too close on a single daemon or host, or too far out on the cluster, can both be equally deceptive when trying to get a complete picture of performance or health of a service like HDFS.

Worse still, we want to know how MapReduce is performing on top of HDFS. Alert thresholds and performance data of MapReduce is inherently coupled to that of HDFS when services are stacked in this manner, making it difficult to detect the root cause of a failure across service and host boundaries. Existing tools are very good at identifying problems within localized systems (those with little to no external dependency) but require quite a bit of effort to understand the intricacies of distributed systems. These complexities make the difference between a daemon being up and responding to basic checks and whether it is safe to walk away from a computer (or go to sleep) difficult to ascertain.

In the following sections, we'll cover what Hadoop metrics are, how to configure them, and some common ways to integrate with existing monitoring services and custom code.

Hadoop Metrics

Hadoop has built-in support for exposing various metrics to outside systems. Each daemon can be configured to collect this data from its internal components at a regular interval and then handle the metrics in some way using a plug-in. A number of these plug-ins ship with Hadoop, ready for use in common deployment scenarios (more on that later). Related metrics are grouped into a named *context*, and each context can be treated independently. Some contexts are common to all daemons, such as the information about the JVM and RPC operations performed, and others apply only to daemons of a specific service, such as HDFS metrics that come from only the namenode and datanodes. In most cases, administrators find that all contexts are useful and necessary when monitoring for health, understanding performance, and diagnosing problems with a cluster.

The metrics system has evolved over time, gaining features and improvements along the way. In April 2010, a project[1] was started to refactor the metrics subsystem to support features that had been too difficult to provide under the existing implementation. Notably, the new metrics subsystem (referred to as *metrics2*) supports sending metrics to multiple plug-ins, filtering of metrics in various ways, and more complete support for JMX. Work was completed in mid to late 2011 and included in Apache Hadoop 0.20.205 and CDH4 and later. Earlier versions of Apache Hadoop and CDH use the original metrics implementation. For the sake of clarity, we'll refer to the old metrics system as *metrics1* when discussing the specific implementation and use the more general term *metrics* to refer to the functionality of either version.

---

1. See Apache Hadoop JIRA HADOOP-6728 (*https://issues.apache.org/jira/browse/HADOOP-6728*).

Apache Hadoop 0.20.0 and CDH3 (metrics1)

The original implementation of the metrics system groups related metrics into contexts, as described earlier. Each context can be individually configured with a plug-in that specifies how metric data should be handled. A number of plug-ins exist including the default `NullContext`, which simply discards all metrics received. Internal components of the daemon are polled at a regular, user-defined interval, with the resulting data being handled by the configured plug-in. The primary four contexts are:

jvm

> Contains Java virtual machine information and metrics. Example data includes the maximum heap size, occupied heap, and average time spent in garbage collection. All daemons produce metrics for this context.

dfs

> Contains HDFS metrics. The metrics provided vary by daemon role. For example, the namenode provides information about total HDFS capacity, consumed capacity, missing and under-replicated blocks, and active datanodes in the cluster, and datanodes provide the number of failed disk volumes and remaining capacity on that particular worker node. Only the HDFS daemons output metrics for this context.

mapred

> Contains MapReduce metrics. The metrics provided vary by daemon role. For example, the jobtracker provides information about the total number of map and reduce slots, blacklisted tasktrackers, and failures, whereas tasktrackers provide counts of running, failed, and killed tasks at the worker node level. Only MapReduce daemons output metrics for this context.

rpc

> Contains remote procedure call metrics. Example data includes the time each RPC spends in the queue before being processed, the average time it takes to process an RPC, and the number of open connections. All daemons output metrics for this context.

 Metric plug-in class names tend to reuse the word *context*–but to mean something other than the context described thus far. When we refer to *context*, we mean one of the four groups of metrics. We'll use the term *metric plugin* to refer to the class that can be configured to handle metrics.

Although all of Hadoop is instrumented to capture this information, it's not available to external systems by default. One must configure a plug-in for each context to handle this data in some way. The metrics system configuration is specified by the *hadoop-metrics.properties* file within the standard Hadoop configuration directory. The configuration file is a simple Java properties format file and is largely self-explanatory, although a few examples are provided in this chapter. The following metric plug-ins are included with Hadoop:

org.apache.hadoop.metrics.spi.NullContext

Hadoop's default metric plug-in for all four contexts, NullContext is the */dev/null* of plug-ins. Metrics are not collected from the internal components, nor are they output to any external system. This plug-in effectively disables access to metrics, as shown in Example 10-1.

Example 10-1. Using NullContext to disable metric collection

```
# hadoop-metrics.properties

jvm.class = org.apache.hadoop.metrics.spi.NullContext

dfs.class = org.apache.hadoop.metrics.spi.NullContext

...
```

org.apache.hadoop.metrics.spi.NoEmitMetricsContext

The NoEmitMetricsContext is a slight variation on NullContext—with an important difference. Although metrics are still not output to an external system, the thread that runs within Hadoop, updating the metric values in memory *does* run. Systems such as JMX and the metrics servlet (described later) rely on this information being collected and available to function.[2] There's almost no reason not to enable this plug-in for all contexts, for all clusters. The added insight into the system is significant and well worth the minimal overhead introduced. Additionally, updating the metric configuration requires a daemon restart, which can temporarily disrupt service down the road. The only parameter that NoEmitMetricsContext supports is period, which defines the frequency at which collection occurs. See Example 10-2 for an example of a configuration using NoEmitMetricsContext.

Example 10-2. Using NoEmitMetricsContext for metrics collection

```
# hadoop-metrics.properties

jvm.class = org.apache.hadoop.metrics.spi.NoEmitMetricsContext
jvm.period = 10

dfs.class = org.apache.hadoop.metrics.spi.NoEmitMetricsContext
dfs.period = 10

...
```

org.apache.hadoop.metrics.file.FileContext

FileContext polls the internal components of Hadoop for metrics periodically and writes them out to a file on the local filesystem. Two parameters are available (see

---

2. More specifically, JMX will always be able to access the standard JVM instrumented components, but this is different from the jvm context provided by Hadoop metrics.

Example 10-3) to the control the filename to write to (`fileName`) and the desired frequency of updates (`period`) in seconds.

Example 10-3. Using FileContext for metrics collection

```
# hadoop-metrics.properties

jvm.class = org.apache.hadoop.metrics.file.FileContext
jvm.period = 10
jvm.fileName = /tmp/jvm-metrics.log

dfs.class = org.apache.hadoop.metrics.file.FileContext
dfs.period = 10
dfs.fileName = /tmp/dfs-metrics.log

...
```

Practically speaking, `FileContext` is flawed and shouldn't be used in production clusters because the plug-in never rotates the specified file, leading to indefinite growth. Truncating the file doesn't work because the JVM will continue to write to the open file descriptor until the daemon is restarted. During that period of time, disk space on the local filesystem will continue to evaporate and it won't be immediately clear as to why (the classic anonymous file situation). The other major problem is that a unique file name must be given for each context and when multiple daemons live on the same machine (such as worker nodes), additionally across daemons. This setup is a pain to manage; as an alternative, consider using `NoEmitMetricsContext` and the metrics servlet, or Hadoop's JMX support.

`org.apache.hadoop.metrics.ganglia.GangliaContext` *and* `org.apache.hadoop.metrics.ganglia.GangliaContext31`

Hadoop includes first-class support for integrating with the popular open source performance monitoring system Ganglia (*http://ganglia.sourceforge.net/*). Ganglia was built by a group at the University of California, Berkeley, specifically to collect, aggregate, and plot a large number of metrics from large clusters of machines. Because of its ability to scale, Ganglia is a fantastic system to use with Hadoop. It works by running a small monitoring daemon on each host called `gmond` that collects metrics locally. Each `gmond` process relays data to a central `gmetad` process that records data in a series of RRD (*http://oss.oetiker.ch/rrdtool/*), or *round-robin database* files, which are fixed-size files that efficiently store time series data. A PHP web application displays this data in a simple but effective view.

The `GangliaContext` is normally configured, as in Example 10-4, to send metrics to the local `gmond` process using the **servers** property in *hadoop-metrics.properties*. Like `FileContext` and `NoEmitMetricsContext`, a **period** parameter specifies how frequently data is collected.

Example 10-4. Using GangliaContext for metrics collection

```
# hadoop-metrics.properties

jvm.class = org.apache.hadoop.metrics.file.FileContext
jvm.period = 10
jvm.servers = 10.0.0.191
# The server value may be a comma separated list of host:port pairs.
# The port is optional, in which case it defaults to 8649.
# jvm.servers = gmond-host-a, gmond-host-b:8649

dfs.class = org.apache.hadoop.metrics.file.FileContext
dfs.period = 10
dfs.servers = 10.0.0.191

...
```

The difference between `GangliaContext` and `GangliaContext31` is that the former works with Ganglia 3.0 and older and the latter supports versions 3.1 and newer. For more information about installing and configuring Ganglia, see the project website (*http://ganglia.sourceforge.net*).

JMX Support

Because Hadoop is a Java-based system, supporting JMX (*http://bit.ly/JMX_oracle*) is a relatively simple decision to make from a development perspective. Some monitoring systems, notably those written in Java themselves, even have first-class support for JMX. JMX is nice because it supports self-describing endpoints that enable monitoring systems (or any JMX client) to discover the available *MBeans* and their *attributes* (which would be analogous JMX-speak for a context and its metrics). JMX terminology, its RPC stack, security, and configuration, however, are tricky at best and downright convoluted the rest of the time. Nevertheless, if you know it, or already have a monitoring system that is natively JMX-aware, it's a perfectly valid option for integration.

JMX functionality is related to the metric plug-ins in a slightly unusual way. Internal MBeans in Hadoop rely on a metric plug-in that has an update thread running to collect data from the system. With the default `NullContext` plug-in, for instance, although it's possible to connect a JMX client to any of the Hadoop daemons and see a list of MBeans (see Table 10-1), their attributes will never update, which can be confusing and difficult to debug. Enabling any of the metric plug-ins that have an update thread (`NoEmitMe tricsContext`, `GangliaContext`) will cause MBeans to show the correct information, as you would normally expect.

Table 10-1. Hadoop-supported JMX MBeans

MBean Object Name	Description	Daemon
hadoop:service=NameNode,name=FSName-systemState	Namenode metadata information.	Namenode
hadoop:service=NameNode,name=NameNo-deActivity	Activity statistics on the namenode.	Namenode
hadoop:service=NameNode,name=NameNo-deInfo	Descriptive namenode information.	Namenode
hadoop:service=DataNode,name=DataNo-deActivity-*hostname-port*	Activity statistics for the datanode running on *hostname* and *port*.	Datanode
hadoop:service=DataNode,name=DataNo-deInfo	Descriptive datanode information.	Datanode
hadoop:service=DataNode,name=FSDataset-State-DS-*ID*-127.0.0.1-*port-timestamp*	Datanode storage location statistics (dfs.data.dir) and information.	Datanode
hadoop:service=JobTracker,name=JobTracker-Info	Descriptive jobtracker information.	Jobtracker
hadoop:service=TaskTracker,name=TaskTrack-erInfo	Descriptive tasktracker information.	Tasktracker
hadoop:service=*Service Name*,name=RpcActivityForPort*1234*	RPC information for *ServiceName* port *1234*.	All
hadoop:service=*Service Name*,name=RpcDetailedActivityForPort*1234*	Detailed RPC information for *ServiceName* port *1234*. Tends to not be particularly useful.	All

REST Interface

The other common (and some might argue, slightly more modern) method of getting at metric data is by way of a single-call REST/ JSON servlet running in each daemon's embedded web server. The ubiquity of HTTP-based services, bevy of JSON parsing libraries, and the simplicity make it an extremely compelling option for many. Downsides to using REST/JSON include the lack of standardization and discoverability, HTTP overhead, and requirement for custom polling code to do something with the JSON blob returned from the service.

There are actually two such servlets: the original metrics servlet that lives at */metrics* and its updated replacement at */jmx*. Both provide similar functionality—an HTTP GET request that produces a JSON format response—but they work in very different ways. The */metrics* servlet uses the Hadoop metrics system directly, works only with metrics1, and is available in all versions of CDH3 as well as Apache Hadoop until version 0.20.203 (where it stops working due to the switch to metrics2). The newer */jmx* servlet, on the other hand, exposes Hadoop's JMX MBeans as JSON (which, as you learned earlier, get their information from the metrics system). This servlet is available in CDH starting with CDH3u1 but does not exist in Apache Hadoop until version 0.20.205.

Using the metrics servlet. If a metric plug-in with an update thread is configured, pointing an HTTP client at the path */metrics* will yield a plain-text version of the metric data. Using the `format=json` query parameter, one can retrieve the same content in JSON format:

```
[esammer@hadoop01:~ ]$ curl http://hadoop117:50070/metrics
dfs
  FSDirectory
    {hostName=hadoop117,sessionId=}:
      files_deleted=100
  FSNamesystem
    {hostName=hadoop117,sessionId=}:
      BlockCapacity=2097152
      BlocksTotal=9
      CapacityRemainingGB=24
      CapacityTotalGB=31
      CapacityUsedGB=0
      CorruptBlocks=0
      ExcessBlocks=0
      FilesTotal=33
      MissingBlocks=0
      PendingDeletionBlocks=0
      PendingReplicationBlocks=0
      ScheduledReplicationBlocks=0
      TotalLoad=1
      UnderReplicatedBlocks=1
  namenode
    {hostName=vm02.localdomain,sessionId=}:
      AddBlockOps=1
      CreateFileOps=1
      DeleteFileOps=1
      FileInfoOps=12
      FilesAppended=0
  ...
```

Adding the query parameter `format=json` gives us the same information, but in JSON format:

```
[esammer@hadoop01:~ ]$ curl 'http://hadoop117:50070/metrics?format=json'
{"dfs":{
  "FSDirectory":[
    [{"hostName":"hadoop117","sessionId":""},{"files_deleted":100}]
  ],
  "FSNamesystem":[
    [
      {"hostName":"hadoop117","sessionId":""},
      {"BlockCapacity":2097152,"BlocksTotal":9,"CapacityRemainingGB":24,
       "CapacityTotalGB":31,"CapacityUsedGB":0,"CorruptBlocks":0,"ExcessBlocks":0,
       "FilesTotal":33,"MissingBlocks":0,"PendingDeletionBlocks":0,
       ...
```

Using the JMX JSON servlet. Designed as a replacement to */metrics*, the */jmx* servlet produces logically similar output, but the data is sourced from Hadoop's JMX MBeans instead of the metrics system directly. This is the preferred servlet going forward, as it works across both metrics1 and metrics2 based releases. Unlike */metrics*, this servlet does not support text output—only JSON. Its output should be self-explanatory:

```
[esammer@hadoop01:~ ]$ curl http://hadoop117:50070/jmx
{
  "name" : "hadoop:service=NameNode,name=NameNodeActivity",
  "modelerType" : "org.apache.hadoop.hdfs.server.namenode.metrics.NameNodeActivtyMBean",
  "AddBlockOps" : 0,
  "fsImageLoadTime" : 2756,
  "FilesRenamed" : 0,
  "SyncsNumOps" : 0,
  "SyncsAvgTime" : 0,
  "SyncsMinTime" : 0,
  "SyncsMaxTime" : 70,
  "JournalTransactionsBatchedInSync" : 0,
  "FileInfoOps" : 0,
  "CreateFileOps" : 0,
  "GetListingOps" : 0,
  "TransactionsNumOps" : 0,
  "TransactionsAvgTime" : 0,
  "TransactionsMinTime" : 0,
  "TransactionsMaxTime" : 1,
  "GetBlockLocations" : 0,
  "BlocksCorrupted" : 0,
  "FilesInGetListingOps" : 0,
  "SafemodeTime" : 40117,
  "FilesCreated" : 0,
  "FilesAppended" : 0,
  "DeleteFileOps" : 0,
  "blockReportNumOps" : 0,
  "blockReportAvgTime" : 0,
  "blockReportMinTime" : 0,
  "blockReportMaxTime" : 3
}, {
  "name" : "java.lang:type=Threading",
  "modelerType" : "sun.management.ThreadImpl",
  "ThreadContentionMonitoringEnabled" : false,
  "DaemonThreadCount" : 29,
  "PeakThreadCount" : 38,
  "CurrentThreadCpuTimeSupported" : true,
  "ObjectMonitorUsageSupported" : true,
  "SynchronizerUsageSupported" : true,
  "ThreadContentionMonitoringSupported" : true,
  "ThreadCpuTimeEnabled" : true,
  ...
```

Apache Hadoop 0.20.203 and Later, and CDH4 (metrics2)

Starting with Apache Hadoop 0.20.203, the new metrics2 system is included and must be used. From the perspective of an administrator, the most noteworthy change is the method of configuration and some of the nomenclature. Many of the concepts and functionality of metrics1 are preserved, albeit in a more general capacity.

One of the primary drawbacks of metrics1 was the one-to-one relationship of context to plug-in. Supporting a more generic system where metrics could be handled by multiple plug-ins was necessary. In metrics2, we refer to metrics sources and sinks. The former are components that generate metrics; the latter consume them. The terms are analogous to the relationship between a context and its configured plug-in in the older metrics1 system. Components of Hadoop that wish to produce metrics implement the `MetricsSource` interface or use a set of simple Java annotations; those that wish to receive and process metric data implement the `MericsSink` interface. The framework, based on the administrator-provided configuration, handles getting the metrics from sources to sinks.

By default, all metrics from all sources are delivered to all sinks. This is the desired behavior in most cases—to deliver all metrics to a single file, or to Ganglia, for example. When more elaborate routing of data is required, one can filter metrics by the context to which they belong, as well as other so-called tags. Filters can be applied to a source, record, or even metric name. Note that the more specific the filter, the greater the overhead incurred during metric processing, as you might expect.

System configuration is done by way of the *hadoop-metrics2.properties* (note the subtle number 2 in the name) file in the standard Hadoop configuration directory. Like its predecessor, *hadoop-metrics2.properties* is a Java properties file, but it uses a few special conventions to express defaults and overrides. In Example 10-5, a simple metrics2 configuration file is shown.

Example 10-5. Sample hadoop-metrics2.properties configuration file

```
# hadoop-metrics2.properties

# By default, send metrics from all sources to the sink
# named 'file', using the implementation class FileSink.
*.sink.file.class = org.apache.hadoop.metrics2.sink.FileSink

# Override the parameter 'filename' in 'file' for the namenode.
namenode.sink.file.filename = namenode-metrics.log

# Send the jobtracker metrics into a separate file.
jobtracker.sink.file.filename = jobtracker-metrics.log
```

Each property name in the configuration file has four components: prefix, type, instance, and option, in that order. For instance, in the property namenode.sink.file.filename, namenode is the prefix, sink is the type, file is the instance, and filename is the option. These components can be replaced by an asterisk (*) to indicate that an option should act as a default. For more information on the advanced features of metrics2, see the Javadoc (*http://bit.ly/javadoc_packagesummary*).

What about SNMP?

Most system administrators have encountered the Simple Network Management Protocol (or SNMP) at one time or another. SNMP, like JMX, is a standard for extracting metrics from a service or device and is supported by many, if not all, monitoring systems. If JMX could be called cryptic, SNMP borders on alien, with equally obtuse terminology and a long history of security issues (this is theoretically resolved with SNMPv3, but it's still exceedingly complicated). Hadoop has no direct SNMP support and no defined MIB module. Users are encouraged to use JMX, as it offers similar functionality and industry adoption, if they'd rather not write custom code to interface with the JSON servlet.

Health Monitoring

Once Hadoop is properly configured and integrated with your monitoring system of choice, the next step is to decide which metrics are important and which aren't. Even more so, the question of which metrics most accurately represent the health of a given service is the critical question. Because there are dependencies between services, it usually makes sense to model this relationship in the monitoring system to quell spurious alerts. For instance, if HDFS isn't available, it probably doesn't make sense to ring the alarm for MapReduce. There are, however, a handful of metrics for each service that act as the canary in the coal mine, so to speak.

Metric selection is only half the battle when configuring monitoring systems. Equally important are the thresholds we establish to indicate alert conditions. The problem with monitoring in general is that on any active system, as soon as a measurement is taken, it is immediately outdated. Assume for a minute that a host check reveals that the disk containing the namenode metadata is 93% full. It's unclear whether this is alert worthy because on a 1TB disk, this means that almost 72GB is still available. Knowing the total size of the disk is necessary, but it doesn't reveal the full story because we still don't know the *rate* of growth. If disk space is consumed at a rate of 1GB per day on average, 72GB is more than sufficient and shouldn't yield an alert. Always remember that the rate of growth must also factor in the rate of attrition of old data, which in some cases can be independently controlled. Aggressive log pruning is a good example of compensating for resource consumption by reducing the retention rate of other data that may exist on the same device.

So what does all of this mean when establishing alert thresholds? Here are some basic rules:

- All thresholds are fluid. As cluster usage and resource consumption changes, so too should alert thresholds.
- For new clusters, start with a conservative value for a threshold, measure usage, and refine over time. Remember that utilization patterns can occur at different intervals. For example, it's not uncommon to have a significant bump in activity

for clusters primarily used for analytics during office hours, at the end of the month, the end of the quarter, and the end of the year.

- A high signal-to-noise ratio for alerts is absolutely critical. Overly sensitive alerting will desensitize an operations team to the criticality of the event, and it fatigues staff.

Host-Level Checks

The host on which the various daemons run must have the requisite local disk capacity, free memory, and minimal amount of CPU capacity. Some services require significant (read: as much as possible) network bandwidth; others are far more sensitive to latency. Here, we'll focus on what checks should be in place on any Hadoop cluster.

Most Hadoop daemons use the local disk in one way or another. Historically, many of the daemons have not taken kindly to exhausting the available storage resources on a host. In the case of the namenode, for instance, it was trivial to accidentally corrupt the metadata by filling the disk on which the edit log was stored until recent versions (which admittedly only reduce the chance, not eliminate the possibility). Although the level of maturity of the software has increased over time, better still is to not test such scenarios.

Recommendation: Monitor local disk consumption of the namenode metadata (`dfs.name.dir`) and log data (`HADOOP_LOG_DIR`) directories. To estimate the immediate rate of growth, use a 14-day rolling average and alert when the remaining capacity is below 5 to 30 days' capacity, depending on how long it normally takes you to mitigate the situation. The low end of five days is recommended to provide enough overlap for long weekends.

Datanode (`dfs.data.dir`) directories differ from most others in that they exist to permanently store huge amounts of data. When a datanode directory fills to capacity, it stops receiving new blocks. If all datanode directories become full, the namenode will stop placing blocks on that datanode, effectively treating it as read-only. Remember that if you choose to colocate MapReduce local data and datanode data on the same devices, you should properly configure `dfs.datanode.du.reserved` to ensure capacity remains for task temporary data (see `dfs.datanode.du.reserved` on page 96 for more information). MapReduce local (`mapred.local.dir`) directories have spiky usage patterns, and as a result, their capacity can be difficult to monitor in a meaningful way. All data in these directories is transient and will be cleaned up when no longer needed by running jobs, whether they succeed or fail. Should all volumes supporting `mapred.local.dir` become invalid due to capacity exhaustion or disk failures, the tasktracker becomes unusable by the system. Any tasks assigned to that node will inevitably fail and the tasktracker will eventually be blacklisted by the jobtracker.

Recommendation: Monitor `dfs.data.dir` and `mapred.local.dir` directories' volumes SMART (*http://en.wikipedia.org/wiki/S.M.A.R.T.*) errors and capacity, but avoid alerting at this level, if possible. Instead, opt for higher-level checks on the aggregate HDFS and MapReduce service level metrics for alerts, and warnings for individual hosts and disks. To put it another way, a disk failure in a worker node is not something that an administrator should wake up for unless it has an impact on the larger service.

Physical and virtual memory utilization are of concern when evaluating the health of a host in a cluster. Each daemon's maximum heap allocation (roughly) defines its worst-case memory footprint. During configuration, the sum of the memory consumption of all daemons should never exceed physical memory. Provided that this is true, and there's nothing else running on the hosts in a Hadoop cluster, these machines should never swap. Should a host begin swapping, a ripple effect can occur that drastically decreases performance at best—and causes failures at worst.

Recommendation: Monitor to ensure that the number of pages (or amount of data in bytes, whatever is easier) swapped in and out to disk, per second, does not exceed zero, or some very small amount. Note that this is not the same as monitoring the amount of swap space consumed—a common mistake. The Linux kernel is not obliged to re-claim swap space previously consumed, until it is needed, even after the data is swapped back in, so monitoring the utilization of the swap file(s) or partition(s) is almost guaranteed to generate false positives.

Processor utilization—specifically, load average—is one of the most frequently mis-understood metrics that people monitor on hosts. The CPU load average in Linux is the average number of processes in a runnable state on a machine, over a rolling window of time. Normally, three discreet values are given: the 5-, 10-, and 15-minute averages. A contrived, "perfect utilization" example of this would be a 5-minute load average of 1.00 on a single-core CPU, meaning that over the last five minutes, the core was fully occupied by a running process. Modern server CPUs have between four and eight physical cores (at the time of this writing) and can support a perfect utilization of a number greater than 1.00. In other words, you should fully expect, and target, the load average of a Hadoop worker node to be roughly equal to the number of cores, either physical, or virtual if you have a feature such as Hyper-Threading enabled. Of course, it's rare to achieve such perfection in the real world. The point is to absolutely not set alert thresholds on load average on a large Hadoop cluster unless you wish to regularly swim in a sea of false alerts.

Recommendation: Track CPU metrics such as load average for performance and uti-lization measurement, but do not alert on them unless there's an unusually compelling reason (hint: there isn't).

Network bandwidth consumption is similar to CPU utilization in the context of mon-itoring. Ideally, this is a metric we track because it tells us something about the behavior of HDFS data ingress and egress, or running MapReduce jobs, but there's no prescribed upper limit at which it makes sense to alert. Latency, on the other hand, can cause some services to fail outright, which primarily affects HBase, where a region server becoming even temporarily disconnected from its ZooKeeper quorum can cause it to shut down and possibly even precipitate a cascading failure, but it's still a point of concern. The

RPC metrics from the individual daemons provide better insight into the observed latency, so we measure it there.

Recommendation: Network latency checks are best measured by looking at the total RPC latency, as reported by the daemons themselves, because that's what we're really interested in. Bandwidth utilization is interesting from a performance perspective and can help detect (or eliminate) possible bottlenecks (something we'll look at later).

Arguably, a host-level check of process presence is a common, simple, check performed to measure health. Unfortunately, the mere presence of a Hadoop process isn't a reliable indication that a service is alive or healthy because of the distributed nature of the system. It's very possible for a daemon to be alive and running but unable to communicate with other nodes in the cluster, for whatever reason. The uncertainty of this method of monitoring, coupled with the fact that Hadoop does provide meaningful metrics from each daemon, means that process presence checks are probably best skipped in Hadoop clusters. Skipping them also reduces the amount of potential noise generated from process-level restarts during maintenance operations, which is a nice side effect.

Recommendation: Skip process presence checks altogether when monitoring hosts, instead deferring to daemon and service-level metric checks as described later in this chapter.

All Hadoop Processes

All Hadoop processes are Java processes and as a result, have a common set of checks that should be performed. One of the most important checks to perform, especially in the instances of the namenode and jobtracker, is the available heap memory remaining within the JVM. Using the JMX REST servlet, for example, it's possible to discover the initial, maximum, and used heap (Example 10-6). Unfortunately, determining the health of a process is not as simple as just subtracting the used heap from the max because of the way garbage collection works. The amount of *used* memory is always less than or equal to the committed memory and represents the amount of heap that actually used by objects. The *committed* memory is the current size of the heap. That is, the amount of memory that has been allocated from the operating system and can be immediately consumed by objects if it is needed. Committed memory is always less than or equal to the maximum heap size. Should the amount of used memory exceed (or need to exceed) the amount of committed memory, and the committed memory is below the max, the amount of committed memory is increased. On the other hand, if an application attempts to grow its usage beyond the current committed memory, but the committed memory cannot expand anymore due to the max, the JVM will run out of memory, resulting in the dreaded OutOfMemoryError.

Example 10-6. Sample JVM memory JSON metric data from the namenode

```
{
    "name" : "java.lang:type=Memory",
    "modelerType" : "sun.management.MemoryImpl",
    "Verbose" : false,
    "HeapMemoryUsage" : {
      "committed" : 1234829312,
      "init" : 1584914432,
      "max" : 7635533824,
      "used" : 419354712
    },
    "NonHeapMemoryUsage" : {
      "committed" : 47841280,
      "init" : 24313856,
      "max" : 136314880,
      "used" : 47586032
    },
    "ObjectPendingFinalizationCount" : 0
  }
```

It is very common for the amount of used memory to increase over time until it comes extremely close to the committed or even maximum thresholds and then to immediately jump back down as the result of a garbage collection event, and it is perfectly normal. In fact, this is how it is supposed to work. It's also why monitoring memory can be difficult.

One option for monitoring a dynamic heap like this is to measure the median used heap over a set of samples rather than the absolute value at a point in time. If the median remains high for a period of time (which needs to be long enough for at least one full garbage collection to occur), it's probably not going to change and an alert should be triggered. Alternatively, if you are concerned about false positives and you want to ensure that a full garbage collection has occurred, there are metrics to expose the number of full garbage collection events per pool that can be combined with a check of the median.

Recommendation: Perform heap monitoring on the namenode, jobtracker, and secondary namenode processes using the technique described.

In addition to the amount of memory available, some applications are sensitive to the duration of garbage collection events. This tends to plague low-latency services, especially where, because the JVM spends a long time dealing with garbage, it's unable to service requests in a timely manner. For an application such as the namenode, this can be particularly disruptive. Being unable to answer a request for even a couple of seconds can be the same as not answering it at all. Included in the JVM-level metrics, you will find metrics for each memory pool that indicate both the number of garbage collection events as well as the average time each took.

Recommendation: Monitor the average time spent performing garbage collection for the namenode and jobtracker. Tolerance for these pauses before failure occurs will vary by application, but almost all will be negatively affected in terms of performance.

HDFS Checks

One of the advantages of HDFS is that the namenode, as a side effect of keeping track of all datanodes, has an authoritative picture of the state of the cluster. If, for some reason, the namenode becomes unavailable, it's impossible to perform any HDFS operations. Whatever the namenode sees is what clients will see when they access the filesystem. This design saves us the otherwise difficult task of correlating the events and state information of the datanodes, leaving no room for nondeterminism in health checks.

Earlier, a general recommendation was made to prefer service-level health and metric checks. Using the aggregate view from the namenode, we see a more complete picture of HDFS as a service. Most of the critical health checks performed use the metric data produced by the namenode. In the following sections, we'll use the output of the JMX JSON servlet because of its readability, but you should be able to access this data using any of the methods described earlier. Within the namenode's metrics, you will find an MBean called `Hadoop:service=NameNode,name=NameNodeInfo`, shown in Example 10-7, which contains high-level HDFS information.

Example 10-7. Sample NameNodeInfo JSON metric data from the namenode

```
{
  "name" : "Hadoop:service=NameNode,name=NameNodeInfo",
  "modelerType" : "org.apache.hadoop.hdfs.server.namenode.FSNamesystem",
  "Threads" : 55,
  "Total" : 193868941611008,
  "ClusterId" : "CID-908b11f7-c752-4753-8fbc-3d209b3088ff",
  "BlockPoolId" : "BP-875753299-172.29.121.132-1340735471649",
  "Used" : 50017852084224,
  "Version" : "2.0.0-cdh4.0.0, r5d678f6bb1f2bc49e2287dd69ac41d7232fc9cdc",
  "PercentUsed" : 25.799828,
  "PercentRemaining" : 68.18899,
  "Free" : 132197265809408,
  "Safemode" : "",
  "UpgradeFinalized" : false,
  "NonDfsUsedSpace" : 11653823717376,
  "BlockPoolUsedSpace" : 50017852084224,
  "PercentBlockPoolUsed" : 25.799828,
  "TotalBlocks" : 179218,
  "TotalFiles" : 41219,
  "NumberOfMissingBlocks" : 4725,
  "LiveNodes" : "{
    \"hadoop02.cloudera.com\":{
      \"numBlocks\":40312,
      \"usedSpace\":5589478342656,
      \"lastContact\":2,
```

```
      \"capacity\":21540992634880,
      \"nonDfsUsedSpace\":1287876358144,
      \"adminState\":\"In Service\"
    },
    ...
  "DeadNodes" : "{}",
  "DecomNodes" : "{}",
  "NameDirStatuses" : "{
    \"failed\":{},
    \"active\":{
      \"/data/2/hadoop/dfs/nn\":\"IMAGE_AND_EDITS\",
      \"/data/1/hadoop/dfs/nn\":\"IMAGE_AND_EDITS\"
    }
  }"
}
```

This output is slightly reformatted for readability, and only a single datanode is shown in the LiveNodes map, but it should otherwise be self-explanatory. Some fields contain strings that are in turn distinct JSON blobs. Although this is awkward in the JSON output, it's a side effect of the way the underlying JMX MBeans store these values. If you do decide to use the JMX JSON servlet, expect to encounter this in a few places. In the above example, you can see this in the LiveNodes, DeadNodes, and NameDirSta tuses, for example.

Recommendation: From this data, perform the following critical health checks:

- The absolute amount of free HDFS capacity in bytes (Free) is over an acceptable threshold.

- The absolute number of active (NameDirStatuses["active"]) metadata paths is equal to those specified in dfs.name.dir, or failed (NameDirStatuses["failed"]) paths is equal to zero.

The next set of checks uses metrics found in the Hadoop:service=NameNode,name=FSNa mesystem MBean (see Example 10-8). Here you will find filesystem-level metrics about files, blocks, edit log transactions, checkpoint operations, and more.

Example 10-8. Sample FSNamesystem JSON metric data from the namenode

```
{
  "name" : "Hadoop:service=NameNode,name=FSNamesystem",
  "modelerType" : "FSNamesystem",
  "tag.Context" : "dfs",
  "tag.HAState" : "active",
  "tag.Hostname" : "hadoop01.cloudera.com",
  "MissingBlocks" : 4725,
  "ExpiredHeartbeats" : 2,
  "TransactionsSinceLastCheckpoint" : 58476,
  "TransactionsSinceLastLogRoll" : 7,
  "LastWrittenTransactionId" : 58477,
  "LastCheckpointTime" : 1340735472996,
  "CapacityTotalGB" : 180555.0,
  "CapacityUsedGB" : 46583.0,
```

```
"CapacityRemainingGB" : 123118.0,
"TotalLoad" : 9,
"BlocksTotal" : 179218,
"FilesTotal" : 41219,
"PendingReplicationBlocks" : 0,
"UnderReplicatedBlocks" : 4736,
"CorruptBlocks" : 0,
"ScheduledReplicationBlocks" : 0,
"PendingDeletionBlocks" : 0,
"ExcessBlocks" : 0,
"PostponedMisreplicatedBlocks" : 0,
"PendingDataNodeMessageCount" : 0,
"MillisSinceLastLoadedEdits" : 0,
"BlockCapacity" : 8388608,
"TotalFiles" : 41219
}
```

You may notice redundant information between NameNodeInfo and FSNamesystem like the former's Total and the latter's CapacityTotalGB (albeit in a different unit). In fact, if you look closer, there's even redundant information in FSNamesystem itself (see TotalFiles and FilesTotal). All of these numbers are computed using the same snapshot of the metrics and, as a result, should be consistent with one another.

Recommendation: Create health checks for the following:

- The absolute number of missing (MissingBlocks) and corrupt blocks (Corrupt Blocks) are lower than a acceptable threshold. Both of these metrics should be zero, ideally.

- The absolute number of HDFS blocks that can still be allocated (BlockCapacity). This is the maximum number of blocks that a namenode will track before it refuses new file creation. It exists to prevent accidental out of memory errors due to over-allocation. Increasing the namenode heap size automatically adjusts the total number of blocks allowed.

- The result of the current epoch time minus the last time a namenode checkpoint was performed (LastCheckpointTime) is less than three days. In the previous example, LastCheckpointTime is 1340735472996 or Tuesday, June 26th 11:31:12 PDT 2012. Assuming that the current time is 1341356207664 or Tuesday Jul 03 15:56:47 PDT 2012, this yields 620734668 or approximately 7.1 days because $(1340735472996 - 1341356207664) / 1000 / 60 / 60 / 24 = 7.1$. Note that epoch timestamps generated by Java are expressed in milliseconds, not seconds—hence the division by 1000 in the example.

MapReduce Checks

As with HDFS, most of the monitoring of MapReduce is done at the master process— in this case, the jobtracker. There are two major components to monitoring MapReduce: monitoring the framework and monitoring individual jobs. Job-level monitoring is not a good fit for most monitoring systems and can be incredibly application specific. Instead, we'll focus on monitoring the MapReduce framework.

Using the same JMX REST servlet as we did earlier, let's take a look at some of the available metrics in Example 10-9.

Example 10-9. Sample JobTrackerInfo JSON metric data from the jobtracker

```json
{
  "name" : "hadoop:service=JobTracker,name=JobTrackerInfo",
  "modelerType" : "org.apache.hadoop.mapred.JobTracker",
  "Hostname" : "mo507",
  "Version" : "2.0.0-mr1-cdh4.0.1, rUnknown",
  "ConfigVersion" : "default",
  "ThreadCount" : 45,
  "SummaryJson" : "{
    \"nodes\":8,
    \"alive\":8,
    \"blacklisted\":0,
    \"slots\":{
      \"map_slots\":128,
      \"map_slots_used\":128,
      \"reduce_slots\":48,
      \"reduce_slots_used\":0
    },
    \"jobs\":3
  }",
  "AliveNodesInfoJson" : "[
    {
      \"hostname\":\"hadoop01.cloudera.com\",
      \"last_seen\":1343782287934,
      \"health\":\"OK\",
      \"slots\":{
        \"map_slots\":16,
        \"map_slots_used\":16,
        \"reduce_slots\":6,
        \"reduce_slots_used\":0
      },
      \"failures\":0,
      \"dir_failures\":0
    },
    // Remaining hosts omitted...
  ]",
  "BlacklistedNodesInfoJson" : "[]",
  "QueueInfoJson" : "{\"default\":{\"info\":\"N/A\"}}"
}
```

Aggregate cluster metrics are provided as JSON blob in the SummaryJson field. The total number of nodes currently alive, total map slots available and used, total reduce slots available and used, and total job submissions are also available.

Recommendation: Perform the following cluster-level checks:

- Check whether the number of alive nodes is within a tolerance that still allows your jobs to complete within their service-level agreement. Depending on the size of your cluster and the criticality of jobs, this will vary.

- Check whether the number of blacklisted tasktrackers is below some percentage of the total number of tasktrackers in the cluster. A blacklisted tasktracker is one that is alive but is demonstrating repeated failures across jobs. This number should ideally be zero, although it's possible to trigger false positives if a user or a system rapidly submits a series of poorly written jobs that ultimately fail. On the other hand, such a result is almost certainly indicative of a problem that should be dealt with as well, although not specifically a cluster issue.

You can see that like the namenode, the jobtracker reports all of its workers (tasktrackers, in this case) and their status. These are hosts from which the aggregate cluster information is taken. Be careful not to over-monitor individual tasktrackers, as it's not unusual to have intermittent failures at scale. You may optionally choose to monitor for `dir_failures`, which represent a directory in `mapred.local.dir` that has been ignored by a tasktracker, which is usually a sign of a impending (or complete) disk failure within the machine. If a datanode shares the same underlying device, expect this to impact it as well. The `failures` field is a counter of the number of task failures that occurred on that specific tasktracker. It's common for some number of failures to occur, so it's hard to provide a concrete recommendation as to a specific threshold. Instead, you can optionally monitor the deviation of the tasktracker's number of failures from the average over the others.

## CHAPTER 11

Backup and Recovery

Data Backup

After accumulating a few petabytes of data or so, someone inevitably asks how all this data is going to be backed up. It's a deceptively difficult problem to overcome when working with such a large repository of data. Overcoming even simple problems like knowing what has changed since the last backup can prove difficult with a high rate of new data arrival in a sufficiently large cluster. All backup solutions need to deal explicitly with a few key concerns. Selecting the data that should be backed up is a two-dimensional problem, in that both the critical datasets must be choosen, as must, within each dataset, the subset of the data that has not yet been backed up. The timeliness of backups is another important question. Data can be backed up less frequently, in larger batches, but this affects the window of possible data loss. Ratcheting up the frequency of a backup may not be feasible due to the incurred overhead. Finally, one of the most difficult problems that must be tackled is that of backup consistency. Copying the data as it's changing can potentially result in an invalid backup. For this reason, some knowledge of how the application functions with respect to the underlying filesystem is necessary. Those with experience administering relational databases are intimately aware of the problems with simply copying data out from under a running system.

The act of taking a backup implies the execution of a batch operation that (usually) marks a specific point in time, copies a subset of the total data to a second location, and records the success or failure of the process. Whether applications can continue working during the copy phase depends on how they manage data and the features offered by the filesystem. Many enterprise filesystems support advanced features such as snapshots to minimize the window of time required to get a consistent capture of the data on disk and decoupling it from the time required to copy said data elsewhere. Today, HDFS doesn't support snapshots, although the community is working on this feature as part of the Apache HDFS JIRA HDFS-233 (*https://issues.apache.org/jira/browse/HDFS-233*). It is a little simpler working with HDFS, however, because of the write-once semantics of files. Short of replacing a file, it is possible only to append to an existing file or write a new file altogether.

There are two primary approaches to backup today. The first is the distributed copy tool, or distcp for short, which copies HDFS data in parallel either to another location within the same cluster, or between clusters. Another common approach is an architectural solution to the backup problem that involves writing incoming data to two clusters from an application. Each has advantages and disadvantages, and they lend themselves to different situations.

Distributed Copy (distcp)

Hadoop includes the distcp utility, which is, effectively, a MapReduce job that performs parallel copies of HDFS either to the local cluster or to a remote cluster. Users of the rsync utility will notice similarities in the feature set of distcp and should feel at home with how it works. For others, much of the help text is self-explanatory (see Example 11-1). In Apache Hadoop 1.x and CDH3 releases, distcp is a subcommand of the hadoop command, whereas later versions include it as a subcommand of mapred.

Example 11-1. DistCp help text

```
[esammer@hadoop01 ~]$ hadoop distcp
java.lang.IllegalArgumentException: Missing dst path
  at org.apache.hadoop.tools.DistCp$Arguments.valueOf(DistCp.java:830)
  at org.apache.hadoop.tools.DistCp.run(DistCp.java:881)
  at org.apache.hadoop.util.ToolRunner.run(ToolRunner.java:65)
  at org.apache.hadoop.util.ToolRunner.run(ToolRunner.java:79)
  at org.apache.hadoop.tools.DistCp.main(DistCp.java:908)

distcp [OPTIONS] <srcurl>* <desturl>

OPTIONS:
-p[rbugp]               Preserve status
                        r: replication number
                        b: block size
                        u: user
                        g: group
                        p: permission
                        -p alone is equivalent to -prbugp
-i                      Ignore failures
-log <logdir>           Write logs to <logdir>
-m <num_maps>           Maximum number of simultaneous copies
-overwrite              Overwrite destination
-update                 Overwrite if src size different from dst size
-skipcrccheck           Do not use CRC check to determine if src is
                        different from dest. Relevant only if -update
                        is specified
-f <urilist_uri>        Use list at <urilist_uri> as src list
-filelimit <n>          Limit the total number of files to be <= n
-sizelimit <n>          Limit the total size to be <= n bytes
-delete                 Delete the files existing in the dst but not in src
-mapredSslConf <f>      Filename of SSL configuration for mapper task

NOTE 1: if -overwrite or -update are set, each source URI is
        interpreted as an isomorphic update to an existing directory.
```

```
For example:
hadoop distcp -p -update "hdfs://A:8020/user/foo/bar" "hdfs://B:8020/user/foo/baz"

    would update all descendants of 'baz' also in 'bar'; it would
    *not* update /user/foo/baz/bar

NOTE 2: The parameter <n> in -filelimit and -sizelimit can be
    specified with symbolic representation.  For examples,
      1230k = 1230 * 1024 = 1259520
      891g = 891 * 1024^3 = 956703965184
```

The URLs referred to by the distcp help text (seen in the previous extract as `<srcurl>` and `<dsturl>`) are the same as one would use when referring to an HDFS or local file-system path. That is, to copy data from the HDFS cluster managed by namenode A to the HDFS cluster managed by namenode B, we'd use the command hadoop distcp hdfs://A:8020/path/one hdfs://B:8020/path/two as in Example 11-2.

Example 11-2. Performing a simple copy with distcp between clusters

```
[esammer@hadoop01 ~]$ hadoop distcp hdfs://A:8020/path/one hdfs://B:8020/path/two
```

Note that it's perfectly valid to copy data to the same cluster, but under a different path, as shown in Example 11-3.

Example 11-3. Performing a copy with distcp within the same cluster

```
[esammer@hadoop01 ~]$ hadoop distcp hdfs://A:8020/path/one hdfs://A:8020/path/two
```

In fact, it's possible to omit the scheme and host portions of the URLs if the default from the client's fs.default.name parameter is sufficient. In Example 11-4, we assume that fs.default.name is set to *hdfs://A:8020/*.

Example 11-4. Performing a copy with distcp within the same cluster using the default scheme

```
[esammer@hadoop01 ~]$ hadoop distcp /path/one /path/two
```

When the utility runs, it creates a list of files and directories to copy based on the source URL and creates a MapReduce job with a fixed number of map tasks, each of which works on a set of files. The -m option controls the number of mapper to spawn for a given job. By default, distcp assumes that you want to perform a basic copy for which the destination doesn't exist. If the destination does exist, you must tell distcp how you want it to behave with respect to existing data. You may optionally overwrite any existing files with the -overwrite option or attempt to update or freshen the data with -update. Updating existing data uses the size of the file, but also a CRC32 checksum, to decide what files have changed. This task can take some time, so it's possible to disable the CRC32 checksum calculation with the -skipcrccheck option. The -delete option, like rsync's --delete option, attempts to delete any files in the destination that do not exist in the source path. Combined with the -update option, this option makes distcp behave like a file synchronization utility. In most cases, it's desirable to preserve the owner, group, permissions, and other file attributes when performing a copy, although doing so requires superuser privileges on the destination cluster because you're writing files as users other than the effective user of your process. As for the permissions required to read the files on the source cluster, you must, of course, have at least read access to the files you wish to back up or be the super user.

There are, however, a few limitations to using `distcp` for backups. Because it runs as a MapReduce job, `distcp` does chew up map slots and has all the same associated overhead therein. Each map task in the job is essentially an HDFS client of the remote cluster, and all the same HDFS write path semantics apply. Notably, each client—which in this case, is any worker node in the cluster—must be able to write to each datanode in the remote cluster directly. This setup creates an $N \times M$ communication pattern requirement between the two clusters, where N is the number of source cluster nodes and M is the number of destination cluster nodes. Environments that do not permit full $N \times M$ communication between clusters either will not be able to use `distcp` or will experience a ton of pain trying to configure SOCKS proxies appropriately (which, ultimately, may not be able to withstand the amount of data transfer). Depending on the network infrastructure, this may or may not be a problem. It's also important to control the number of map tasks and data transferred appropriately, lest you saturate any private data center interconnect.

When using the *hdfs://* schema to connect to clusters, each cluster must be running the same version of the Hadoop software. If this is not the case, *webhdfs://* should be used instead; it uses an HTTP-based, version-agnostic protocol to transfer data. This benefit does come at some cost to performance, but presumably being able to transfer the data slower is better than not being able to transfer it at all. One final option is to use the *httpfs://* protocol, which, like *webhdfs://*, uses HTTP, but instead of using the embedded web server in each datanode, it uses a dedicated HDFS HttpFS proxy daemon to communicate with the cluster. Both *webhdfs://* and *httpfs://* require some additional, minor configuration.

Parallel Data Ingestion

Traditionally, we think of the data flow as an application to master storage, and then master storage to slave or backup storage as a batch job, at a fixed interval. In fact, that's what the preceding section describes, and it makes sense for a few reasons. This model is simple for application developers to deal with and allows backup to be controlled in a central manner. Backup is outside of the developer domain, a problem for someone else to contend with, and largely transparent. For operations staff, this is the source of many consistency questions: where exactly is the opportunity to take a consistent picture of the data, given different applications? A different perspective on the backup problem is to instead handle it explicitly at the application level, where the consistency semantics are well-known. Treating backup as a first-class problem to be handled by the application forces the problem into the spotlight, where it can be dealt with explicitly and controlled.

So what does that mean? Trivially, have each application responsible for data ingestion write to two discreet clusters, completely eliminating the separate backup process. Although it's possible to make two write operations, normally this is done by having applications write to a durable service that in turn delivers events to two different places. This approach decouples the application write from the cluster writes, acting as a queue, similar to a messaging system. For this method to be feasible, the application must be sure to deliver to the ingest service, which delivers to each cluster asynchronously so that blocking does not occur. Additionally, for the application to know that the data will safely delivered to each cluster (eventually), the ingest service must be durable. In some cases, this durability can be traded for speed, although that wouldn't be appropriate for revenue-bearing events.

You could build this setup yourself; however, a number of open source systems in the Hadoop ecosystem provide exactly this functionality. One of these systems is Apache Flume. Flume can be configured to listen to various data sources like RPC interfaces— for instance, writing received events to one or more channels, which are ultimately connected to sinks. Channels are effectively a queue, and can be reliable, in which case they store data durably on disk before attempting delivery, or not, in which case they only store events in memory while they shuffle it along as fast as possible. Sinks take events from channels and do something with them. The most popular of the sinks is the HDFS sink, which writes events into HDFS in various configurable ways. Flume's ability to "fan out" and duplicate events to separate channels, each of which may go to separate clusters, is one way to deal with the problem of backup, that is, avoiding it as much as possible by rethinking the problem.

Flume isn't a perfect fit for all use cases. It is specifically built for streaming data sources that produce data as discreet events. Primarily, this means log files or things that look like that: syslog events, log4j messages, and so forth. Refer to the Flume website (*http://flume.apache.org/*) and documentation for more information about its intended set of use cases.

When plain old files need to be uploaded to HDFS, the parallel write technique can still be used. Rather than have processes write files directly to HDFS or call the `hdfs dfs -put` command directly, write the file to a designated directory on a local filesystem somewhere. Use a polling process to scan this directory for new files and create hardlinks (not symlinks) into a set of directories that act as a queue for each cluster. When the hardlinks are all successfully created, the original entry in the first directory can be deleted. A poller for each cluster can now run asynchronously, scanning only its directory for new files to upload. When the file is successfully uploaded, it can be deleted. The hardlink decrements the reference count on the data on disk, and after all clusters have copied and deleted their respective pending hardlinks, the data is removed from the local disk. This approach makes sense for cases in which data should be uploaded to multiple HDFS clusters reliably and removed from the staging or incoming area.

Using these techniques, the only remaining data that needs to be backed up in a traditional fashion is that which is generated as a result of MapReduce jobs within HDFS.

Although some of this data is critical and should be backed up using `distcp` and other traditional cluster-to-cluster copy techniques, it's possible that much of it can be regenerated from the raw source data that was replicated on ingestion. With the total cluster processing power of MapReduce, regenerating the data in the event of catastrophic failure may be possible in a reasonably small amount of time, and although it's not the most fun way to spend an afternoon or two, it may be a calculated risk.

Parallel writes to multiple clusters have the added benefit of drastically reducing the window of time between discreet backup operations. Data is much fresher in both clusters, and this approach also opens the possibility of running read-only or ad hoc analysis jobs on the otherwise backup-only cluster. Another nice side effect is that by streaming data throughout the data to two clusters, the costly, large, batch network operation of a full or incremental backup is amortized throughout the day. This way tends to be easier to manage and control and reduces the risk of a large backup "eating its tail" (meaning that the next backup is scheduled to start, but the previous instance is still running). Recovering from the case in which one cluster falls behind happens implicitly, because this technique is based on the idea of queuing. Temporarily disabling backups for maintenance is unnecessary; data destined for a cluster in maintenance accumulates in the queue until the cluster returns to service.

Again, there's no free lunch to be had here. The downside to this approach is that the idea of backups is something developers have to think about. Some (including myself) might argue that this is where the problem belongs, but there are plenty of reasons why this may not be feasible within an organization. Having additional infrastructure for data ingestion like Flume or file queuing means more to monitor.

Namenode Metadata

Without the namenode metadata, there might as well be no data in HDFS. Historically, for mission-critical production clusters, it has been essential to script namenode metadata backup. In Apache Hadoop 1.0 and CDH3, this is done by using two different calls to the *\/getimage* servlet included in the namenode's embedded web server. The first call uses the query parameter `getimage=1` and retrieves the *fsimage* file; the second uses `getedit=1` and returns the *edits* file. In both cases, the data is retrieved at a consistent point from disk, which guarantees that it can be safely restored later. In Example 11-5, we fetch a copy of the *fsimage* and *edits* files via the servlet and then use the `md5sum` command to prove that they are identical to what's on disk in the namenode's metadata directory. This validation step is only for illustration purposes; on an active cluster, it is very likely that the edits file would have changed between the time we fetched it and the time we compared the files with `md5sum`.

Example 11-5. Backing up the namenode metadata (Apache Hadoop 1.0 and CDH3)

```
[root@hadoop01 ~]# curl -o fsimage.20120801 'http://hadoop01:50070/getimage?getimage=1' \
  2>/dev/null
[root@hadoop01 ~]# curl -o edits.20120801 'http://hadoop01:50070/getimage?getedit=1' \
```

```
    2>/dev/null
[root@hadoop01 ~]# md5sum fsimage.20120801 /data/1/dfs/nn/current/fsimage \
    edits.20120801 /data/1/dfs/nn/current/edits
d04d6b0f60cf9603fcc7ff45b620d341  fsimage.20120801
d04d6b0f60cf9603fcc7ff45b620d341  /data/1/dfs/nn/current/fsimage
d944934c10b4f6b5ac8ba5f0490a759b  edits.20120801
d944934c10b4f6b5ac8ba5f0490a759b  /data/1/dfs/nn/current/edits
```

Apache Hadoop 2.0 and CDH4 use a new metadata storage format designed to be more resilient to corruption, as described in "Managing Filesystem Metadata" on page 14. As a result, the /getimage servlet in these versions works a little differently, although it serves the same purpose. To retrieve the latest *fsimage*, you must additionally pass the txid=latest query parameter. Retrieving edit transactions is a bit more complicated because the new storage system uses multiple edits files. It is now necessary to pass a start and end transaction ID. Despite being more cumbersome, this approach allows for incremental transaction retrieval, which can make the backup process more efficient. Example 11-6 demonstrates retrieval of the latest *fsimage* followed by the transactions 17 through 109. If an attempt is made to fetch a transaction range that the namenode does not have, an HTTP 410 error is returned, along with an HTML document containing a stack trace.

Example 11-6. Backing up the namenode metadata (Apache Hadoop 2.0 and CDH4)

```
[root@hadoop01 ~]# curl -o fsimage.20120801 \
    'http://hadoop01:50070/getimage?getimage=1&txid=latest' 2>/dev/null
[root@hadoop01 ~]# curl -o edits-17-109.20120801 \
    'http://hadoop01:50070/getimage?getedit=1&startTxId=17&endTxId=109' \
    2>/dev/null
```

Deprecated Configuration Properties

In Apache Hadoop 2.0 and CDH4, a large swath of configuration properties were deprecated and replaced with properties that have more accurate names. Although the original property names continue to work for standard (non-HA, nonfederated) HDFS deployments and MRv1, users of these versions are encouraged to switch to the new properties. For those who wish to use new features such as HDFS high availability, the new properties must be used. Table A-1 lists the Apache Hadoop 1.0/CDH3 property name and its new Apache Hadoop 2.0/CDH4 counterpart. Property names are ordered by the original name to make reference easier.

Table A-1. Deprecated property names and their replacements

Original Property Name	New Property Name
StorageId	dfs.datanode.StorageId
create.empty.dir.if.nonexist	mapreduce.jobcontrol.createdir.ifnotexist
dfs.access.time.precision	dfs.namenode.accesstime.precision
dfs.backup.address	dfs.namenode.backup.address
dfs.backup.http.address	dfs.namenode.backup.http-address
dfs.balance.bandwidthPerSec	dfs.datanode.balance.bandwidthPerSec
dfs.block.size	dfs.blocksize
dfs.client.buffer.dir	fs.client.buffer.dir
dfs.data.dir	dfs.datanode.data.dir
dfs.datanode.max.xcievers	dfs.datanode.max.transfer.threads
dfs.df.interval	fs.df.interval
dfs.http.address	dfs.namenode.http-address
dfs.https.address	dfs.namenode.https-address
dfs.https.client.keystore.resource	dfs.client.https.keystore.resource
dfs.https.need.client.auth	dfs.client.https.need-auth
dfs.max-repl-streams	dfs.namenode.replication.max-streams

Original Property Name	New Property Name
dfs.max.objects	dfs.namenode.max.objects
dfs.name.dir	dfs.namenode.name.dir
dfs.name.dir.restore	dfs.namenode.name.dir.restore
dfs.name.edits.dir	dfs.namenode.edits.dir
dfs.permissions	dfs.permissions.enabled
dfs.permissions.supergroup	dfs.permissions.superusergroup
dfs.read.prefetch.size	dfs.client.read.prefetch.size
dfs.replication.considerLoad	dfs.namenode.replication.considerLoad
dfs.replication.interval	dfs.namenode.replication.interval
dfs.replication.min	dfs.namenode.replication.min
dfs.replication.pending.timeout.sec	dfs.namenode.replication.pending.timeout-sec
dfs.safemode.extension	dfs.namenode.safemode.extension
dfs.safemode.threshold.pct	dfs.namenode.safemode.threshold-pct
dfs.secondary.http.address	dfs.namenode.secondary.http-address
dfs.socket.timeout	dfs.client.socket-timeout
dfs.upgrade.permission	dfs.namenode.upgrade.permission
dfs.write.packet.size	dfs.client-write-packet-size
fs.checkpoint.dir	dfs.namenode.checkpoint.dir
fs.checkpoint.edits.dir	dfs.namenode.checkpoint.edits.dir
fs.checkpoint.period	dfs.namenode.checkpoint.period
fs.default.name	fs.defaultFS
hadoop.configured.node.mapping	net.topology.configured.node.mapping
hadoop.job.history.location	mapreduce.jobtracker.jobhistory.location
hadoop.native.lib	io.native.lib.available
hadoop.net.static.resolutions	mapreduce.tasktracker.net.static.resolutions
hadoop.pipes.command-file.keep	mapreduce.pipes.commandfile.preserve
hadoop.pipes.executable	mapreduce.pipes.executable
hadoop.pipes.executable.interpretor	mapreduce.pipes.executable.interpretor
hadoop.pipes.java.mapper	mapreduce.pipes.isjavamapper
hadoop.pipes.java.recordreader	mapreduce.pipes.isjavarecordreader
hadoop.pipes.java.recordwriter	mapreduce.pipes.isjavarecordwriter
hadoop.pipes.java.reducer	mapreduce.pipes.isjavareducer
hadoop.pipes.partitioner	mapreduce.pipes.partitioner

Original Property Name	New Property Name
heartbeat.recheck.interval	dfs.namenode.heartbeat.recheck-interval
io.bytes.per.checksum	dfs.bytes-per-checksum
io.sort.factor	mapreduce.task.io.sort.factor
io.sort.mb	mapreduce.task.io.sort.mb
io.sort.spill.percent	mapreduce.map.sort.spill.percent
job.end.notification.url	mapreduce.job.end-notification.url
job.end.retry.attempts	mapreduce.job.end-notifica tion.retry.attempts
job.end.retry.interval	mapreduce.job.end-notifica tion.retry.interval
job.local.dir	mapreduce.job.local.dir
jobclient.completion.poll.interval	mapreduce.client.completion.pollinterval
jobclient.output.filter	mapreduce.client.output.filter
jobclient.progress.monitor.poll.interval	mapreduce.client.progressmonitor.polli nterval
keep.failed.task.files	mapreduce.task.files.preserve.failedtasks
keep.task.files.pattern	mapreduce.task.files.preserve.filepattern
key.value.separator.in.input.line	mapreduce.input.keyvaluelinerecor dreader.key.value.separator
local.cache.size	mapreduce.tasktracker.cache.local.size
map.input.file	mapreduce.map.input.file
map.input.length	mapreduce.map.input.length
map.input.start	mapreduce.map.input.start
map.output.key.field.separator	mapreduce.map.output.key.field.separator
map.output.key.value.fields.spec	mapreduce.fieldsel.map.out put.key.value.fields.spec
mapred.acls.enabled	mapreduce.cluster.acls.enabled
mapred.binary.partitioner.left.offset	mapreduce.partition.binaryparti tioner.left.offset
mapred.binary.partitioner.right.offset	mapreduce.partition.binaryparti tioner.right.offset
mapred.cache.archives	mapreduce.job.cache.archives
mapred.cache.archives.timestamps	mapreduce.job.cache.archives.timestamps
mapred.cache.files	mapreduce.job.cache.files
mapred.cache.files.timestamps	mapreduce.job.cache.files.timestamps
mapred.cache.localArchives	mapreduce.job.cache.local.archives
mapred.cache.localFiles	mapreduce.job.cache.local.files

Original Property Name	New Property Name
mapred.child.tmp	mapreduce.task.tmp.dir
mapred.cluster.average.blacklist.threshold	mapreduce.jobtracker.blacklist.average.threshold
mapred.cluster.map.memory.mb	mapreduce.cluster.mapmemory.mb
mapred.cluster.max.map.memory.mb	mapreduce.jobtracker.maxmapmemory.mb
mapred.cluster.max.reduce.memory.mb	mapreduce.jobtracker.maxreducememory.mb
mapred.cluster.reduce.memory.mb	mapreduce.cluster.reducememory.mb
mapred.committer.job.setup.cleanup.needed	mapreduce.job.committer.setup.cleanup.needed
mapred.compress.map.output	mapreduce.map.output.compress
mapred.create.symlink	mapreduce.job.cache.symlink.create
mapred.data.field.separator	mapreduce.fieldsel.data.field.separator
mapred.debug.out.lines	mapreduce.task.debugout.lines
mapred.healthChecker.interval	mapreduce.tasktracker.healthchecker.interval
mapred.healthChecker.script.args	mapreduce.tasktracker.healthchecker.script.args
mapred.healthChecker.script.path	mapreduce.tasktracker.healthchecker.script.path
mapred.healthChecker.script.timeout	mapreduce.tasktracker.healthchecker.script.timeout
mapred.heartbeats.in.second	mapreduce.jobtracker.heartbeats.in.second
mapred.hosts	mapreduce.jobtracker.hosts.filename
mapred.hosts.exclude	mapreduce.jobtracker.hosts.exclude.filename
mapred.inmem.merge.threshold	mapreduce.reduce.merge.inmem.threshold
mapred.input.dir	mapreduce.input.fileinputformat.inputdir
mapred.input.dir.formats	mapreduce.input.multipleinputs.dir.formats
mapred.input.dir.mappers	mapreduce.input.multipleinputs.dir.mappers
mapred.input.pathFilter.class	mapreduce.input.pathFilter.class
mapred.jar	mapreduce.job.jar
mapred.job.classpath.archives	mapreduce.job.classpath.archives
mapred.job.classpath.files	mapreduce.job.classpath.files
mapred.job.id	mapreduce.job.id
mapred.job.map.memory.mb	mapreduce.map.memory.mb

Original Property Name	New Property Name
mapred.job.name	mapreduce.job.name
mapred.job.priority	mapreduce.job.priority
mapred.job.queue.name	mapreduce.job.queuename
mapred.job.reduce.input.buffer.percent	mapreduce.reduce.input.buffer.percent
mapred.job.reduce.markreset.buffer.per cent	mapreduce.reduce.markreset.buffer.percent
mapred.job.reduce.memory.mb	mapreduce.reduce.memory.mb
mapred.job.reduce.total.mem.bytes	mapreduce.reduce.memory.totalbytes
mapred.job.reuse.jvm.num.tasks	mapreduce.job.jvm.numtasks
mapred.job.shuffle.input.buffer.percent	mapreduce.reduce.shuffle.input.buffer.per cent
mapred.job.shuffle.merge.percent	mapreduce.reduce.shuffle.merge.percent
mapred.job.tracker	mapreduce.jobtracker.address
mapred.job.tracker.handler.count	mapreduce.jobtracker.handler.count
mapred.job.tracker.history.completed.loca tion	mapreduce.jobtracker.jobhistory.comple ted.location
mapred.job.tracker.http.address	mapreduce.jobtracker.http.address
mapred.job.tracker.jobhis tory.lru.cache.size	mapreduce.jobtracker.jobhis tory.lru.cache.size
mapred.job.tracker.persist.jobsta tus.active	mapreduce.jobtracker.persist.jobsta tus.active
mapred.job.tracker.persist.jobstatus.dir	mapreduce.jobtracker.persist.jobsta tus.dir
mapred.job.tracker.persist.jobsta tus.hours	mapreduce.jobtracker.persist.jobsta tus.hours
mapred.job.tracker.retire.jobs	mapreduce.jobtracker.retirejobs
mapred.job.tracker.retiredjobs.cache.size	mapreduce.jobtracker.retired jobs.cache.size
mapred.jobinit.threads	mapreduce.jobtracker.jobinit.threads
mapred.jobtracker.instrumentation	mapreduce.jobtracker.instrumentation
mapred.jobtracker.job.history.block.size	mapreduce.jobtracker.jobhis tory.block.size
mapred.jobtracker.maxtasks.per.job	mapreduce.jobtracker.maxtasks.perjob
mapred.jobtracker.restart.recover	mapreduce.jobtracker.restart.recover
mapred.jobtracker.taskScheduler	mapreduce.jobtracker.taskscheduler
mapred.jobtracker.taskScheduler.maxRun ningTasksPerJob	mapreduce.jobtracker.taskscheduler.maxrun ningtasks.perjob

Original Property Name	New Property Name
mapred.jobtracker.taskalloc.capacitypad	mapreduce.jobtracker.taskscheduler.taskalloc.capacitypad
mapred.join.expr	mapreduce.join.expr
mapred.join.keycomparator	mapreduce.join.keycomparator
mapred.lazy.output.format	mapreduce.output.lazyoutputformat.outputformat
mapred.line.input.format.linespermap	mapreduce.input.lineinputformat.linespermap
mapred.linerecordreader.maxlength	mapreduce.input.linerecordreader.line.maxlength
mapred.local.dir	mapreduce.cluster.local.dir
mapred.local.dir.minspacekill	mapreduce.tasktracker.local.dir.minspacekill
mapred.local.dir.minspacestart	mapreduce.tasktracker.local.dir.minspacestart
mapred.map.child.env	mapreduce.map.env
mapred.map.child.java.opts	mapreduce.map.java.opts
mapred.map.child.log.level	mapreduce.map.log.level
mapred.map.max.attempts	mapreduce.map.maxattempts
mapred.map.output.compression.codec	mapreduce.map.output.compress.codec
mapred.map.task.debug.script	mapreduce.map.debug.script
mapred.map.tasks	mapreduce.job.maps
mapred.map.tasks.speculative.execution	mapreduce.map.speculative
mapred.mapoutput.key.class	mapreduce.map.output.key.class
mapred.mapoutput.value.class	mapreduce.map.output.value.class
mapred.mapper.regex	mapreduce.mapper.regex
mapred.mapper.regex.group	mapreduce.mapper.regexmapper..group
mapred.max.map.failures.percent	mapreduce.map.failures.maxpercent
mapred.max.reduce.failures.percent	mapreduce.reduce.failures.maxpercent
mapred.max.split.size	mapreduce.input.fileinputformat.split.maxsize
mapred.max.tracker.blacklists	mapreduce.jobtracker.tasktracker.maxblacklists
mapred.max.tracker.failures	mapreduce.job.maxtaskfailures.per.tracker
mapred.merge.recordsBeforeProgress	mapreduce.task.merge.progress.records
mapred.min.split.size	mapreduce.input.fileinputformat.split.minsize

Original Property Name	New Property Name
mapred.min.split.size.per.node	mapreduce.input.fileinputformat.split.min size.per.node
mapred.min.split.size.per.rack	mapreduce.input.fileinputformat.split.min size.per.rack
mapred.output.compress	mapreduce.output.fileoutputformat.com press
mapred.output.compression.codec	mapreduce.output.fileoutputformat.com press.codec
mapred.output.compression.type	mapreduce.output.fileoutputformat.com press.type
mapred.output.dir	mapreduce.output.fileoutputformat.output dir
mapred.output.key.class	mapreduce.job.output.key.class
mapred.output.key.comparator.class	mapreduce.job.output.key.comparator.class
mapred.output.value.class	mapreduce.job.output.value.class
mapred.output.value.groupfn.class	mapreduce.job.output.group.compara tor.class
mapred.permissions.supergroup	mapreduce.cluster.permissions.supergroup
mapred.pipes.user.inputformat	mapreduce.pipes.inputformat
mapred.reduce.child.env	mapreduce.reduce.env
mapred.reduce.child.java.opts	mapreduce.reduce.java.opts
mapred.reduce.child.log.level	mapreduce.reduce.log.level
mapred.reduce.max.attempts	mapreduce.reduce.maxattempts
mapred.reduce.parallel.copies	mapreduce.reduce.shuffle.parallelcopies
mapred.reduce.slowstart.completed.maps	mapreduce.job.reduce.slowstart.completed maps
mapred.reduce.task.debug.script	mapreduce.reduce.debug.script
mapred.reduce.tasks	mapreduce.job.reduces
mapred.reduce.tasks.speculative.execution	mapreduce.reduce.speculative
mapred.seqbinary.output.key.class	mapreduce.output.seqbinaryoutputfor mat.key.class
mapred.seqbinary.output.value.class	mapreduce.output.seqbinaryoutputfor mat.value.class
mapred.shuffle.connect.timeout	mapreduce.reduce.shuffle.connect.timeout
mapred.shuffle.read.timeout	mapreduce.reduce.shuffle.read.timeout
mapred.skip.attempts.to.start.skipping	mapreduce.task.skip.start.attempts
mapred.skip.map.auto.incr.proc.count	mapreduce.map.skip.proc-count.auto-incr

Original Property Name	New Property Name
mapred.skip.map.max.skip.records	mapreduce.map.skip.maxrecords
mapred.skip.on	mapreduce.job.skiprecords
mapred.skip.out.dir	mapreduce.job.skip.outdir
mapred.skip.reduce.auto.incr.proc.count	mapreduce.reduce.skip.proc-count.auto-incr
mapred.skip.reduce.max.skip.groups	mapreduce.reduce.skip.maxgroups
mapred.speculative.execution.slowNodeThreshold	mapreduce.job.speculative.slownodethreshold
mapred.speculative.execution.slowTaskThreshold	mapreduce.job.speculative.slowtaskthreshold
mapred.speculative.execution.speculativeCap	mapreduce.job.speculative.speculativecap
mapred.submit.replication	mapreduce.client.submit.file.replication
mapred.system.dir	mapreduce.jobtracker.system.dir
mapred.task.cache.levels	mapreduce.jobtracker.taskcache.levels
mapred.task.id	mapreduce.task.attempt.id
mapred.task.is.map	mapreduce.task.ismap
mapred.task.partition	mapreduce.task.partition
mapred.task.profile	mapreduce.task.profile
mapred.task.profile.maps	mapreduce.task.profile.maps
mapred.task.profile.params	mapreduce.task.profile.params
mapred.task.profile.reduces	mapreduce.task.profile.reduces
mapred.task.timeout	mapreduce.task.timeout
mapred.task.tracker.http.address	mapreduce.tasktracker.http.address
mapred.task.tracker.report.address	mapreduce.tasktracker.report.address
mapred.task.tracker.task-controller	mapreduce.tasktracker.taskcontroller
mapred.tasktracker.dns.interface	mapreduce.tasktracker.dns.interface
mapred.tasktracker.dns.nameserver	mapreduce.tasktracker.dns.nameserver
mapred.tasktracker.events.batchsize	mapreduce.tasktracker.events.batchsize
mapred.tasktracker.expiry.interval	mapreduce.jobtracker.expire.trackers.interval
mapred.tasktracker.indexcache.mb	mapreduce.tasktracker.indexcache.mb
mapred.tasktracker.instrumentation	mapreduce.tasktracker.instrumentation
mapred.tasktracker.map.tasks.maximum	mapreduce.tasktracker.map.tasks.maximum
mapred.tasktracker.memory_calculator_plugin	mapreduce.tasktracker.resourcecalculatorplugin

Original Property Name	New Property Name
mapred.tasktracker.memorycalculatorplugin	mapreduce.tasktracker.resourcecalculator plugin
mapred.tasktracker.reduce.tasks.maximum	mapreduce.tasktracker.reduce.tasks.maxi mum
mapred.tasktracker.taskmemorymanager.moni toring-interval	mapreduce.tasktracker.taskmemoryman ager.monitoringinterval
mapred.tasktracker.tasks.sleeptime-before-sigkill	mapreduce.tasktracker.tasks.sleeptimebe foresigkill
mapred.temp.dir	mapreduce.cluster.temp.dir
mapred.text.key.comparator.options	mapreduce.partition.keycomparator.options
mapred.text.key.partitioner.options	mapreduce.partition.keyparti tioner.options
mapred.textoutputformat.separator	mapreduce.output.textoutputformat.separa tor
mapred.tip.id	mapreduce.task.id
mapred.used.genericoptionsparser	mapreduce.client.genericoptions parser.used
mapred.userlog.limit.kb	mapreduce.task.userlog.limit.kb
mapred.userlog.retain.hours	mapreduce.job.userlog.retain.hours
mapred.work.output.dir	mapreduce.task.output.dir
mapred.working.dir	mapreduce.job.working.dir
mapreduce.combine.class	mapreduce.job.combine.class
mapreduce.inputformat.class	mapreduce.job.inputformat.class
mapreduce.jobtracker.permissions.super group	mapreduce.cluster.permissions.supergroup
mapreduce.map.class	mapreduce.job.map.class
mapreduce.outputformat.class	mapreduce.job.outputformat.class
mapreduce.partitioner.class	mapreduce.job.partitioner.class
mapreduce.reduce.class	mapreduce.job.reduce.class
min.num.spills.for.combine	mapreduce.map.combine.minspills
reduce.output.key.value.fields.spec	mapreduce.fieldsel.reduce.out put.key.value.fields.spec
security.job.submission.protocol.acl	security.job.client.protocol.acl
security.task.umbilical.protocol.acl	security.job.task.protocol.acl
sequencefile.filter.class	mapreduce.input.sequencefileinputfil ter.class
sequencefile.filter.frequency	mapreduce.input.sequencefileinputfil ter.frequency

Original Property Name	New Property Name
sequencefile.filter.regex	mapreduce.input.sequencefileinputfil ter.regex
session.id	dfs.metrics.session-id
slave.host.name	mapreduce.tasktracker.host.name
tasktracker.contention.tracking	mapreduce.tasktracker.contention.tracking
tasktracker.http.threads	mapreduce.tasktracker.http.threads
topology.node.switch.mapping.impl	net.topology.node.switch.mapping.impl
topology.script.file.name	net.topology.script.file.name
topology.script.number.args	net.topology.script.number.args
user.name	mapreduce.job.user.name
webinterface.private.actions	mapreduce.jobtracker.webinterface.trusted

Index

Symbols
* (asterisk) everyone permitted, access control
    list, 156

A
absolute path, 21
access control list (ACL), 156
access switches, 69
access time, 66
ACL (access control list), 156
acl-administer-jobs, 157
acl-submit-job, 157
Active Directory, 164
administrative web interface, 35
administrators, 142
AES-128, 146
AES-256, 146
AFR (annualized failure rate), 213
alert thresholds, 239
allocations tags, 182
alternatives system, CDH, 84
Amazon Web Services power outage, 220
annualized failure rate (AFR), 213
Apache Software Foundation (ASF), 41
APIs, HDFS, 20, 23
appenders, 91
application container, 38
application data, swapping, 62, 124
application master (YARN), 38
Apt repository, 42
apt-get format repository, Cloudera, 81
AS (authentication server), 138
ASF (Apache Software Foundation), 2, 41
atime, 66

attempt of task, 35
authentication
    within Hadoop, 140
    performed before authorization, 136
    and resource allocation, 167
authentication server (AS), 138
authorization
    in Flume, 163
    in HBase, 160
    in HDFS, 153
    in Hive, 159
    in Hue, 161
    inherently service specific, 136
    in MapReduce, 155–159
    in Oozie, 160
    in Pig, Cascading, Crunch, 163
    and resource allocation, 167
    in Sqoop, 161
    in ZooKeeper, 163
automatic failover mode, 16, 100, 111
automatic parallelization, 26
available capacity, 175
AWS, Amazon, 4

B
backup, 249
    distributed copy (distcp), 250–252
    of namenode metadata, 254
    parallel data ingestion, 252
balancer utility, HDFS, 95
bandwidth
    1 vs. 10 Gb networks, 69
    balancing, 95, 204
    datanodes and, 10, 196
    MapReduce and, 33

We'd like to hear your suggestions for improving our indexes. Send email to *index@oreilly.com*.

oversubscription of, 70, 124
reducers and, 128
spine fabric and, 72
utilization of, 241
banned.users, 152
batch data processing, MapReduce as, 32
batch performance, 7
Beeswax, 161
bidirectional data transfer, 3
big data, 5
BigTable, Google, 4
Bigtop, Apache, 89
blacklist, job-level, 37
blade systems, 52, 133
BLOCK compression, 126
block data, balancing HDFS, 202
block locations, 11
    block placement policy, 130
    displaying, 22, 223
    outdated, 13
    and performance, 63
block pools, 19, 113
block reports, 11
    not written to disk, 18
    regarding failed path, 205
    traffic from, 67
block size, 8, 169
block tokens, 139
bonded NICs, 46
bootstrapping namenodes, 108–112
bottlenecks
    diagnosing, 221–224
    and mapred.reduce.tasks value, 128
    and multiple racks, 133
    in processing pipeline, 121
    reducer skew, 52
break out cables, 73
buffer size, 95

C

Capacity Scheduler (cap scheduler)
    choice of, 180, 185–191
    configuration, 187–191
    deprecated memory related parameters,
        187
    new job acceptance, 190
    and physical machine resources, 186
capacity-scheduler.xml, 86, 187
Cascading, 163

Cassandra, Apache, 4
CDH (Cloudera's Distribution Including
        Apache Hadoop), 42
    dependency on Oracle RPM, 56
    downloading Apache Hadoop from, 80–84
    and federation, 113
    FUSE HDFS support, 23
CentOS, 54
    default issues with, 59, 64
    init scripts on, 80
    uid numbering in, 152
centralized account management, 164
cgroups, Linux, 194
checkpoints, 16, 94
Chef, 54, 62, 164, 195
child tasks
    environment variables for, 88
    failures of, 36
Cisco Nexus 7000 series switches, 71
ClassLoader, Java, 87
client ViewFS mount table configuration, 119
Cloudera's Distribution Including Apache
        Hadoop (CDH), 42
    dependency on Oracle RPM, 56
    downloading Apache Hadoop from, 80–84
    and federation, 113
    FUSE HDFS support, 23
cluster-id, 114
clusters, 2, 195
    (see also planning a Hadoop cluster)
    adding storage to, 9
    administrator of, 155
    cluster-level checks, 116, 248
    combining, 135
    compute capacity of, 170
    configuration of, 85, 212
    distribution switch, 71
    hardware requirements, 46, 48
    HDFS maintenance tasks, 196–205
    housekeeping traffic, 67, 71
    managing Hadoop processes, 195
    MapReduce maintenance tasks, 205–208
    one job per MapReduce, 34
    owner of, 155
    sample growth plan for, 50
    size growth projections, 51
    starting/restarting, 11
codecs, pluggable compression, 126
colocated clients, 203

multiple failed datanodes, 14
multiple replicas, 8, 34
multitenancy, 135, 159

N

namenode high availability (NN HA)
    and automatic failover configuration, 105
    basic configuration of, 104
    enabling, 100
    fencing options, 102
    formatting and bootstrapping of, 108–112
    initializing ZooKeeper for use with, 106
    overview, 16
    support for, 48
NameNodeInfo MBean, 244–246
namenodes (NN), 10, 46
    cluster view, 116
    confirming active status of, 110
    directories and permissions for, 55, 61
    and failed paths, 205
    federation, 18, 113–119
    filesystem metadata, 11, 14, 18, 254
    formatting, 99
    hardware requirements, 47
    heap monitoring on, 243
    host-level checks of, 240
    and identification, 57
    and IP address, 225
    and Kerberos authentication, 141, 147
    mapping of, 119
    metric info on, 244
    and permitted machine names, 86
    and ports, 93
    and RPC activity, 97
    single namenode view, 116
    starting or stopping, 195
    unavailability of, 12
    URL for location of, 21, 93
    worker threads/handlers, 96
namespace federation, 18
namespace, global, 119
NAS (network attached storage), 7, 33, 52
Netezza, 3
Netflix postmortem, 220
network attached storage (NAS), 7, 33, 52
network bandwidth consumption, 241
network design, 66
    1 vs. 10 Gb networks, 69
    1 vs. 10Gb networks, 71, 72

bottlenecks, 133
    network partitions, 214, 222
    network usage in Hadoop, 67
    typical network topologies, 69–73
network interface cards (NICs), 46
network latency checks, 242
Nexus 7000 series switches, Cisco, 71
NFS filer, 16, 101
NICs (network interface cards), 46
node manager (YARN), 38
nodes, 34, 46
NoEmitMetricsContext, 232
non-graceful failover, 16
non-ssh based fencing method, 103
non-zero exit codes, 36
noncollocated clients, 67
nonqualified hostname, 58
-norandkey option, 141, 145
North/South traffic, 67, 71
NTP configuration, 56
NullContext plug-in, 231, 234

O

Oozie, Apache, 4, 42, 160
operating system selection and preparation, 46,
    54
    deployment layout, 54
    hostnames, DNS, and identification, 57–59
    software, 56
    users, groups, and privileges, 60–62
Oracle, 3, 5
org.apache.hadoop.hdfs.server.namenode.FS
    Namesystem.audit, 91
org.apache.hadoop.io.compress.DefaultCodec
    , 126
org.apache.hadoop.io.compress.GzipCodec,
    126
org.apache.hadoop.io.compress.SnappyCodec
    , 126
org.apache.hadoop.mapred.CapacityTaskSche
    duler, 187
org.apache.hadoop.mapred.DefaultTaskContr
    oller, 151
org.apache.hadoop.mapred.FairScheduler,
    180
org.apache.hadoop.mapred.JobInProgress
    $JobSummary, 91
org.apache.hadoop.mapred.JobQueueTaskSc
    heduler, 127

org.apache.hadoop.mapred.LinuxTaskContro
ller, 151
org.apache.hadoop.metrics.file.FileContext,
232
org.apache.hadoop.metrics.ganglia.GangliaCo
ntext, 233
org.apache.hadoop.metrics.ganglia.GangliaCo
ntext31, 233
org.apache.hadoop.metrics.spi.NoEmitMetric
sContext, 232
org.apache.hadoop.metrics.spi.NullContext,
232
org.jets3t.service.impl.rest.httpclient.RestS3Se
rvice, 91
orthogonal features, 20
OS user, 137
"other" user class, 154
OutOfMemoryError, 242
output format, 31
output troubleshooting, 216
overcommitting memory, 62
overlapping mounts, 120
overriding properties, 87
oversubscription, 70, 124
owner user class, 154

P

package installation, 78
packets, 13
PAM (Pluggable Authentication Modules), 61
parallelization
    limitations of, 32
    and MapReduce, 171
    parallel data ingestion, 252
parentheses, use of, 103
partitioner, 28
password security, 139, 142, 145
patch releases, 42
path, failed, 205
patterns, troubleshooting, 216
PDUs (power distribution units), 17
Pentaho, 5
performance issues
    access time, 66
    balancing data, 202
    delayed task assignment, 179
    disk configuration, 63
    garbage collection events, 243
    idle spindle syndrome, 94, 121

monitoring performance, 233
"mystery bottleneck", 221–224
oversubscription, 124
swapping, 241
virtualization and, 52
permissions (HDFS), 61, 101, 153
physical (post-replication) size, 169
physical and virtual memory utilization, 241
physical locality of machines, 130
pid directory, Hadoop, 55, 88
Pig, Apache, 3, 42, 80, 159, 163
planning a Hadoop cluster
    blades, SANs, and virtualization, 52
    cluster sizing, 50
    disk configuration, 63–66
    hardware selection, 45–49
    kernel tuning, 62–63
    network design, 66–73
    operating system selection and preparation,
        54–62
    picking a distribution and version, 41–44
Pluggable Authentication Modules (PAM), 61
pluggable compression codecs, 126
plugins, 161, 231
poolMaxJobsDefault element, 184
pools, 19, 174–179, 181, 184
ports
    embedded HTTPS server, 148
    mapred.job.tracker, 121
    namenode, 93
    in secure mode, 147
POSIX, 57, 153
postfix, 57
postmortems, 220
power distribution units (PDUs), 17
preventative maintenance, 219
primary namenode, starting the, 109
primary, Kerberos, 138
principals
    defined, 138
    and hostnames, 143
    MapReduce, 151
    parameter, 147
    unique for each worker, 140, 144
prioritized FIFO queues, 172
process presence checks, 242
processes, starting and stopping, 195
processor utilization, 241
prod-analytics, 114

About the Author

Eric Sammer is currently a Principal Solution Architect at Cloudera where he helps customers plan, deploy, develop for, and use Hadoop and the related projects at scale. His background is in the development and operations of distributed, highly concurrent, data ingest and processing systems. He's been involved in the open source community and has contributed to a large number of projects over the last decade.

Colophon

The animal on the cover of *Hadoop Operations* is a spotted cavy, or lowland paca. The large rodent goes by different names depending on where it lives: *tepezcuintle* in Mexico and Central America, *pisquinte* in Costa Rica, *jaleb* in the Yucatán peninsula, *conejo pintado* in Panamá, *guanta* in Ecuador, and so on. The name comes from the now extinct Tupian language of Brazil, meaning "awaken" and "alert."

The paca has coarse fur and strong legs, at the end of which are four digits in the front and five on the back; pacas use their nails as hooves. Usually weighing in about 13 to 26 pounds, the paca usually has two litters per year.

Overall, this rodent keeps to itself, often described as a quiet, solitary nocturnal animal. They live in burrows that they dig themselves, about seven feet into the ground. Pacas prefer to live near water, which is where they tend to run for escape when threatened. Living in the tropical Americas means a diet of fruit such as avocado and mango as well as leaves, stems, roots, and seeds. These animals are great climbers and gather their own fruit. Considered a pest for farmers harvesting yam, sugar cane, corn, and cassava, the lowland paca are hunted for their delicious meat in Belize.

The cover image is from *Shaw's Zoology*. The cover font is Adobe ITC Garamond. The text font is Linotype Birka; the heading font is Adobe Myriad Condensed; and the code font is LucasFont's TheSansMonoCondensed.

Have it your way.

CPSIA information can be obtained at www.ICGtesting.com
Printed in the USA
BVOW11s0243180214

345245BV00013B/285/P